Little Comrades

LITTLE
COMRADES

LAURIE LEWIS

The Porcupine's Quill

Library and Archives Canada Cataloguing in Publication

Lewis, Laurie, 1930–
    Little comrades / Laurie Lewis.

ISBN 978-0-88984-342-4

    1. Lewis, Laurie, 1930–. 2. Lewis, Laurie, 1930– — Family.
3. Communists — Alberta — Biography. I. Title

HX104.7.L49A3 2011   335.4092   C2011-901303-7

1   2   3   •   13   12   11

Published by The Porcupine's Quill, 68 Main Street, PO Box 160,
Erin, Ontario NOB 1TO. http://porcupinesquill.ca

Readied for the press by Doris Cowan. Cover and interior photographs are
courtesy of the author.

Represented in Canada by the Literary Press Group.
Trade orders are available from University of Toronto Press.

We acknowledge the support of the Ontario Arts Council and the Canada
Council for the Arts for our publishing program. The financial support of the
Government of Canada through the Canada Book Fund is also gratefully
acknowledged. Thanks, also, to the Government of Ontario through the
Ontario Media Development Corporation's Ontario Book Initiative.

Canada
Ontario
Ontario Media Development
Corporation

Canada Council   Conseil des Arts
for the Arts   du Canada

ONTARIO ARTS COUNCIL
CONSEIL DES ARTS DE L'ONTARIO

Why will a spark flare, and kindle a memory long filed away to burn again? It doesn't seem to matter how many years have passed, how many chapters in the book of your life, it's as if the whole time your mind's been working to connect it all, to prove to you everything had its reasons, makes sense in the long run.

Eliza Clark, *Bite the Stars*

For the survivors

CONTENTS

PART TWO

RUNNING AWAY FOR GOOD

PART ONE

NO PLACE LIKE HOME

Oh, we do look like poverty-stricken rural kids.
But my mother said she had taken the washtub outside
because there wasn't enough light in the house
(no such thing as 'flash' yet). She thought we were cute and
made us pose for this shot.

This is my darling bear, and that's my not-so-darling
brother sitting on a wooden train.

1. A WAY WITH SECRETS

A childhood full of pretence; that was how I thought of it. We didn't pretend that our family life was normal. We children knew of no other families, no other standards, so we made no comparisons. It was just the way things were. That's the only thing children know, in the beginning. Our pretence was that we didn't mind it, that we found it an acceptable way to live. Of course we didn't. Not for one minute, not any of us. But that was a secret. Three separate secrets, really, one for each of us, my mother, my brother, me, that we never told each other. Of my father's secrets I knew nothing, or perhaps I chose not to know.

My mother had her way with secrets: she would act as if they didn't exist. She gave us acting lessons.

'Daddy's coming home,' she would say cheerfully, smiling brightly, looking at her two children, blinking. 'Daddy's coming home. Let's wave from the window, so he'll see us. He'll see how happy we are that he's coming home.'

And we children arranged our faces, put on masks of cheerful welcome like costumes we had taken from the drawer, a sweater that didn't quite fit, handed down from a cousin; a plaid scarf in some unsuitable colour for a child, brown maybe. Our arms tight against our bodies; our eyes darting, blinking, looking everywhere but at each other. As if we had already learned the wisdom of the frightened. Don't look. Don't risk the mirror game, where you see your fear reflected back from other eyes, their fear in yours, yours in theirs, multiplying endlessly. We never looked, never spoke the fear. We tried to believe the other actors in the drama.

I was about two years old when Tim Buck first came to visit us, so I don't remember this, but I was told the story: He was the leader of the Communist Party of Canada, an important man, small and energetic, like my grandfather. My mother was typing reports in the kitchen, late into the night and early morning. He asked her: Why aren't you in the Party? and Lawrence, my father, said she wasn't ready but he was teaching her. 'She doesn't need your permission, comrade,' Tim said.

'If she's politicized enough to stay up all night typing for the Party, she's ready to be a member.'

My brother Andy said to me years later, 'In all my life, I always thought of Tim Buck as a friend. A hero, an idol, and a friend, who brought me an apple as big as my head when he came secretly to town. But I think the Party could have tried to control Lawrence a bit more. It wasn't enough just to say "Comrade Lawrence has a violent temper and must learn to control it." They could have done more.'

And just how, now, was Daddy coming home? All we asked, my brother and I, was that he be ordinary. Not a happy hero, not a bellowing bully. Just ordinary. Walking, not stumbling against the door. Just ordinary. Smiling at us, asking how was school today. Ordinary. We weren't asking for a toy or a piece of candy, or, god forbid, a piggyback. Only ordinary.

My brother taught me to keep my mouth shut like he tried to do. He learned to be careful with his mouth, and with his eyes.

'Look at me when I'm talking to you,' my father would say.

Or the other way,

'What do you think you're looking at?'

So you never knew for sure what you were supposed to do, look or not look. Andy was very careful, but it didn't do him much good. He got whacked around just the same.

I thought I'd be an actress when I grew up, just because I had so much practice.

When you're poor you're at the bottom of the ladder, and you have to live however you can. The poorest, the cheapest, place to live is a furnished room. In the Depression you could rent one by the week – cash in advance, of course – so it was just about the cheapest thing you could do. Except a flophouse, where you could pay just one night at a time. Just a place to sleep, that's all, and only for men. But the men were sleeping under bridges, out in the open, trying to stay warm somehow, building little fires, but trying not to get caught. Riding the rails to other towns, looking for work.

Sometimes in the room you could have a hot plate, so you could heat some soup or have a cup of tea, but cooking wasn't allowed. The strangest kinds of place, people lived. Office buildings, where there were no offices any more. Old stores, out of business because no one could buy anything. Any old space. Empty garages, warehouses.

My parents rented a two-bedroom house for $15 a month. That was 1932. I was two. There are three or four pictures of me with my brother taken in the back yard of that house. In one of them he is handing me a cookie. In another I am wearing a sunsuit made of some kind of netting, and I am hugging a large stuffed bear. Andy is sitting a few feet away from me, next to a wooden truck. We look as though we might be happy. I'm so glad to see that picture, those toys. You have no idea how happy it makes me, just to see that bear. I didn't even know I had a bear like that.

Years later, when we looked at the photograph, my mother told me that the bear belonged to the neighbour; that I was given it to play with now and then. I was very glad to know that. I'd hate to think I had such a wonderful bear and then forgot about him.

This was before baby-sitters: people took their children with them everywhere, or left them at home and asked a neighbour to look in. People came to our house or apartment, usually for Party meetings, Party business. Sometimes I was a show-off when I was a little kid – I had two things I did at parties. I'd stand up on a chair and do an imitation of Carmen Miranda – with a lampshade or something on my head to represent a bowl of fruit. And I'd sing and wave my hips about like she did. *Chicky-chicky boom, chicky boom.* I guess I must have seen a movie. And the other thing I did, still standing up on the chair, was recite the opening of the *Communist Manifesto*. A four-year-old, probably wearing my flannelette nightie, standing up on a chair in the living room: 'Workers of the world, unite! You have nothing to lose but your chains.' I'd lift up my fist on the word *unite!* Everyone would laugh, applaud. I liked that.

My mother told me stories:

Calgary, that would be in about 1934 or '35. I'd take you with me while Andy was in school. Ben's house was where the typewriter was, and I had a key. I used to go there to type the notices and the reports. I'd type directly onto a stencil, right onto a mimeo sheet – oh, the ego then. No such thing as a first draft, just write it as it comes.

When I was finished I'd hide it for the comrade who would do the mimeographing. I'd roll it up into the window blind in the kitchen, and then I'd leave. I didn't even know who it was that came to get it. Next thing I knew, it would be printed.

But it was all illegal, so it was very secret. The law was called Article 98, passed in 1924, soon after the Russian Revolution. The other countries, including Canada even, were afraid that their workers would rise up too. And especially in Canada after the Winnipeg strike. So it was illegal to go to meetings, to pass out leaflets, to organize workers, like we were doing.

Sometimes Ben would be there at the house, sometimes not. He was organizing the unemployed workers then – the U.M.M.A., the unmarried men. Those were the ones who would get sent away to camps. Ben and I liked each other a lot, kidded around. I guess I had a bit of a crush on him. You'd sit on the floor, like I told you to. Just waiting and watching. You always took everything in.

Then, one day, when I went there Ben was gone. They had taken him. They took all the active communists they could find. We'd been organizing people for protest rallies, for demonstrations, for trying to get the government to help the unemployed, trying to get relief – that's what welfare was called then. And there wasn't any. The prime minister said 'Not one red cent for relief.'

Ben went to jail then, I think, or to internment camp, and I never heard of him for over fifty years.

This was before the trek, before the boys came through Calgary on boxcars, on their way to Ottawa, they thought.

2. PINK

Christmas. It must have been Christmas. There could be no other reason for these gifts. My mother was annoyed, angry even. This woman at the door with gifts, had my mother asked for this charity? She must have. Two young children – I was four, I think, and my brother was six. My father was away somewhere, that's all I knew. Everyone was unemployed, looking for work, in 1934.

Gifts for the children: for me, a doll carriage, for Andy a truck. The carriage was filled with things that weren't for me – food things. My mother lifted each bag, each package. She had to say thank you to the woman who brought these gifts. What could she say? A bag of flour. A pound of lard. Whatever could she say? A can of cocoa, dark and bitter. She must have been trying to imagine a Christmas dinner from these things, perhaps had hoped even for oatmeal, for beans, for sugar. Else why would she have asked? Would she have humiliated herself just for these reminders of the bare cupboards? To make empty pie crusts, fried dough?

She should have been grateful. It was something. With her proud good manners she said, 'Thank you for these things. For the children, I am grateful.' She would not prompt us to *say thank you to the nice lady.* Her own humiliation was enough; she wouldn't make us share it.

I was instantly in love with the doll carriage, it was wicker, it was pink; it was perfect for a little girl. I didn't even notice that it wasn't new. Someone had repaired it and painted it pink. I loved it, my fingers curled around the wooden bar on the handle.

When the carriage was empty and the stranger was gone I pushed it around the room. My mother watched me, then found a piece of cloth, tied a string around it to make a tadpole sort of doll, drew a face with pencil. I pushed the carriage forward, pulled it back; a flash of pain screamed from my leg. A protruding nail had scratched my thigh – a perfect crescent moon, a thin line of red – just a scratch bubbling on my skin. My mother sat with me and cried; she cried more than I did. I was a good excuse. She used the heel of her shoe to pound the nail down into the wood, fiercely.

This was my first scar. Just a scratch. The perfect crescent moon grew on my thigh as I grew. When my skin tanned, the moon showed pale and silver. It has never left me. It is always the pink carriage. It is always my mother's desperation. It is always a warning: be wary of the gifts of strangers.

One of the oddest things about childhood – Memory. How can these memories last fifty, sixty, seventy years? Some tiny chemical in the brain forms a kind of scar, like a mark on the skin, that will be there forever. These memories are locked into flesh, ready to reveal themselves when we poke at them. Always tied to the time they were made, always the sound, always the voice of that moment.

Calgary

SUPPORT THE
YOUTH OF CANADA
GIVE HELP TO MARCHERS ON
OTTAWA

1200 B.C. Relief Camp Strikers will arrive in your city tonight.

Already the advance guard has arrived and held a meeting in the Labor Temple where a number of prominent citizens were present and assured us of their support. Women's organizations agree also to help us.

The purpose of the march to Ottawa is to lay our case, the case of the thousands of youth of Canada before the Federal authorities and to bring pressure to bear on the government to abolish the slave camps and to provide work with wages so we may live like human beings.

We expect to be in your city three days. We expect that during this time it will be necessary for us to appeal to everyone to give us their full support not only morally but financially. At the meeting last night a delegation was despached to interview the Mayor requesting relief and accommodation for the strikers while they remain in the city. Plans are being laid for a picnic for Sunday afternoon at the St. George's Island and also for a 10 minute broadcast over CFAC about 7 P.M. We invite all political, economic, cultural and church organizations to give us their support in our just fight for the abolition of the present relief camp system.

We have established the headquarters at the Labor Temple, 229-11th Ave. E. and phone M1759.

Send all donations care of RELIEF CAMP WORKERS, RELIEF COMMITTEE, to the above address.

Note: The broadcast will take place Friday, June 7th at about 7 p.m.

Issued by: RELIEF CAMP STRIKERS
PUBLICITY COMMITTEE

Facsimile reproduction: Artful Codger

Flyer calling for contributions to help
the 'On to Ottawa' march (reproduction).

3. LEARNING TO LIE

I was six years old when I learned how to lie. My brother taught me.
Everyone said he was really good at it. So Andy taught me, but I don't
think he knew he was doing it. We always fought with each other, so
he wouldn't ever really deliberately teach me anything. But I knew he
told silent lies – testing the wrath of God to see if there was a lightning
bolt out there ready to flatten a kid who's just trying to keep out of
trouble. That was a time before the lies became really necessary. He
was almost eight years old.

We had just come from Calgary and my mother was trying to find
a job in Vancouver. My father was in Prince Rupert looking for work –
that's what my mother told us to say. Andy and I had been plunked
with our father's parents on their farm near White Rock. It was the
middle of the Depression, although we didn't know that then, in 1936.
Didn't know we were in the middle of anything, just hard times.
Didn't know anything before the hard times, and didn't know they
would ever end.

In the mornings my grandfather drove to his carpentry job and on
the way he delivered cans of milk to the dairy pick-up station and
dropped us off at school. After school Andy and I always walked home
along the trail between the fields and the woods – three miles along
the dark overgrown pathway – where Andy tormented me with stories
that a wild bull was loose in the area (that wasn't really a lie), and I
looked for raging beasts lurking behind every shrub. At almost six, I
was afraid of a lot of things.

My grandmother was always up early to milk the eight cows, and
the cans from the evening's milking had cooled all night in a deep tank
of water. The metal cans, heavy with milk, rested in the waterhole
next to the barn, in a deep wet space that I found terrifying. Whenever
I had to go through the cooler shed I pushed myself back against the
wall, far away from the dark hole. I was afraid of falling in, but felt
drawn to the edge. The hole seemed to murmur frightening things and
I thought there might be a person deep down in the well. I knew what
the hole would do to a person, how you would never get out, but spend
your whole life wetly in the echoing dark.

My grandmother Charlotte packed lunches for us to take to school, jam sandwiches, the same kind she had made for each of her own ten children. Twenty years of jam sandwiches, the red jam staining slabs of white bread. All the farm wives made the same kind of bread, using the same recipes, mostly, baked in the same big black cookstoves. My grandmother made the kind of squared-off oblong loaves with rounded tops that are still around today. She cut thick slices for breakfast and for lunches and for tea. That was honest homey bread. There's nothing much but truth in one of those loaves. Nothing but truth in a jam sandwich.

Every school day she wrapped the sandwiches neatly in waxed paper, with a double fold on top to seal them and triangles like tent flaps at the ends. She put the two sandwiches in a brown paper bag, soft from re-use, and handed it to Andy. He was my big brother, so carrying the bag was his job.

'Now you take care of your sister at lunch and give her a sandwich, you hear me, Andy?'

We rode in the back seat of the car; it was a 1929 Durant, and the front seat next to the driver had been taken out to make room for four ten-gallon cans of milk. Our grandfather drove to the highway intersection where a wooden platform had been constructed as a pickup spot for the local dairy. On the way there, the full cans thudded heavily against each other in the car, the metallic sound muffled by the rich milk inside. When he lifted them onto the platform we could tell by his grunts how heavy the cans were. The empties from yesterday he lifted easily into the car. The lids were off and dangled noisily against the side of the cans, fastened to the handles with a short chain. The cans rattled and clanged against each other as the car turned toward the school at last. Every day we thought we'd be late, but he always got us there. He said, 'I'll get you there on time. Don't you be bothering me.'

Here in the country everything was strange and different, scarier to me than the apartment near Calgary's Chinatown where we had been living before my father went away. The schoolhouse was set into an acre of yard, with two neat rows of outhouses at the back and a large open shed to hold the winter's supply of firewood. A couple of swings dangled from wooden frames. Trees and shrubs edged the clearing. The children in the schoolyard all knew each other, had known each other for years. It was my first year at school and I was shy and frightened. Lonely. I missed my mother.

Inside the school there was just one big room with maybe four rows of desks, wide aisles in between. Students in all the grades were there in that room, up to grade eight. The teacher walked up one aisle and down the other, looking at what everyone was doing. I sat in the first seat of the first row. In the seat behind me sat the one other first grader – Milton. The kids called him Milkweed.

Whenever I finished my work I had to teach Milton. He wasn't as scared as I was in first grade, because he had been there last year too. I loved learning things, and loved helping Milton. I just listened and watched and tried not to get noticed, looking at Milton working with his yellow pencil. When I finished with him, I could listen to the lessons for the other grades, reading, arithmetic, history. I especially liked it when the teacher or one of the big kids read stories and poems out loud. They read things like 'I wandered lonely as a cloud ... '

On the day I learned to lie, as we left the car in the morning Andy was daydreaming as usual – that's what they always said: *I suppose he was daydreaming as usual* – and the brown lunch bag was left on the back seat. At the noon recess Andy told me: No sandwiches, No lunch. 'And don't cry, you little twerp. And don't tell anyone.'

I sat on the big grey steps of the school, exactly halfway up and halfway down, at the side right next to the railing, and holding it for comfort.

At lunchtime I usually took my sandwich and sat in a green cave under the bushes, but I was afraid to go in there when I had no lunch. I knew that children were starving in China and I wondered how long it would take me to starve to death. I didn't think I would die before teatime, anyway, but perhaps I would lapse into a coma. That was something I had heard from my mother once in Calgary, just before her father died, 'He lapsed into a coma.'

The teacher came down the steps. She always ate her lunch in the schoolroom – where she could have some peace and quiet, she said – and then she usually went for a little walk.

'Have you finished lunch already?'

'No, Miss Harris,' I said, not even thinking about telling a lie.

'Well, don't you think you should eat it instead of dawdling here on the steps?'

That raspy lump formed in my throat and I could feel my chin start its quivering. How could I not tell the truth? How could I not cry? So I had to tell. Oh, I knew Andy would be so angry.

'Well, I'll see what I can do. Go and find your brother, please. He must be hungry, too.'

She walked down the road and around the corner to the house by the river. When she came back she had two sandwiches wrapped in waxed paper, just the way my grandmother did it, the little foldover and the tent flaps. They were jam sandwiches too, red jam like Grandma's, and tasted delicious.

But I was shocked. Jam and butter. There was butter on that sandwich! Even at six years old I knew what a 'cash crop' was. My grandparents got paid money for these things, so they were precious. Apples were a cash crop, except the scabby ones, which we ate. Eggs were a cash crop, that's why Andy and I had half a fried egg each at supper, and my grandfather had a whole one. So was milk – and butter. We *never* had butter on sandwiches.

After school, when we started to walk home, Andy was very angry.

'You're a dope. You know that? A dope. You had to go and tell, didn't you?'

My throat got raspy again and tears tried to get out.

'Get away from me,' he told me. 'You walk home alone. Go on.'

'It's not fair. You ate your sandwich, too. And anyway, it's not my fault. Miss Harris made me tell.'

'You're not supposed to tell things. Don't you know *anything?* Dummy.'

He made me walk all the way alone, far in front of him along the trail, under the big trees, in the dark wet shadows where the wild things were. The trail was very long – each step so small, just one after the other. I looked behind me to see if he was there, but I saw only shadows. Andy usually walked ahead of me, calling back, 'Hurry up, you twerp. Come on, step on it.' I'd call out to him, 'Wait for me, Andy, wait for me.' And I would try to run fast to catch up with him. But that day I couldn't see him at all; I looked far far ahead for the brightening that would tell me the road was near. Soon, soon, please let it be there.

When I reached home, my grandmother met me in the lane. She had found the lunch bag in the car when Granddad got home from work. 'I was so worried,' she said. 'What did you do for lunch? And where's Andy?'

I started talking right away. I told her all about the children starving in China and about being rescued by Miss Harris, and the jam sandwich from the lady by the river.

'Did you have enough to eat?' she asked. 'Was it a good sandwich?' She worried about everything. I saw her thin old face and raggedy hair bending over me. But suddenly my mouth just stopped.

I didn't tell about the butter. About the cash crop.

'Sure, Grandma, it was nice,' I told her. And I hugged her around her apron.

Andy came up the lane then, turning in from the road. He stood right next to me, silent and watching, waiting for trouble. He was used to being in trouble though, so maybe he didn't mind too much. He just stood there, looking at me. So all of a sudden I didn't tell about him making me walk home alone. He hadn't even told me not to tell on him, but I knew. I didn't tell about being alone and scared, about walking the dark trail by myself.

'It was a good sandwich, Grandma. Really, but not as good as yours,' I told her.

Once I learned, I got really good at not telling. In the years of growing up I didn't tell a lot of people about a lot of things. Later, there were things I *should* have told – told someone. But that year when I was six I discovered a power in knowing something secret, private; a way of having thoughts when nobody knows. And in that space of 'not-telling' I found a person that might be me.

Sometimes the thoughts I stored up were as simple and smooth as butter; sometimes as frightening as the wild things in the woods. Or dark and wet as the waterhole into which my grandmother would lower herself on the pulley, one despairing autumn day late in her life, wearing her winter coat to keep out the cold.

She scared herself too good, she said, and had to hang on all afternoon until her husband came home. And she hollered out to him.

'I need you in here, John. Would you come.'

'Are you daft, woman,' he said when he pulled her out.

And that's the truth that she never told to her children, but only to my mother. Just a bit daft that day, that's what she said.

4. FINDERS KEEPERS

While my father was away my mother took care of Andy and me. She made sure we had food and clothes and went to school and learned our manners. After she found a job we shared a furnished apartment in Vancouver with her friend Milly. It had two rooms, one of them with a hot plate sort of kitchen, and there was a bathroom down the hall. It was good. Two women, two kids, just living in those two rooms. No one shouting, no yelling, no drinking. Pretty good. Milly had the roll-out bed in the living room; it could divide into two parts and Andy slept on the cot. I slept in the big bed with my mother. My mother had a part-time job in an optometrist's office and Milly taught tap-dancing. Step brush brush, step step, Step brush brush, step step, she showed me.

In my mind the room is a large one, but maybe it just seemed so because it was very empty. There was a big wooden wardrobe for our clothes, and four drawers down the side of it. I think there was a table and four chairs. There must have been. We must have had a hotplate, but I really don't remember it. I don't remember eating anything except Aylmer's tomato soup, toast, and oatmeal. Porridge, we called it. But we must have eaten something else!

A protest march of the Single Unemployed Protective
Association, in Vancouver, 1935.

Once we went to visit my mother's friend Dora. She had three children and a vegetable garden. Now, there's one problem with living in an apartment, you can't have a vegetable garden. But at Dora's we all sat around a big table in a real dining room and ate a lot of kinds of vegetables, little baby ones, potatoes, carrots, beets, beans, and peas I remember, with a sauce made with milk. Oh, it was so good. We ate and ate, all of us. These tiny vegetables had to be thinned from the garden so that the others could grow big and there would be a plenty to eat later. I thought that was a really good system of gardening.

Andy and I spent a lot of time together. We'd just wander around the city. Neither one of us had any friends of our own to play with, mostly because we were new in the city. We were used to being always new in the neighbourhood, and we never stayed long enough in one place to make friends. Partly all this moving around was because of the Depression, when people moved from place to place if they found work. Partly, at least lately, it was because of political things.

Andy was two years older, so he was supposed to take care of me after school if our mother wasn't home, or even if she was and she sent us out to play. Mostly I stayed at home after school, near my mother, but sometimes she'd say, 'Why don't you go outside and play?' The streets around the apartment building were good for exploring, for finding things to play with. One place we lived was over a shoe repair shop. One was over a Chinese laundry. Sometimes I went out into the back alley, just to be by myself. There was a grey striped cat, skinny and eager, pushing at me all the time. I'd hold her on my lap and pat her. One day I met a man in the alley.

The man looked poor, like everyone else. His brown pants were rumpled, and his brown wool sweater had a little hole in it, just about where his heart would have been.

He sat on a wooden bench, leaning against the side of a shed in the alley. He called to me, 'Hello there. I haven't seen you around here before.'

'We just moved here,' I told him, hanging on to the cat and not looking at him.

'Where do you live?' he asked me.

'Just over there,' I waved down toward the middle of the block.

'Where did you come from?' I thought that was probably one of the things that I wasn't supposed to talk about, so I just shrugged as if I was dumb or didn't care. He told me that he lived over in the next street, but he liked to sit out here in the alley, where it was private. I understood that. That's what I liked too, that it was private and safe.

In the alley the man was there. In the next days we talked about cats and things. He told me I was a pretty little girl, and we started to like each other. I didn't remember anyone telling me I was pretty. So I liked that.

One day he asked me if I'd like to sit up on the bench with him. He said, 'Would you like to sit up here, honey?'

I'd never heard the word honey like that. My parents didn't talk that way. I remember I thought maybe he was a poet – I knew about poetry from my mother. Maybe he was describing my hair. Honey-blond hair. Honey-coloured, how pretty that would be. Better than mousy. I remember thinking that. I sat beside him that day.

I visited the man a few more times. Once he called me honey again, and I let him put his pale shaky hand into my panties. But I didn't go back again, after that. And I never told anyone. Never ever. I was so ashamed. I'd get a licking if I told.

My brother got a lot of lickings when my father was around. That's what it was called then: getting a licking. Andy could never behave himself. I remember my mother used to plead with him. 'If you won't stop I'll have to tell your father.... Please, don't make me have to tell him. You know what will happen.' I always knew he was going to get it anyway, no matter what he did. No matter what he said. I guess he knew too. He'd stand there glaring, holding his fists at his sides, he'd never back down, never cry. Once he was so scared he wet his pants.

When my brother got beaten, I always hid somewhere, behind the couch or something, trying to get out of the way where no one would notice me. I persuaded myself that it was his fault if he got it. *It's his own fault. He won't behave himself.* I learned to duck. I just kept my head down; I didn't make trouble. I was a very good girl. And I knew how to keep secrets.

Sometimes Andy went out first and I said I wanted to stay home. Then later I would ask 'Can I go out and play?' That way I got to go by myself. That was something I was just learning to work out. Stay close to home, my mother always said. I wasn't allowed to go downtown with him; he did on his own on Saturdays. Or if he was playing hookey. And on Saturdays it was my job to help my mother clean the house.

One of the places Andy took me was the junkyard. There was everything there. Broken washing machines and old cars, mostly. The old cars were the most fun. We sat together in the front seat if it wasn't broken and he pretended to drive and I said 'Be careful, dear' and he said 'Who's driving this car, me or you?' We looked in the glove compartment and under the seats and sometimes we even found money – pennies or a nickel sometimes. Dirty and stuck to the floor, but still good money, you just have to clean it up.

If you lifted up the back seat, you never knew what you were going to find under there. That's where most of the good stuff was. Sometimes an old liquor bottle. Rye, something like that, the flat kind of bottle that could slide behind the seat. If there was a drop or two Andy would lick at the end of the bottle. Cigarette packages, squashed and empty, Sweet Caporals, Player's.

But I got bored and besides it was messy and I didn't want to get my dress dirty because my mother would be annoyed that she'd have to wash and iron it. It wasn't my school dress, it was my extra, but still, I wasn't supposed to get dirty.

Andy had a magic knack of finding things in the dumpy cars. Brand new things, too. My mother would say, 'Where did you get that padlock?' and he'd say, 'I found it in the old car lot.' You could tell she didn't believe him, but what could she say? She couldn't just say he was lying. 'If I find out you stole it, there's going to be trouble, so you'd better not be lying to me.'

'No, honest. I found it.'

She was suspicious, but she couldn't prove anything. Not till later when he got caught filching from the five-and-ten.

One time we were in the lot and we were looking under the back seats of a lot of cars but didn't find anything useful.

'Andy, I want to go home. I don't like all this messy stuff.'

But he said, 'Come on, just one more. Let's try that one, over there.'

'No, Andy, I'm tired, really. I want to go home.'

'Oh, come on. Just one more. I'll look in the front and you look in the back seat and then I'll take you home.'

So I scrambled up into the back and lifted up the seat and you'd never guess what I found.

'Hey, Andy, look at this. A powder puff, a brand new powder puff.'

It was still in cellophane that crackled when I squeezed it. Puffy and pink. Part of the mysterious world of women, I knew.

'Well, that's amazing. I wonder how it got there. Probably just slipped out of some lady's purse. Aren't you glad you looked?'

'Oh, I love it. Can I keep it, Andy?'

'Sure. What would I want with it? Look around and see if there's anything else.'

So I poked around some more and there was a key chain with a whistle hanging from it and a red flashlight. Andy wanted to keep those, and I didn't care. That wasn't my kind of stuff. We weren't supposed to say 'stuff' but that's what it was anyway.

When we got home I showed my mother the powder puff. I said she could have it for a present if she wanted to, but she let me keep it, which made me very glad. But when Andy showed her his things she looked at him straight in the face for a long time. She put her hand flat on the table and leaned down to him.

'Now, that's just about enough, Andy. I don't want you *finding* any more things.'

'But I didn't find them, *she* did,' he said. 'She's the one that found them. Ask her.'

And I piped right up.

'That's right, mama, I found them, honest.'

'Andy,' she said. 'No more. Do you hear me?'

So if he ever found anything else, he never told her and he learned to keep it hidden somewhere. He had a lot of secret places, Andy did.

5. LOSERS WEEPERS

Oh, when you are a child it is dreadful to see your mother cry. Impossible that the one who comforts you should be weeping. I stand at my grandfather's coffin and rise on my tiptoes to look over the rim. The sleek white satin bed holds the man who was always kind, who never shouted. And I think that he loved me, even though I was just a little girl. He was a carpenter and now no longer smelled of wood shavings. One day he made wooden curls for my hair, pushing his plane along the edge of new clean wood just hard enough to make the wood curl up in thin slices. He sat me up on his workbench and held a pale wooden curl up to my pale straight hair. 'See,' he said, 'you have ringlets.' And he let me see my reflection in a mirror. 'Just like Shirley Temple,' he said. My mother laughed and I laughed and he laughed. And now he was in the box, very neat and very still, and my mother stood beside me and tried not to cry. On my tiptoes I could just peek over the edge and see his white moustache and the dimple in his chin that was just like mine.

My uncle Bill pushed my mother out of the way and picked me up. He held me over the coffin, and said, 'Kiss him. Kiss your grandfather!' But I started to cry too, and my mother took me away. My brother Andy came and sat down with us. He didn't have to kiss Granddad and he didn't have to cry. He was almost eight, looking very grown up in trousers and a white shirt from his cousin Alfred and a tie and jacket from cousin Arthur. My mother and I cried together.

In the summer after her father died, that was when my mother decided to move to Vancouver. Running away from misery again. Running from her loneliness, from her hard unforgiving family. She thought that my brother and I could stay at my grandparents' farm while she looked for a job and a place to live in Vancouver. She was a good planner, and she took good care of us.

She was busy going to meetings and working to raise money and get supplies for Dr Norman Bethune and his blood transfusion unit, to help the people in Spain.

When Tim Buck came to Vancouver my mother talked to him, as always.... At the end of 1936 he was encouraging volunteers to go to Spain. She told me he was a lot like her father, 'a good man'. The government had passed a law forbidding Canadians to fight or join the army on either side in Spain. But Comrade Tim said, 'Every man must decide for himself in the light of his own conscience.' My mother said he wasn't advising the men to break the law, just telling them to make up their own minds and take the consequences. If the volunteers went to Spain the Canadian government wouldn't give them any assistance. But the Party was there to help. My mother raised money, a nickel at a time. It took a hundred nickels to buy a train ticket to Halifax, she told me. A lot of nickels to help the comrades get to Spain.

The comrade I remember best is Red, he was a favourite with Andy and me. He was called Red not because of his politics – only the newspapers called the comrades Reds, that wasn't a word we ever used in our house – but because of his hair. Andy and I called him *Red, Red, Cabbage Head* and he used to play tag with us sometimes and he'd bounce me on his knee and call me his little sweetheart. When Red volunteered to go to Spain my mother said he had to have a medical checkup first, because they didn't want to send boys who were sick or weren't strong enough. And the doctor could sign his passport application, too.

We went sometimes with my mother to the train station in Vancouver, and I know that we went there when Red left. When the boys were leaving for Spain they'd go just one at a time from their towns, and later make groups of ten when they got to France. We weren't inside the station, but outside, near the tracks, and in my memory everything was made of cement, except there were some wooden benches. It seemed to me that the train came out of a tunnel, but I think that was probably just the part of the train station, a ramp or something. Andy and I stood quietly, fearfully, because we knew he was going away to the war in Spain and he might be killed. But also, when we were out in public we were not supposed to talk about Spain, because it was illegal. Not the talking, the going to. And we couldn't call him Cabbage Head then, but he grinned at us. Oh, I remember he was so skinny and had this thin, thin head, not at all like a cabbage, and red hair that was sort of curly but now he had it cut very short, and shaped up around his ears and at the back of his head. One of the other comrades was a barber and he gave Red a good haircut at our place just a couple of days before he went away. The barber said he would have liked to go to Spain too, to fight. But he was too old and besides, he at least had a bit of a job, barbering. Most of the boys going to Spain didn't have jobs. They had come right out of the camps where the unemployed unmarried men were staying during the hard times.

The Communist Parties of a lot of other countries arranged for volunteers too, from Germany and Italy and Russia and France. We learned bits of other languages from learning the songs of the volunteers. Learning languages, I'll never forget it. When you're six or seven years old you can learn just about anything, I thought. The Spanish Civil War was my introduction to languages and to geography too, I suppose. In Spanish we learned 'No Pasaran', They Shall Not Pass and 'Los Quatros Generales', The Four (Insurgent) Generals; in German, 'Freiheit', Freedom and 'Wir sind die Moorsoldaten', We are the Peatbog Soldiers.

And there were a lot of people who were worried about war coming. We listened to the radio all the time, there were news reports from Spain every day. England was worried about the Communists, so were Germany and Italy. France was worried about the Fascists, so was Russia. A lot of reporters were there, in Madrid or other cities. A lot of writers were there. Hemingway and Dos Passos. George Orwell. There was a blockade by England, Germany, to stop any supplies from getting through to the government of Spain. 'Non-intervention' they called it. But the German and Italian planes bombed the cities.

I was in my new pyjamas that I got for Christmas and Andy was sitting at the table finishing his homework. The radio was on for the evening programs – we listened to 'Fibber Mcgee and Molly' and the news reports from Europe. It was a small radio on the table. Two wooden knobs like headlights, and a cloth-covered opening where the sound came out. I was just standing beside my mother, leaning against her leg where she sat in her chair. The leading news was 'the fall of Madrid'. My mother pulled me up onto her lap and hugged me. She was crying in her soft sobby way, stroking my hair. 'The bombs, the bombs,' she said. 'The German planes are bombing everywhere. It's a terrible terrible thing to bomb civilians. The city is burning.'

Andy looked up. 'Does that mean the Fascists have won?'

She was vehement. 'No. No. We are still fighting.'

But she was crying as though she could see the future.

I see by my missing tooth that this photo was probably
taken in 1936. My mother sent a print of it to my father
while he was in the Soviet Union. The wounded expression
on Andy's face shamed my father, at least briefly.

6. BECOMING A SECRETARY

Secrets about politics were always there. From the time I was four years old I knew that my family was different. Knew that I wasn't to talk about things to people I didn't know, people my parents didn't know, kids at school, teachers. People who weren't part of the Party. I grew up with the Party in my head. It meant the Communist Party, the way the Movement meant the Labour Movement, working people and those who were involved with organizing unions and helping working people. My parents were part of that. They taught me not to talk about what I might hear at home or at meetings. Not talking to strangers meant something special in our house, it meant watch out for the RCMP.

My father was away for about a couple of years. We kids got in trouble when my mother went out at night to a political meeting, because Andy and I would get into a fight. We always fought, but I never really knew what it was about. Nothing, probably. Boy/girl. Eight/six. Worlds apart. The landlady had to come in to make us be quiet because we were hollering and yelling, and when my mother came home she gave us the very dickens. 'You should be ashamed of yourselves. What will people think of you? What will they think of me? You know how you are supposed to behave. I'm ashamed of you. It's up to you to be responsible well-behaved kids when I'm out at a meeting. That's the least you can do for the Party.'

The political work was very important. Andy and I knew that. Our parents were *the vanguard of the working class*. They worked all the time. Going to meetings, to protests, distributing leaflets, organizing people, trying to raise money. When you're in the Party you dedicate your life to this work – the work of helping the poor. Of leading them to a better life, leading them to socialism.

Secrets about family life, by which I mean about drinking or violence, became connected to political secrets. The truth would reflect badly on my father, so these things, the drinking and the violence, were political secrets, not ever to be mentioned. Not by us, not by my mother.

These are words children know: *smack, whack, spanking, licking, whip, punch, beat.* We understand each word precisely: the difference between a licking and a beating is the implement used and the part of the body affected. A licking is done, is *given*, with a leather belt usually, although a razor strop can also serve. A licking is on the buttocks and back of a child. If you have to take your shirt off, it's a whipping. A whipping is deliberate. It has to be planned. The implement must be grasped. A beating is done with the fists and is usually performed on the front of the child, often about the head and face; the two people face each other, clearly see each other. A beating comes from temper, from anger. Boys are beaten more often than girls. Andy and I knew all of this.

I saw the first time Andy got beaten, the first time my father's open hand closed into a fist, the first time the whack on the face changed to a punch. Andy answered back, that's what caused it. Well, he *knew better*, so why didn't he keep his mouth shut, like he always told me to? I think my father was surprised too.

My brother, later, remembered almost none of this. I was the small observer in this house, the one who saw everything.

It was 1938 when my father came home from two years of study in the Soviet Union, sent home because of the war everyone knew was coming. My mother, my brother and I moved to Edmonton and he came there to meet us there. We were staying in a couple of furnished rooms. But my mother hadn't been able to get an apartment yet – she had no money, of course.

First day home – excitement, getting to know our father again. He brought a brooch for my mother, some kind of smooth Russian mineral, and a book. The book was *Tom Jones*, the story of a 'worker hero', by Henry Fielding, published in the Soviet Union, in English. The memory of what gifts he brought for us, his children, has died of neglect.

We gathered in the living room to praise the returning hero. He told us what he learned in the Soviet Union: *peevo*, beer. *Spaseeba*, thank you. *Nyie gahvaroo paruski*, I don't speak Russian. *Nyie paheeymayoo paruski*, I don't understand Russian.

With two years' practice, he said *peevo* very well. And *wodka*. That should have been a warning to us.

When my father came back from the Soviet Union he was made head of the Party in Alberta. Andy thought the title was wonderful: Secretary General. It sounded like king of the world. I couldn't spell it yet, secretary. But I learned. It starts just like secret, which is what it meant probably. Someone who could keep secrets, or who was a secret, who could know things and not tell. I guess my father could do that then.

Then we – our family – lived in Edmonton with the Morrises for a while. 'The Central Committee sent them out to live with us, to keep an eye on your father in his new job,' my mother said. Sonya Morris was worried about her son Bobby's health and she used to make carrot juice for him. Vitamin A was much in the news. Good for poor eyesight – perhaps. She'd grate the carrots and then put them in a cheesecloth bag and squeeze and squeeze. You can't imagine how hard that was. 'Can I try it, Sonya? Let me try.' Of course I couldn't get one drop of juice. She'd get a little glassful, and he wouldn't drink it. This was in 1938, right after they came back from the Soviet Union. They were like strangers to him. Bobby seemed so angry with them all the time.

Sonya and Leslie were in the Soviet Union for about five years. My father Lawrence had also just returned. We shared a house – two mothers, four children, two political dads with new jobs. Eighteen dollars a month was what my father got paid by the Party. We were luckier than a lot of people.

I remember standing in the kitchen. There was a big white stove against the wall across from the window, and a door at the end of the room out to the back yard. The floor was worn linoleum. A kitchen table in front of the window, and a matching buffet to hold dishes.

The two mothers (this is my mother's memory):

'Ellen, it pains me to see the Party leadership driving around in new cars when times are so bad.'

'Yes, but Lawrence says we have to modernize the Party's image. We are more than a party of the poor and unemployed, we must be a party of authority and substance, he says, ready to govern.'

The first day we went to school my mother told Andy to take me, since he was eight-almost-nine. I don't know why she didn't come with us. I don't know why, but I'm sure there was a reason. It wasn't because she had a job. My father 'didn't want his wife to work',

Elsie Anderson's Theatre Group, Edmonton, March, 1938. (My mother's chosen name in later life was Ellen Stafford. When she was at Banff in 1938 her name was Elsie Anderson.) Shown here are the cast and production staff of *Transit*. Left to right: Victor Senko, Cecil Feldman, 'Chuck' Yakimchuk, Jack Milner, Fred Kostyk, Sally Milner, Sam Yakimchuk, Rose Milner, Jack Alexander, Berger Hanson, Harry Weitz (assistant director), Elsie Anderson (director), Helmer Hober, Jack Nicholson.

Political camp. This is, I believe, the only photograph in which our whole family appears. My father is on the left, in the back row. My mother is in the centre, and my brother and I are seated together in the front row.

so she didn't. She had signed us up at school, she said. And we had always gone to school alone, so we had no reason to be nervous or afraid. But since we were new, we had to go to the office.

At the office a woman asked Andy all the questions and he answered for himself and for me too. Our names, surname and Christian names. I knew we weren't Christians, of course, because our parents had taught us all about being communists. *Religion is the opiate of the masses,* Lawrence said. It was from one of his books. My mother told me what it meant: 'When people go to church they become contented and passive and they don't fight for their rights the way they should in these hard times.' She taught me a funny song:

Long-haired preachers come out every night
Just to tell you what's wrong and what's right
But when asked about something to eat
They will answer in voices so sweet:
Work and pray, live on hay
You'll get pie in the sky when you die.
Work and pray, live on hay
You'll get pie in the sky when you die.

I thought that was so funny. Work and pray, live on hay. I laughed and laughed, just like a little kid. We didn't live on hay, not really. (Lettuce once, remember the lettuce; it's almost like hay. My mother said if you sprinkle a little sugar on it, it tastes just like peaches. It didn't. Not in the least, although I tried very hard to imagine it. But that was only once; we certainly didn't have lettuce for dinner *every* day.) But we didn't have pie either. So my parents said they were atheists, which meant there wasn't a God up in the sky to take care of you; people just had to take care of each other.

Still, Andy knew just what to say. He just told the lady: Alan and Laurie. (Andy was just his nickname, so he had to tell his real one.) I'm glad he was there to answer questions because I was just learning about communism, so I would probably have tried to explain about not being Christian instead of just saying what she wanted to know. And our address. I had learned that too, but Andy had it down pat. Every time we moved we had to learn a new one and he was so good at it.

Mother's name, Ellen; father's name, Lawrence. Occupation: they meant my father, of course; mothers didn't have occupations then. Or maybe a few of them had jobs away from home, but no one asked. Occupation. I'll never forget how Andy put his head up, so proudly and said the whole title: Secretary General of the Communist Party of Alberta.

It was a bad year for me. I came down with scarlet fever and the whole house was quarantined. No one could leave. My mother got someone to take a message to the two fathers, to tell them not to come home – if they came home, they couldn't leave again for weeks. My mum soaked sheets in disinfectant and hung them in the doorway of my room. She wore a mask over her face when she came in to see me. To feed me, wash me. In my fever the room became a tent in a burning desert, white hot. But in a few days, because of the fear of infecting the other children, I was taken away to an isolation hospital that had been set up to deal with the epidemic.

'You were there for two months,' my mother said. 'And when you came home you came down with mumps. You picked it up in the hospital, apparently. So that took another two weeks. You were pretty sick, but at least you were at home.'

I was eight years old, so I missed a lot of school. But eventually I

Edmonton School 1937.
I am in the centre in the second row.

started getting caught up again. Then appendicitis started; I would tell my mother, 'The elastic on my panties is too tight. It hurts me.' She'd loosen it, but I still complained. Eventually, off to the doctor I went, and into the hospital to have my appendix removed.

My brother was jealous of the attention and the ice cream I got, so he began developing his own symptoms and eventually followed me into surgery. Afterwards he said, 'Half the time I was only making it up.'

That was the last of my illness for a while. My mum had probably been pretty worried about me that year, but at least during the time I was sick she managed to keep my father from bashing me about – mostly because I was away from him.

Later the principal tried to kick us out of school because Andy was always arguing with his teacher about political affairs, 'What do you think of your Russsky friends, now?' he'd say, and Andy would say, 'I think they're doing just fine.'

One day when I was at school an office lady came to the door of the classroom and whispered to my teacher, who looked at me very sadly. Why was she sad? She called me and I went to stand in front of her. She said very quietly, privately, so that the whole class didn't hear, 'You're to go with Miss Calder.' The reason I remember her name is that she was named Calder and she had called me. We walked down the hall together, past all the coats hung on hooks, to the principal's office.

There was a window with bubbly glass that you couldn't see through, so you never could know what was happening inside, and letters painted in black with a gold outline. Principal. Inside there was a lady with a typewriter, then Miss Calder sent me through another door. Andy was standing in there. We just looked at each other and I went to stand beside him. But the principal told me, 'Sit over there,' so I did. He hadn't finished yelling at Andy yet, I suppose. I wondered what Andy had done this time.

Andy stood in front of the big wooden desk, the principal stood behind it frowning at Andy. A green blotter in a leather frame filled most of the top of the desk, and a shallow wooden box at one side had papers in it. Andy, so proud, but I knew he was scared. I could see his tight hands at his sides, just the way he stood in front of our father sometimes when he was getting yelled at. Really stiff.

'What's all this about the Communist Party?'

Andy told him, 'That's what our father does, sir. That's his work.'

Now, you see! I could never have done that. I didn't know about saying *sir*.

'So what do you think of your Russian pals now? They aren't doing too well against the Finns. They're getting whipped.'

'I don't think they're doing so badly,' Andy said, giving up on the *sir*.

He stood in front of him, his thin arms held in close against his sides, his hands in small fists. Just standing there, being ten years old.

'You two get out of here. We don't want any of that Red Bolshie propaganda in this school. Just go home. Take your Bolshie talk and go back to Russia.'

I cried all the way home. 'I don't want to go to Russia.'

Andy said, 'Oh, shut up you little idiot. Now we don't have to go to school.'

'But I want to go to school. I want to.'

I can't remember how it came out. My father just loved a chance to go and shout at someone, so he may have gone to the school and shouted at the principal. Maybe my mother went to the school and told them about the law that children have to go to school. Or maybe we moved to a new house soon after that, and Andy learned the new address, and we went to a new school and he learned to say: 'Father's occupation, carpenter.'

7. MY FATHER AND LILLIAN GISH

My mother told me: 'Sugar. That was your father's first big success as a union organizer, 1931, I think. Lawrence went to southern Alberta to organize the sugar-beet workers. Got them all into a union. You should have seen how they were being exploited. Children even, working in the fields. There was a big push on for the One Big Union, O.B.U., we called it. In the States it was the I.W.W. – the Wobblies. People forget what a mess it was before the unions. The bosses could do anything, and you had no rights at all. None.'

It was a cold day, and he wore a windbreaker over his sweater. He went down on the bus and someone met him and they drove out of the town, not far. It was evening and the farmworkers' camp was full. Some of the men with families, the wife and kids, no place else to live anyway.

'Your father told them they weren't alone. There were other workers at other farms. There were people who would help, would put the screws on the bosses for a change. The power would come from working together, from workers joining together in a union.'

Lawrence's family had come to Canada from Scotland: his father had been a shipyard worker. With his brothers he learned to sing the proud song of a Glaswegian drunk: 'I belong to Glasgow, good old Glasgow town ... but when I get a drink on a Saturday night, Glasgow belongs to me.' The boys shouted and stomped. The Saturday night booze-up custom was well established in his family: sometimes he started his boozing on Friday, to get a jump on the others. They were proudly competitive about how much they could drink. The next day they'd compare hangovers – who had the worst, what they drank and where. All of them vigorous, argumentative, authoritarian. Predatory, preening. They grew up squabbling, shouting, punching. Trying to outdo each other. Their mother said: *'Hidje yur whisht,'* which meant, more or less, Be quiet, shut up. Their father said: 'I'll draw my han' off yur jaw,' which meant he'd slap his hand on your jaw first, then he'd draw it off.

My father was the third child in a string of ten. He hated his name. 'Lawrence' was a stuck-up name, he said, a sissy name. He held it against his parents that they had given him such a moniker, with no middle name to choose from, to better himself. All his brothers had middle names. His brothers had proper first names too, real men's names: George, Bert, Dave, John, Roy.

'Lawrence! What kind of name is that for a man like me?' He had been named after a neighbour in the town where they used to live, where he was born. He didn't look like any of his brothers: his hair was different, his eyes were different. He glowered over the injustice of his name, his face. He was the smartest of the lot too, which he interpreted darkly, wondering where his sharp mind had come from. He suspected his mother of everything but that. Adultery, yes, but not intelligence, never that.

He was one of the lucky ones: late in the Depression he had a job. He was paid a small salary by the Party. In his official portrait his hair is slicked back with Brylcreem, in the style of the thirties. His long jaw is closely shaven, glossy. He is blond, blue-eyed. Lean and, I have to admit it, handsome. Wearing a suit – trousers with suspenders, a white shirt. The jacket double-breasted. A hat – fedora. You hold the crown between your thumb and forefinger to make the indents on each side, the brim curves lightly down in front, up at the back. Some kind of tie, wide.

The photograph was taken by the Party, something the newspapers could use when they reported on a meeting. And that the RCMP used later, when they were hunting for him. In the picture he looks very stern. These were not times when politicians dared to smile. Life was grim; the voters were not amused. The photograph is excellent: his mouth is firm, his jaw thrust forward slightly, his eyes look into the near distance, fixing someone across the room with a look that would be called forceful. Full of something more than confidence – righteousness, maybe. A man ready and able to command. You could almost see him in a uniform.

A picture. Lawrence, up on a stage, standing at the podium. Acknowledging the applause. The words of his speech, neatly typed by my mother, would be available for the newspaper reporters so that they could be accurate in their stories of this dynamic young Party leader.

During his time in the Soviet Union he learned the custom of the performer applauding the audience, responding to their ovation.

He does this now, a man of the people. Standing centre stage looking strong but humble, applauding back to the audience as they stand cheering him. His family is in the front row. Pretty wife, two young children. They stand with the audience, proud of this father, of course. Proud of the political speech he has delivered with such vigour.

He gestures to his wife and she guides the children to the steps, up onto the stage. The three of them stand beside him awkwardly. The children shy, embarrassed. Andy holds his right hand up in what looks like a salute, but he's just shielding his eyes from the spotlight so that he can look up at his father's face glowing with the idealism of this magnificent political movement. He is proud to be the son of such a man. Beneath his brown argyle sweater, under his grown-up shirt and tie, his back carries the scars of his father's recent teachings in the uses of power.

When my brother and I played together, we fought. It seems to be the way we played.

We were squabbling over possession of a broomstick – a good toy – both of us hanging on to it, shrieking at each other, shouting.

The room, as I remember it, was big and empty. Had we just moved in, moved to another town again? There was no furniture. I picture the front door. My father opening it, coming in, bumping on the side of the doorway as he comes through. He can barely stand up; he's drunk. I don't remember him speaking at all. An angry face. He has great speed when he's angry, snatches the broomstick from our hands and starts flailing at us. The broomstick hits my shoulder, Andy's back, comes around again and smashes my arm. I'm screaming. My mother rushes in from the kitchen, 'Stop it! Stop it!' she says, 'Are you crazy?' There is no place to hide.

When I was grown up I watched a late-night movie – early Lillian Gish – silent, flickering, black-and-white images. A bone-thin girl, terrorized by the brutal father, who bullies her, slaps her, threatens her. Toward the end of the movie, he picks up a stick, a club, and chases her around the room. She ducks and runs and weaves around the small room as he comes after her. I sat staring at the blinking black-and-white screen. The girl cries out; the subtitle flashes: 'Don't do it, Daddy. Don't do it.' The image returns and she crouches and cowers in the corner as he swings the stick. 'Don't do it, Daddy. They'll hang you for it.'

I saw my own image duck and weave and turn in my mind as my father swung the broom handle at me, at my back, at my legs, again and again. My mouth whispered the words, *Don't do it, Daddy.*

8. JELL-O

I was going into a restaurant with my family. My mother and father and my brother. They waited for me while I threw up at the curb. I had appendicitis and I would throw up a lot until after my operation.

We all sat down at a table – a booth – in the restaurant. The table was cluttered; some other family had just left; we slid in along the benches. My brother and my dad on one side, with my brother trapped in the corner – he hated that – my mother on the other side, with me sliding in beside her. The youngest in the family, and the shortest too, I can see what no one else sees. Just under the edge of the plate, right in front of me: two bits. I thought someone must have lost it. It was just lying there on the table, under the edge of the plate. I was very quick. No one saw me. I had it in my pocket before my mum even finished tucking her skirt under her. I don't think I'd ever had so much money. I knew I should give it to the lost and found. But I didn't. I think it was the first time I ever stole anything, and I don't even know what happened to it. Maybe I told Andy. Maybe he bought me some candy and kept the rest of the money himself. I don't know.

At the restaurant I didn't eat anything but Jell-O. My father had Salisbury steak with mashed potatoes and peas. My mother had fish and chips; Andy had a grilled cheese sandwich and some of her chips. 'Why don't you have something to eat?' my mum would coax me. But I knew if I ate anything I'd just have to throw up. So I only ate things that were easy to throw up. Like Jell-O. Maybe it was supposed to be a party before I went to the hospital.

When they cut open my belly to take out the appendix it made a long scar with big stitches across it that always made me think of a railway track. After the operation I ate more Jell-O, and ice cream. That's what kids eat when they're sick, even today. My mother and Andy came to visit me. I had to stay there for over a week, because some other kind of infection started, right where they cut me open. Andy would tell me stories about what he had been doing while I was away and I'd say 'Oh, don't make me laugh, please don't make me laugh, it hurts so much.' And I'd laugh and it hurt my stitches and I'd cry and laugh both at the same time. That was my brother and me, right there!

That scar is big and long. When my doctor looked at it recently, she said, 'They certainly made a mess of that one, didn't they.' I said, 'It was a long time ago.' She told me, nowadays the scars are tiny, what they call bikini incisions.

The long scar on my belly means: Take the consequences; throwing up is terrible, so be careful what you eat. It means: laughter sometimes hurts, but it's worth it. It means, if you wear a bikini it reveals a lot about your past.

9. GOING UNDERGROUND

We moved to Calgary. In the summer of 1939 we lived in an apartment near Chinatown, my mother, my father, Andy and me. The comrades came to our house to talk about what was going on in Europe, discussing the threat of Fascism, the fall of Madrid. Some of the boys were coming home from Spain. The Munich pact: 'They are just *giving* Czechoslovakia to Hitler!' The Russian-German pact: 'It's necessary, that's all. England won't help Russia if Germany invades.'

For a birthday present Andy gave me a jar of minnows that he caught down by the river.

'Happy birthday, kiddo.' He was excited about catching them. 'If you take care of them, you can see them turn into frogs.'

This was the birthday that came just before the start of the war and other troubles. I think that was in Calgary. Yes, I'm sure it was Calgary. My mother gave me a special treat that was half a cantaloupe filled with ice cream and some dark red cherries around the edge. I had never had anything like that before in my life, and it was so beautiful. Andy got one too and we sat at the table in front of the window where she put a tablecloth on and everything. It was really delicious and you had to scoop the cantaloupe with your spoon. But really I didn't feel too much like eating, so I asked my mother to finish it for me. And then she could taste how good it was too. The ice cream was a bit melty by then.

The minnows that Andy gave me were supposed to grow into frogs and I was supposed to watch them. But by accident I poured them down the sink after a couple of days. I was mortified. It really was an accident, they were just there sitting in the jar and I was helping with the dishes and oops, there they went, but Andy thought I didn't appreciate his present. Well, I certainly did, because I liked to get presents even if it was something I didn't like, and I would never, never have thrown them out. Oh, well. So he was mad at me. He said he'd never give me another present, and then the next thing, right before school started, there was the war.

But before the war, there was a great mess all over Europe, with all the countries trying to decide which side to be on. Would they fight Germany, or would they fight Russia? That's what my mother said. Which was the worst enemy, Communism or Fascism? Russia said no one would help her if Germany attacked. England wouldn't, certainly. Help the Communists? Don't be ridiculous. And then Russia and Germany made a pact. Molotov, that was the Russian, and Ribbentrop, that was the German, agreed not to fight each other. And no one knew what to think. My mother said, 'Well, Russia needs time to prepare for war. War with Fascism will come, that's a real certainty, but the pact will give Russia time to prepare.'

I remember the day war was declared. The ninth of September, 1939. Two weeks after my ninth birthday. I heard the newspaper boy calling outside the window. That's what they used to do – call out the headlines. 'Extra. Extra. Canada declares war on Germany. Get your paper. Extra Extra. War declared in Europe.' It was the end of summer, right after Labour Day.

Pretty soon the comrades started to arrive. They always got together to talk politics. They were thrilled about the war. 'At last we can really fight the Fascists,' they said. And up the stairs came Ned, in uniform already. (We kids had given him the secret nickname of Bouncing Ned because of the way he walked.) 'I've enlisted. First thing this morning. I'm going. Off to fight the Fascists, isn't it great? No more appeasement.'

Oh, how everyone stared and talked and some of the comrades congratulated him. He strutted around the kitchen in his uniform.

'Just wait a while,' my father said. 'Wait till we see what the Party says.'

Everyone talked at once. 'It's time to teach the Fascists a lesson.'

'Yes, I know. But cool down a bit and think about it before you rush off to enlist.'

And the Party, the Party. No one knew what to do. They changed their plans every two minutes, from what I heard, but no one actually said that.

My father couldn't go to war. He had a wife and kids. The young comrades – the unmarried ones – rushed off to join up.

Comrade Leslie was there early one morning. Six o'clock, it wasn't even light yet. He'd been out all night.

He came to warn my father: 'The RCMP's on a rampage.'

My mother poured a cup of tea for him. Andy and I stood there in our pyjamas.

'All the comrades who joined the army are being rounded up. There's talk of concentration camps somewhere – using the old Depression camp in Kananaskis to keep the boys locked up.'

My mother tried to make sense of it. 'But look at the Party's anti-Fascist record. We've been against Hitler from the beginning.'

'Sure. We know that. But it doesn't matter. We're war enemies now, the same as the Germans, because of the pact with Moscow, and they'll be after all the leadership.'

He took my dad's arm and pulled him down into a chair at the kitchen table. 'Look, Lawrence, Sonya and I are going into hiding for a while. We're going to send Tommy to his grandparents again. You'd better disappear too, or you'll be in jail. They're looking for Tim, of course, but he's safe. The other leaders are going underground too.'

'Okay, okay, I understand. I'll go. What about Ellen and the kids?'

We were standing right there, my mother and Andy and me.

'Well, you can't all disappear together. You'd be too easy a target. You and Ellen will have to go separately, and you'd better put the kids somewhere.'

Ellen leaned against the kitchen stove, her hand over her mouth. Andy and I just stood there listening, like we always listened to everything. Always ready to do what we were told.

10. THE LITTLE COMRADES

While the RCMP was hunting for our parents my brother Andy and I stayed with strangers. If my father had been found, they'd have shipped him to a prison camp, like the other communist leaders, so my parents went underground in 1939. When I imagined them in hiding, I saw dark earthen basements with spiders and centipedes, damp and scary.

My father and a comrade dug a hole in the back yard of a safe house and planted a sack full of books. All the books in the house had to be hidden before my parents went underground – anything that seemed incriminating. *Das Kapital* and the *Communist Manifesto*, of course, and *The Conditions of the Working Class in England.* But even books by good old American authors. Steinbeck, *Of Mice and Men, The Grapes of Wrath.* Subversive, the lot of them. And all my mother's library of favourite Russian authors – Tolstoy, Chekhov, Dostoyevsky. Even *Crime and Punishment* was subversive.

Living in a communist family meant that our ordinary lives were not like those of other children. My brother and I called our parents' friends by their first names, not Mr or Mrs Whatzit, the way children did in the real world. We called the comrades George or Steve or Harry. In the Party, formal titles were *vestiges of bourgeois ideology;* the Party was *egalitarian,* my mother explained. That meant everyone is equal. Except kids, we knew that. We still had to do what our parents said. From them we had to learn discipline and obedience. Everyone in the Party learned that too.

When there was a meeting or when our parents talked about someone who wasn't there, they'd say Comrade Paul or Comrade Ted, so that it was clear they were talking about the person's political identity. My father was Comrade Lawrence and my mother was Comrade Ellen.

When it was time for my parents to go underground, Andy and I were sent to the home of Mrs Sketchley, across the street from a large open park or woodland, up a hill about three blocks from a streetcar line. Ellen had asked a druggist on the other side of the park if he knew anyone who took in boarders and didn't mind children. That's how she got Mrs Sketchley's name. Ellen's success in getting this information from someone who didn't know who she was convinced her that she had left no trail. It wasn't a boarding house, Mrs Sketchley just took in lodgers occasionally to make a little money. She wasn't a comrade so we always called her by her formal lady's name; so did Ellen.

My mother explained everything to us. The RCMP was looking for my father, so he had to hide, and she had to hide so that they couldn't make her tell where he was or put her in jail, and we kids had to not know anything so that we couldn't tell anything. We had to be very grown up and responsible, she said, and behave ourselves. That was the best thing we could do for the Party in these difficult times. She took us to Mrs Sketchley's on the streetcar and then went away and we didn't know when we would see her again.

Mrs Sketchley liked children, she said, and had a grown-up daughter of her own who came to visit sometimes. Her husband was dead, I think. She took in boarders in her spare room, so Andy had that room and I slept in the bed with her. That was not something I liked. She was very fat and I'd never shared a bed with a big person before, only occasionally slept in a bed with my mother, who was very small and thin. I was very small and thin too and I was afraid Mrs Sketchley would roll over and squash me. She liked puddings and said she was really glad to have someone who appreciated them the way she did. Sometimes she made small pancakes for a special Sunday tea, little flat golden ones about three inches across and sprinkled with sugar. I never had so much pudding in my life.

I was in grade four at Haultain school that year. She had to sign my report card, 'M. Sketchley'. I wasn't a very good pupil, I'm afraid; my report card was full of 'could do better'. I got Ds in Self Reliance and Neatness.

In Mrs Sketchley's bedroom I found a small wooden doll's bed, and a doll with blond hair painted in curls around its face. I'd never seen anything like it before in my life. It was hidden behind the skirt of Mrs Sketchley's dressing table. I was playing with it when she came into the room. 'Oh, no,' she said. 'No no no you can't play with that.' She took it away and put up on the top shelf of the wardrobe. 'I'm sorry, dear,' she said. I didn't know what to make of it and tried hard not to cry. I didn't have any toys. Maybe they were underground too.

Across the street at the edge of the hill was a dug-out cave where Andy helped me make a house. We dug ledges for us to sit on and dug niches into the dirt wall, like shelves to put things on. I put up pieces of broken dishes, or I picked some flowers and put them in a medicine bottle, and we made books out of folded-up school paper and put them on the shelves. Andy wrote messages in the books in a secret code he made up, in case anybody found them. It was like our own *underground*, where we could share our parents' lives, the spiders and centipedes, the damp and fragrant earth, even though we didn't know where they were. That was a good discovery, the cave. It made the unknown underground less frightening.

In the spring there were flowers that came up all over the hillside, crocuses, purple and yellow like the ones in Vancouver. Here in

Calgary they were covered with a soft white fuzz, like a fur coat to keep them warm in the cold Alberta spring.

When we were at Mrs Sketchley's I met the RCMP in person at last. I had heard about them for years, just listening to my parents talk, listening to the comrades. Andy and I were playing on the street outside the house and the two men came up to us, one talking to Andy, the other to me. I knew right away they were RCMP. It was almost as if my mother was right there warning me. It was just like she said, they wore careful suits with shirts and ties like men did when they were dressed up for not going to work. They wore hats and had shiny shoes. They were not 'working men', I could see that. The one who talked to me was tall and thin; everything about him was thin, a long thin nose, a thin moustache over a thin mouth. And a thin blue tie. When he was talking to me he bent over but I couldn't really see his face then. He was the size of a real person and I was just a little girl looking his tie in the face.

He asked me where my father was and I told him 'I don't know' because I didn't, but I knew I mustn't tell him anyway. And my mother, where was my mother, he asked, and it was the same answer for the same reason. But the next question was trouble. I knew as soon as he said it. 'When did you last see your mother?' I didn't know how to answer it, since I had seen her just three or four days before, when we had a secret meeting on the streetcar at the bottom of the hill.

Mrs Sketchley took us down the hill that day but she didn't say what for. 'It's a surprise,' she said. And we waited at the streetcar stop. She told us then, 'Your mother will be on the streetcar. You have to be very good and not call attention to yourselves. Just get on and walk to the back as if you see her every day.' One streetcar came along and she said, 'No, not that one,' and then another, and I saw she was looking at the last window when it stopped. A long red streetcar with the electric pole reaching up to the cable line overhead.

'This one,' she said and she put streetcar tickets into our hands and pushed us up the steps. We were very quiet and good, like we knew how to be, and walked right to the back of the car. Andy led the way and I don't think anyone noticed us at all. We were just ordinary kids. We sat with our mother and talked. She said she missed us very much and asked us about school and how we were and that sort of thing. I didn't tell her about getting Ds at school, I was too ashamed. I sat on one side of her and Andy sat on the other side and we talked together all the way out to the end of the line. The streetcar turned around and we went back along the same street. Then my mother said we would have to get out at the next stop and Mrs Sketchley would be there to meet us. She told me, 'Now don't cry! You mustn't make a scene or I won't be able to meet you this way again. The RCMP is still looking for us.'

Andy and I got off the streetcar when it stopped and there was Mrs Sketchley. I ran to her and tried to stretch my arms around her big body. She hugged me, but it was no good, I really needed to cry.

So now there was the RCMP tall guy right in front of me asking me when was the last time I saw my mother and I couldn't tell him, but I knew he'd keep on asking me, and I was scared. I might tell on my mother by accident, I might become a stoolie by accident. I knew I had to stop him from asking me again. I looked at his face up there above the tie and I started to cry. 'I want my mother.' I let my emotions loose and sobbed at him, 'I want my mother, I want my mother.'

He started to back away from me. I could see he didn't know what to do with a crying girl. So I just kept crying, not little sniffly sounds like I usually make, but big strong noisy crying. I just opened the gates to hysteria. I could see Andy out of the corner of my eye wondering what was going on. He'd never seen me do anything like that before. And then he started being a kid too. 'You leave her alone, you big bully.' Ten years old and he started pounding my tall guy's chest. 'You leave my sister alone.'

The two guys left. 'Okay, kids, forget it, just forget it, okay?' they said.

Andy and I stood close together and I kept on gulping and wailing while we watched them walk down the hill, talking, looking back at us. When they were out of sight, Andy and I looked at each other and sort of smiled. He put his arm across my shoulder.

'Good going, comrade,' he told me.

'You too, comrade,' I told him back.

11. SNEAKERS

The river. I was with my brother at the river, the creek, where we played along the edge. 'Don't get all wet, now,' my mother said when we left. 'Andy, you take care of her.' I bet he was sick of hearing that. But today we weren't fighting. We had taken our shoes off – sneakers – and put them under the dogwood on the bank. We walked in the water, stepping on the big round boulders near the shore. Our feet tried to bend around the bulges, slid into the spaces. Andy had rolled up his pant legs, up above his knees, and he was going out from the shore. I tucked my dress up into the legs of my panties to keep it dry. My feet were freezing cold. This icy water had come down from the mountains, seeping along the ragged banks, sucking out the red earth. I didn't even feel the jagged piece of glass that sliced my toe from nail to joint. The blood rushed out to show me, plumes drifting downstream. I backed up toward shore to sit down; I had to pull my dress out of the panties and lift up the back so I didn't sit on it. Keep it clean. I lifted my foot out of the water and blood rushed everywhere. I couldn't even tell where it was coming from.

Of course I yelled to Andy. He was angry: 'You little fool, now look what you've done.' I wasn't really crying – he hated it when I cried. But I could tell he was scared. There was a lot of blood. If I got hurt when I was with him, it was his fault, maybe. He was afraid he'd get a whipping, but he knew we had to go home.

He helped me put my sneakers on. One foot was fine; dried with my sock, the shoe on. Not the other foot; there was blood all over. Andy got some leaves from the bush and wrapped up my toes, put the sock on. He loosened the laces in my shoe and spread it wide open so I could get my foot in, my heel hanging over the back. 'Lean on me,' he said and we started to walk home. I could see the blood start to stain through my white sneakers. New ones, too. All through the front, over the inside toe. Dark red ooze.

Andy didn't get a whipping, because he helped me and didn't do anything stupid. My mum took me for stitches. When we got back home we put my sneaker into soapy water. 'Use cold water because of the blood,' my mother said. I washed the shoe and tried to bleach it.

When it was dry I put white shoe cleaner on it, but the blood was always there, brown deep into the canvas. I could always see it.

The scar on my toe was very thin and neat. I didn't really mind it. It was always my brother helping me. It meant, *use cold water if you're bleeding.* It meant, learn to live with accidents; cover them up as best you can. But they'll always show.

12. RUNNING AWAY

Running away from home. We all did it. My brother the most: the most often, the most successfully. Perhaps he had the least baggage, the fewest ties. When he was just a baby there was nothing he could do to save himself, but when he got old enough to find his way to the corner Andy ran away.

Afterwards he had to learn it was no use. Someone would always find him, or he would return of his own volition, what else could he do? And he always got it worse when he came back, for running. He was a kid who was always in trouble. He couldn't win for losing, Andy.

Running away. My whole family: my mother, my brother, me.

My brother Andy and I ran away together once, when I was just a little kid, oh maybe I was five. For a whole day we lived on raw carrots and small white turnips from someone's garden. We were up on a hill close to the viaduct where we could stand at the cement edge and look down on the cars on a busy street. Everyone seemed to have a place to go, walking or driving cars. We lay down on the edge and stuck our heads over. Andy talked about spitting on people's heads but he didn't do it. It wasn't a good idea to draw attention to ourselves.

We could have stayed away longer but it began to get dark, so he thought I wanted to go home, at least that was what he said. Maybe he was the one who wanted to go home. All I know is I wanted some water to wash the carrots. And I didn't like going to the bathroom out in the woods; I thought Andy peeked at me when I went in the bushes to pee.

We talked about going home, or about going off somewhere on our own. I said, 'We're too young, Andy. We need them.' He said, 'They need us more than we need them.' I had no idea what he meant. But he was known to be a smart boy.

We both got a licking for running away. His was worse than mine, because he was seven and was supposed to know better and he certainly shouldn't have taken his little sister with him, teaching her disobedience. After that, he didn't take me with him.

One time Andy was away for four days. My mother was frantic, but she couldn't call the police. If you were a communist you couldn't trust the police. She asked all around the neighbourhood, asked everyone. Andy spent his days wandering around downtown, trying to sneak into movies, or down at the dump just poking around looking for useful stuff. He spent his nights in the hall bathroom of the building where we lived, as though keeping an eye on us to make sure we didn't move away and leave him behind.

He stole food from milk wagons and bakery delivery vans – cinnamon buns were his favourite, he said later, then jelly rolls after that. He finally let himself be found. He was bored, more than anything. He couldn't think where to go. He had no place to go. He was ten. That was just after my father got back from being away.

I remember that building. It was never made for apartments; it was for offices. The place where we lived was an office suite. We used the waiting room for our living room. That was where my father kicked the Christmas tree over because he was so angry at my mother just because she decided not to cook Christmas dinner since he wasn't home. One room had a stove and a sink in it. That was the kitchen where our mother cooked our meals, except she didn't cook Christmas dinner, she took us out to a restaurant because my father didn't come home from the Christmas Eve party until it was already the nighttime of Christmas Day and the day was all over and we had opened our presents and everything. And then he came home late and he had brought a guy with him to have a good Christmas dinner he promised him, with the wife and kids even if it was ten o'clock at night. And we kids were already in our beds in one of the offices that we used for bedrooms. But we woke up and came out into the waiting room when he started hollering at my mother. He was angry because she had 'shown him up', he said, in front of his friend that he had promised dinner to.

My father had been gone for two years, studying in the Soviet Union. Studying Marxism, political theory and the rights of the working class, dialectical materialism: we all had a hard time getting used to each other again. Andy had forgotten how to do what he was told. To behave. You have to learn how to behave yourself, that's the key. I didn't run away, but I got sick and managed to stay sick for nearly a year: scarlet fever, mumps, chicken pox, appendicitis.

When my mother ran away she always had to take us kids with her, and that made it all a lot more difficult. The next summer, when I was about nine years old, she bolted. My brother was spending that summer in Calgary with cousins. Maybe she was getting him away from my father, I didn't think of that at the time. But it made it easier for her to run away, having only one child to take care of.

In the years that my father was away, my mother was the one who decided everything for the family; she was the one with the responsibility and she could manage it. She had a part-time job, she shared a couple of furnished rooms with another woman. She went to meetings, took on Party work, raised money for sending the MacPaps to Spain, went for picnics with the kids, visited friends, invited friends home for spaghetti. Whatever she wanted, whenever she wanted, as long as she could pay for it somehow. She didn't make much money, but she was the one who figured out what was the best thing to do and she did it. Independence.

When he came home, everything changed. Now she had to ask him about everything, and mostly he'd say no. That summer the Party was planning a political school at a camp outside Calgary. He would be attending as a speaker and she wanted to be a delegate. She felt she had earned the right to be treated like a real person, not just his wife. But he said no.

'I don't want my wife getting special treatment.'

'It's not special treatment, Lawrence. The organizers want me to go. I was involved in Party work all the time you were away.'

'I said no, Ellen! Two functionaries in one family won't work. Your job is to be my wife and to help me. I'm back now, and I'm the one who makes those decisions. And I say I don't want you attending.'

So much for her precious freedom and independence.

So she left. While he was out at work she packed a suitcase and we walked to the bus station.

'How much is the fare to Macleod? One adult and one child. One way.'

She went to her mother's little house in Macleod, but her mother was recuperating from gall bladder surgery. Ellen and I shared the little bed that used to be hers when she was a girl. She wanted to go to Calgary to look for a job, but I hung on her, her mother was sick, what could she do?

She took me to Lethbridge with her, on the bus, with money her mother gave her. And we stayed with the Chaffee family.

Ted Chaffee was a friend, a *Party sympathizer*, and one of the people who thought Ellen was bright and capable. He was a bore, lecturing like some teacher all the time. *Pontificating*, Ellen said. A mouthful of a word, full of little pointed bits. What a perfect word to learn that day. But he knew a lot, I could tell. The house was dark and smelled of wet dog.

I read some wonderful books while we stayed at that house. Heavy books in red bindings with gold on the front; Books of Knowledge, some history, some science, some Greek myths. I remember Sisyphus rolling a big stone up the hill and it would always roll back down, over and over again. I certainly knew what that felt like; like things couldn't ever change, you just had to keep on pushing the same old rock up the same old hill. But while we were at the Chaffees' and I had all those stories to read, I thought things were pretty good. They made a bed for me on the living room couch and in the middle of the night I'd get up and turn on the little lamp. I'd find the next book in the series and read another myth. The Golden Oranges, or were they golden apples?

Ted Chaffee persuaded Ellen to think about learning Pitman shorthand. 'You'll always be able to make a living,' he said. His wife said nothing. Maybe he didn't want his wife to make a living.

My father drove to Lethbridge to get her in a brand new Chrysler he'd made the Party buy for him, cream coloured, with lots of chrome. What a fuss when he parked it in front of the house, the neighbours looking. He explained to Ellen, 'I told them that it's important to upgrade the image of the Party. We are no longer only an organization of the poor and unemployed. We must be ready and able to govern; we need to look more formal, more capable.' It certainly was a capable car.

'Lawrence, I'm not going back with you the way things are,' she told him.

'We can talk about it, can't we? You know I want you to come home.'

My father stayed so they could talk things over. The Chaffees camped out in the back yard in their trailer and my mother and father slept in the bedroom. I knew then that she'd go back to him. She always went back after they talked things over in bed.

On the couch in the living room I didn't feel like reading. I put a pillow over my face and held it there, trying to suffocate myself. *Two's company, three's a crowd*, I told myself. They had each other, they didn't want me. Over and over again – all night it seemed – I kept trying to kill myself. *Two's company, three's a crowd*. My lungs wouldn't let me do it. I'd turn over and put my face in the pillow, a cushion over my head, hold it down. Try again. I fell asleep of course, or maybe unconscious. But my lungs rescued me.

We all went to the political camp, the whole family. Andy and I hung around outside the big tents where the comrades sat on hard wooden benches in their shirtsleeves, listening, talking. The Fascists, the fall of Spain, a war to come, strategy and tactics. Organizing the unorganized.

The dry prairie grass crunched under my brown sandals; I squatted beside the gopher holes – a city child on the long curving hills, under the screaming sun. Andy tied a lasso for me and laid it with his great cunning around one of the holes. He put the end of the rope in my hands, taught me to wait and watch, to yank the rope at the right moment. Eventually in the hot afternoon, the sun scorching the top of my head, I caught a gopher. I led him around for hours, my little pet on a leash, and eventually he stopped struggling to escape, stopped trying to run away. My little pet, I thought he'd be my friend then. I stooped to pat him and he bit my hand, ran, jumped. Away, away, and dived back into a hole, to his home underground.

In one of my mother's flights from my father she moved to Vancouver in 1942. My father came after her and gave her a cocker spaniel puppy, which she called 'Happy'. Was she, I wonder?

In Vancouver, probably 1943. My friend Lorraine and I took Happy's puppies to the front yard for an outing. My frizzy hair is the result of what was then called by its full name, a 'permanent wave'. I hated my straight hair. So did my mother. 'Your hair is just like your father's. I hated his hair,' she said.

13. NOT REALLY CONFESSING

The Party was underground for about two years, because of Russia being on the wrong side at the beginning of the war. And the war wasn't going so well. Germany was winning all over Europe – Belgium, France, Holland, all the way from Norway to Greece. I was ten years old and almost exactly on my birthday France surrendered to Germany. And Britain was getting bombed. In Canada the RCMP was everywhere. The undercover agents would be one of the crowd, fitting in; maybe your best buddy even. For my father, a drinking buddy, the one who always said, 'Come on, Lawrence, have another one. You're not the kind of guy to let your wife boss you around. What's the harm in having a little fun?' Sitting in the beer parlour, the smell of stale beer and cigarette smoke soaking into their clothes. Just getting relaxed. Talking, a few beers. A bit of bragging, what's the harm? It makes you feel good among your buddies. They would be interested, eager to know everything. To hear his advice, his plans. He was a great talker, my father.

She ran away again, my mother, to Vancouver. Andy and I both went with her this time, on the train. She left my father back in Alberta, where no one would talk to him because he had disgraced the Party and been expelled. *Drunken hooliganism*, they said. I knew it was a disgrace, but I loved the sound of those words. The dance of the consonants in my mouth, with the spiky k, the long refreshing ghostly howl of the double oo in the middle, then sliding over the top of the hill and down to the bottom of the ism. What a game! And besides, it meant my father got what he deserved. The words were like a punch in the face.

My mother found a small furnished apartment, because she had left everything behind in Calgary, just got on the train with two suitcases and two children. It wasn't much of an apartment, not much furniture. Andy slept on the couch in the living room and I shared the bed with my mother. But my father came after her again.

What I remember is waking up in the night with the bed jolting and, still in my sleep really, I said, 'Stop bouncing the bed, stop bouncing it.' And my mother saying 'Shush now, Laurie. Go back to sleep.' And my father made a deep grumbling sound, and she said 'Just wait a minute dear, she'll go back to sleep.' And then I did, but I woke up again. I didn't say anything because I didn't want my father to get mad at me. He sounded mad. 'Why can't she sleep on the floor? She's just a kid, she won't know the difference.' I didn't want to sleep on the floor, so I kept my mouth shut. My brother Andy always said keep your mouth shut if you don't want to get in trouble. He should know, he was always in trouble whether he kept his mouth shut or not. After a while it stopped bouncing. The bed. That was a secret I never told anyone.

My mother found a bigger apartment and my father moved in to live with us again and brought his friend Steve Cory Campbell, whose wife was left in Calgary to have her baby before she could travel.

'He was a Negro but didn't look it,' my mother said. 'Then what made him Negro,' I asked, 'if he wasn't dark?' 'You just knew,' she said. I always puzzled over that.

But in the meantime, my father bought two small beds for me and Andy, and Steve slept on the couch in the living room and Andy and I had to share a room with a blanket hung in the middle. My father bought my mother a puppy. She named him Happy.

And then when Germany invaded Russia, all the politics changed again. Now Russia was on the right side in the war, and Joseph Stalin became Uncle Joe, and the Russians were the good guys, so the Canadian Communists were out of jail again, and even legal. The Party started up again under a new name, Labour Progressive Party. My parents' political life picked up all the usual round of meetings, this time in support of the war effort, which meant supporting Russia. My father got an important job with one of the shipyard unions, my mother wrote for a newspaper, Andy and I were in school.

I was not a girl who could run away, not then. I didn't have the courage. But whenever I played hookey from school, which wasn't very often, that was a kind of flight. I'd take the streetcar downtown to Simpson's or Hudson's Bay, whichever appealed to me at the moment and I'd live in a little fantasy world. My favourite place was the ladies' waiting room outside the women's washrooms at the Hudson's Bay. I think it was Vancouver, but it could just as easily have been Calgary;

they run together in my mind. The room was full of white wicker furniture: sofas and chairs with flowered cushions, little desks with writing paper and pens in the drawers, the words Hudson's Bay Company in Old English print across the top. Sometimes I'd write letters to imaginary people, perhaps a nice aunt or a cousin, a girl friend. Sometimes I'd be feeling miserable and sorry for myself and I'd write a letter to my mother: *Dear Mama, I'm sorry if you have been worried, but I have run away....*

Of course I couldn't really run away then. I didn't have money to take care of myself and I was too young to get a job. Except I did have a job after school, taking care of a little kid until her mother got home from work. I had to get the girl – I think her name was Beth or Becky – at her school and walk her home. Then I'd give her a cookie '(And have one for yourself too,' her mother said) and I'd read to her for a bit and then she'd play in the yard. The apartment was on the ground floor, I remember that. There was a father but I never saw him. At four-thirty I had to peel some potatoes and put them in a pot with water and salt and put them on the stove at five: 'Start the supper,' her mother said. That was part of what I was getting paid for. I got ten cents every day. That's fifty cents for the week. I was trying to save up money for my independence, like my mother was.

What I liked was to go into the bathroom and try on all her lipsticks. She had about four different colours and I'd try them all, and she had a necklace of bright red discs like tiddly-winks that I think maybe I swiped. I don't remember for sure, so I'm not really confessing to this.

14. LUMPEN

There was linoleum on the floor of my room and wallpaper with green leaves and lilacs. My bed, a dresser, a bedside table. It's important to have a bedside table for a lamp and your book. When you're old enough, you have a clock. All my life I would have a lamp, a book, a clock. From now on.

I had the radio on in my room that morning. It was on the dresser. I was making my bed, changing the sheets, so it must have been Saturday morning. And I heard 'Pennies from Heaven' on the radio. I didn't remember ever hearing it before, but somehow I knew all the words. I still remember them. Bing Crosby singing about money falling from the clouds. It didn't occur to me that the pennies might not be real, might represent happiness or love or dreams. For me they were only money, real money. That was everyone's dream then.

This room was on the second floor; it had a window that looked out over the back alley. I think this may have been the room where my father beat me for the last time. I don't remember getting beaten ever after, which is not to say that it didn't happen, only that I don't remember. The thing about being beaten when you're a kid is that you really don't remember all the times. It's possible not to remember any of it, just not remember it at all. My brother Andy – who turned into a shuffly old man bragging into his vodka, just like my father became – to the day he died he didn't remember. He knew, though, because I told him. His mind would never let him remember the beatings, but I remembered.

'Lumpen, that's what they are.' My father was talking about the neighbours who lived down the back lane from our apartment. They had two kids that went to my school. I almost knew what *lumpen* meant. Something to do with the kind of work they did and their politics. Lumpen Proletariat was the whole name.

'I don't want you to have anything to do with them,' he said.

They invited me to the park for Sunday afternoon. This was in Calgary. There was a big holiday picnic. 'No, you can't go with them,' my father said. I was ten or eleven years old. The war with Germany had started, and even Russia was in it now, so being a communist was okay. My father did political work, all the time, every day, making the world a better place for mankind, just as he'd done since before I was born.

I told the neighbours I couldn't go with them – 'My brother is going to take me,' I said. I thought maybe I'd see them there, but I couldn't say that. I didn't say that. I *know* I didn't say it. The boy had a crush on me. I was all nervous and edgy. Tantalized. They liked me.

When I got home there was a scene in my room. That room, the one I remember.

My father had seen me walking home with those neighbours and thought I had disobeyed him. I tried to tell him that I didn't *go* with them, I really didn't, that they just walked home with me when I couldn't find Andy. I was just being polite, I tried to tell him. They walked me home, that was all.

But it was no use. He said I had to get a licking for disobeying him. 'You've got to learn that what I say goes.' That's what he said. And he pulled down the window shade.

I had already begun crying, little sniffly crying, I was so scared. He unbuckled his belt and drew it out of the loops. Held the buckle in his right hand, wrapped the belt one turn around. The leather hung, swinging in front of my eyes, the round end snake-like, waving back and forth. I could see the holes – the line across in front of the fourth hole where the buckle fastened. The seconds took hours; I was staring at the snakey brown belt, hypnotized by fear.

He told me to turn around. 'You don't want me to hit you in the front, do you?' he said.

I had a quick vision of my brother Andy's face mashed red and purple last Christmas. It was better to turn around. Bend over.

The first swipe with the belt pushed me forward across the bed. The leather strap stung against my legs. I heard myself scream. My back. I screamed every time. Flash of cold, blaze of heat. Caught my breath and screamed.

Each mark was exactly belt-shaped, but larger, blurred around the edges where the blood vessels ruptured and bled into pale skin.

I learned to obey. I was a very good girl. I would be good until I was old enough to leave home and be as bad as I pleased.

The word is polluted now. *Lumpen*. Scarred in the dictionary of my mind, containing this memory. Always this room, this pain. Always the round end of the belt, my father's arm moving. Always the linoleum and lilacs.

15. PAYDAY

Friday nights, payday, we would wait for my father to come home, to bring money so we could have dinner. When he got home, I was sent out to the grocery store – not my brother, because he always lost the change or said the storekeeper didn't give him any. I was much more responsible; a good girl, everyone said so. I bought potatoes and a pound of round steak and a can of corn niblets. That was our special dinner for Friday night. Sometimes we had ground round, because it was cheaper. My mum didn't like to buy hamburger. 'It's all fat,' she'd say. 'Ground round is better value for your money.' I liked saying it, like a poem: a pound of ground round.

We were all living in a second floor flat.

I had my books on the table in the living room, doing homework, and a mayonnaise jar filled with wild roses from the railway tracks, picked on the walk home from school. We each had a streetcar ticket for school every day – well, five for a week; to ride one way and walk the other. I tried to walk both ways so I could save up tickets for an emergency. Mostly we rode the streetcar in the morning. I was always ready before Andy but my mother made me wait for him; I thought she didn't want me to go alone, but it was probably that if Andy was alone he'd play hookey – never get to school at all. When we got out on the street he'd say, 'Come on, let's play hookey. We could go down by the river. Or we could go downtown to the 5 & 10, maybe snitch something.' 'Not me, Andy, I want to go to school.' 'Oh, Little Miss Goody-Goody.' He always called me that.

So this day, Andy teased and I cracked. Fury: my father's temper broke loose in me. I was always afraid of that temper, always afraid it would rage up and lash out the way my father lashed out. I threw the jar of flowers at him, hard. I guess it was a good thing Andy ducked, or it would have really hurt him. The jar went sailing right over his head, crashing through the front window, glass clattering on the roof of the front porch. The sound of the crash broke the ball of fury in my mind. 'Now you'll get it,' said Andy. 'Breaking the window! You'll get a licking for sure.'

That was when I ran away. Oh, I couldn't stand to get another licking. I couldn't stand it. I was already crying, just thinking about it. I put on my jacket and left. I used my emergency streetcar ticket to get downtown. It wasn't dark yet. I walked and walked through the downtown streets and finally found the bus station. I knew I was going to leave town, go off on my own somewhere and start my life. I was about eleven years old, trying to figure out how to make a new life for myself on my own. I could be a waitress, I thought.

It was late at night when I finally gave up and asked someone for a nickel to make a phone call. I started to cry just telling a stranger I had to phone home. Oh, I was such a crybaby. My brother was right.

When my mother answered the phone I told her, 'I'm afraid to come home. I'm afraid to get a licking.' So she came to the bus station to get me, and I didn't get a licking. Andy yelled at me the next day: 'It's not fair. *You* break the window and *I* get a licking.' He was right, it wasn't fair.

My mother must have done something, found some magic words to say to my father that he really heard. Or maybe just giving Andy a licking then was enough, maybe he didn't need to beat up on *two* kids. I never got another licking and I never ran away again. Not until my mother and I ran away together. For good.

16. THE MORAL QUANDARY

'It's a moral quandary,' my mother said. I frowned at her and she tried to explain. 'I mean that I don't know what's the *right* thing to do. It's a real dilemma.' Oh, I loved her words! There we sat, just eating breakfast, and she served up to me *quandary* and *dilemma* with my toast.

The moral quandary had to do with strawberries. Here it was, early June in Vancouver, and the strawberries were ripening in the fields of the Japanese farmers.

Once Japan came into the war on Germany's side, it really was a World War, not just a European one. The Party was against the expulsion of the Japanese from the West Coast. The Canadian government, she told me, had passed some kind of law back in January, that all the Japanese had to move away from the Pacific Ocean. They were actually being shipped away, and put into some of the camps where the unemployed men had stayed during the Depression. Everything they owned was just taken from them. So, all during that spring, Vancouver was moving the Japanese people out, how many thousands my mother couldn't tell me. They turned the stadium at Hastings Park into a place where the police just herded people. 'One suitcase apiece and that's it.' I went down there on the streetcar to see what was going on, but I couldn't get near. The place was full of cars that were being left behind, boxes and suitcases, people holding on to each other, crying.

We were at war with Japan, I knew that. I remembered years and years ago, even before the war, when I was just a kid learning to read, the words *Made in Japan* meant that I shouldn't buy it. Even when I was trying to find a present for my mother for ten cents. The Party was boycotting Japanese things, even the oranges at Christmas that year.

'And didn't the Japanese invade China?' I asked my mum.

'That's the Japanese government, and the army,' she told me. 'This is different. These people, these families, a lot of them were born here. This is their life, right here in B.C. They are Canadians, so the government shouldn't be able to just take their farms away like that. Just lock them up somewhere. It's horrible.

'It's like what Hitler is doing to the Jews,' my mother said. 'Just because they're Jews.'

So, on the one hand, the strawberries belonged to the Japanese farmers, not to us. But on the other hand, we had permission to take them. And, besides, and this was the really important thing, it was immoral to waste food. And there were those strawberries ripening in the fields. And the other thing we didn't really talk about, was that we were still hungry! So hungry for some kind of treats. First the Depression, then rationing, When was the last time we had strawberry jam? The fruit was ripening, and on the radio they said that anyone could go and pick anything ... fruit, vegetables, it was all just there, and it was free.

Sugar was rationed, of course, but my mother had some coupons she had been saving, and some from Gladys.

So my father's friend George drove us all out to Abbotsford. My mum, my brother, and me, with George's wife, Gladys. George and Andy in the front seat with my father, and Gladys, Mom and me in the back seat. (They said I could sit in the front seat between George and my father, but even with my father there I didn't want to be squashed up next to George, so I just went all sulky and they let me sit in the back. I didn't have words then for the kind of man George was. The uneasy sexual emanations. *Lecherous* came later to my vocabulary. I didn't even understand the word 'groping' yet.)

Picking strawberries is very hard. They grow right down on the ground, and you have to kneel in the dirt. Boy, did my knees hurt! And my neck, because you have to sort of scrunch your head down to look under the leaves to see where the strawberries are. Oh, but juicy!

When I first started picking I ate some, of course, and got strawberry juice all over me.

George and Lawrence didn't get down on their knees to pick any, but they would take the small pots and empty them into the big pots, at least at first. Mostly they stood around and smoked cigarettes and talked. Then they went to sit on the bench under a tree. They always talked politics. This was a period when it was acceptable to be a communist, when the Communist Party was legal, and even ran candidates in elections, so there was a lot of complicated political talk to be done by a lot of people. The men didn't have time for women's foolish concerns like strawberry jam.

We had some kind of containers – a big soup pot and a roasting pan, and a big enamel dishpan, I remember, and a couple of saucepans and bowls. Remember, this is before plastic! So we picked into the small containers and then poured the strawberries into the big ones. 'Be careful, be careful,' my mother said. 'Don't bruise them.' Because her big plan was that when we got home we would each have a bowl of strawberries and cream with the big fat berries, before we had to get down to the work of making jam.

I remember the hot sun on the back of my neck, and the imprint of the hard dirt into my knees. Between the pain in my neck, and the sore knees, pretty soon I started to be really tired of this excursion, and even the sweet, tart, juicy berries I could pop into my mouth were not enough to make me cheery about it. The first half hour or so wasn't bad, but after that … ouch. I guess we picked for a couple of hours. And then we had to somehow fit all those pots and pans into the car and all of the people too. For the trip back they made me sit in the front seat because I was smaller than Andy, and George and my father wouldn't be so squished. When I was climbing into the car I put my foot right into a washbasin full of berries that was on the floor, and I cried and cried. But my mother said it was okay. She said we had to wash the berries anyway, and they needed to be squashed for the jam.

So that was the way the moral quandary turned out. My family had strawberries, and the Japanese families got sent away to camps.

17. GETTING THROUGH THE WAR ON THE HOME FRONT

When we lived in Edmonton, King George and Queen Elizabeth had come to Canada and went on a tour right across the country, cheering us all up and maybe giving us a reason to want to help England in the war. We had an apartment over a store, right on the main street. My mother put pillows on the window sill so we could lean out and wave at them. The Queen's dress was pink and frilly, just as it should be, and the King wore a kind of uniform with lots of gold on it. I was disappointed that they weren't wearing their crowns, even though I knew that they wouldn't wear them outside. Not crowns, not on the street.

There were jobs for all the men once the war started in Europe. During the Depression there was no money to help the poor, but now the government had lots of money for soldiers, to pay for their uniforms and their guns, to feed them and send them away to Europe. Everyone had jobs now, now that there was a war. Once the men were in the army, women got jobs doing all the things men used to do, driving trucks, pumping gas, working in factories. Everything.

I was ten when my brother and I moved back to Vancouver with my mother – after my father was disgraced in Calgary. But no, that's wrong: he disgraced himself, nobody did it for him. The Communist Party expelled him. My mother was ashamed, and my brother too. Andy had been so proud to be the son of an important man. Now he didn't know what to think, now that the Party had thrown Lawrence out.

My mother got a part-time job with a newspaper – some typing, some writing – and we lived on the ground floor of a house near the cemetery. In Vancouver, the ground floor is just that, on the ground. No basement. But the apartment was okay. Two bedrooms and a living room/kitchen all in one. There was an old black wood stove and my mother had to learn how to work it. Because Vancouver was a lumber town there was a lot of sawdust, and the old wood-burning stoves had been adjusted with metal hoppers welded onto the side of the firebox, for holding the sawdust. It gave a steady even heat, my mother said, and was really good for baking. After dinner she rubbed the top of the stove with a piece of waxed paper to make it really black and shiny.

At the side of the house, there was a fenced yard with hydrangeas, white ones like snowballs. That was where Andy and I played with Happy, the new puppy that my father gave to my mother when he came to live with us again. A cocker spaniel puppy with long ears like curly blond hair, brown eyes, and a grinning happy mouth. At night the puppy whined in her little box-bed. My mother wrapped a clock in a towel and put it into the bed – I don't know how she thought of it – and Happy quieted right down. The ticking sound must have been comforting to that lonely puppy in a new home without her mother to cuddle up with.

My father got work at the shipyard. He carried a lunch pail to work every day, with two thick sandwiches and a piece of pie that my mother made and a thermos of tea. He was taken back into the Party despite his disgrace – the Party in Vancouver didn't care about anything that happened in Alberta. He soon had a job with the union. Shipwrights and Boilermakers. My mother kept her job, but now she had all that extra work, things like washing my father's overalls, scrubbing the dirty work clothes in the bathtub. But she was always there when we got home from school.

The war gave everybody jobs, so the hard times were over. Single men went into the services – army, navy, or air force, whichever seemed to suit their personalities. Everyone worked, to try to win the war against Germany, and it was important now to help the Russians, because that's where all the fighting was. The United States wasn't in the war yet, but some Americans came up to Canada and joined the Canadian Air Force. And women, too, were going into the army and the air force. I don't know about the navy. My brother Andy was desperate to join up, but he was just about fourteen – and small for his age to boot.

The front lawn was full of dogs when I got home from school. The porch too. I couldn't say how many. Two on the porch nudging each other. Snarling. Four or five smaller ones shoving around on the lawn. One thin old mutt lay sprawled out on the sidewalk, belly on the cool cement, just watching. Waiting his chance.

'Get away, get away.' I pushed past them and jiggled my way in through the door, nudging the dogs away with my feet. Brown shingle siding, wide steps up to the sheltering front porch. A typical Vancouver house.

My mother was inside with a pail of water. She opened the door and sloshed the water onto the nearest dog, who retreated down a few steps.

'What's going on, Mom? Why are all those dogs out there?'

'They're trying to get at Happy.'

'Get at?' A frightening thought. An attack?

'I guess she's come into season. She's old enough to have puppies.'

'How do they know?'

'They must have picked up her scent when I took her out this morning. They've been there all day. I've been trying to shoo them away, but they all keep coming back.'

'What are we going to do?'

She tried to reassure me.

'It should last only for a few days. Tonight we can scrub the porch and the steps and that might put them off the track. Then we'll just carry her a bit of a way down the block when we take her out. And pick her up when we come back. So her scent won't lead them to the house.'

'Happy doesn't smell any different to me.'

'A dog's sense of smell is better than people's. You know that.'

Happy was whining around, trying to get out the front door.

'Get away, Happy. Go on. Laurie, take her down to the basement and shut the door. And make sure the door to the back yard is locked.'

When I got back upstairs I went right back to asking questions.

'Could she have puppies some day? Could we let her have puppies?'

'Some day, yes. But not with any of those scruffy mongrels out on the street. She deserves better than that.'

She stepped outside and threw another pail of water on the dogs and they scattered.

Now that both our parents had jobs we had moved to a house. When you have a dog and two kids, the family needs more room. In the new house we all had our own bedrooms – Andy didn't have to sleep on the pull-out couch any more. There was a living room and a proper dining room – the first ever that I remember – three bedrooms and a bathroom on the second floor, and a real basement. The basement was useful to us because Happy could stay there in bad weather when we were all out during the day. In good weather she stayed out in the yard of course.

In the kitchen there was an icebox and a stove with a sawdust hopper. This one was much more modern than the old black one, it was up on legs and was covered with cream-coloured enamel. The oven door had the name scrolled on in pretty writing, Findley. The sawdust was kept in the basement, and it was Andy's job to scoop it up into a pail and fill the hopper every evening so it would be ready for the next day. My mother always had to nag him. Always. Seemed he couldn't remember a darn thing. He was born for trouble, Andy.

Food was scarce, because most of the good things had to be sent overseas to the soldiers. The special things were rationed, only so much per week: meat, eggs, butter, sugar. Cigarettes, of course. And alcohol, that was rationed too. But still, we had a lot more food than we'd had during the Depression. These were good times starting; at least there was money to buy food. But women still had to be smart cooks to get by on what was available.

My mother had a recipe for a dessert called an eggless pudding. No eggs, no butter. But it did need sugar and flour and raisins. Not much else in it, I don't think, but some baking powder to make it rise. Sometimes I'd make it myself, standing at the stove stirring the sugar and water and raisins together and pouring the mixture on top of the dough. When it was baking the dough rose up to the top and the syrup made a sauce at the bottom. It was a wonderful end to Sunday night dinner.

My father was on his best behaviour because my mother had agreed to live with him again, or to let him live with us. I don't know quite how that worked. Instead of going out drinking he'd stay home at night and listen to the radio. Lying on the living room couch snoring. But if you changed the station he'd wake up and say, 'I was listening to that.' His favourite program was *Front Page* or *City Desk* or something like that, about a newspaper, with Lorelei Kilbourn. He loved her voice, he said. Soft and husky like she was smoking a cigarette. We listened to Jack Benny, of course, and *The Shadow*, *Fibber McGee and Molly*, and Edgar Bergen with Charlie McCarthy and Mortimer Snerd. The idea of a ventriloquist on radio may seem silly now, but in those days we were innocent and trusting. We knew Mr Bergen wouldn't cheat, that even if we couldn't see him, he wouldn't move his lips when he did Charlie or Mortimer.

Sometimes my father would invite his friends over to the house for dinner and afterwards they'd sit in the living room and drink rye and ginger and smoke Player's or Sweet Caporals. When it got late and they were pretty drunk the women would get tired of all that talk talk talk, and they'd put the radio on and get the men to dance. They were all too old to jitterbug, but once I tried to show them how. My father's friend George danced with me. My father gave me a taste of his drink, that's where I got the nerve. My mother got a headache and went upstairs to bed and she didn't speak to me all the next day.

The next time Happy came into season, we had learned our lesson and whenever we took her for a walk we carried her for about half a block so that the male dogs wouldn't pick up the scent. Same thing when we came home. Picked her up and carried her for the last half block. We'd see all the dogs milling around, fighting each other, down the block, but they couldn't find her. My mother knew she'd have to have Happy spayed sooner or later, but we all thought we'd like to let her have puppies first. 'But not with that gang of mangy strays,' my mother said. So she contacted someone who had a male cocker spaniel and took Happy for a visit. She didn't want them to be mating in our house because we kids were 'altogether too curious', she said.

For the next nine weeks we watched Happy fill out around the middle. Bulging sides, two rows of big red nipples on her belly. Andy was always rolling her over to rub her nipples until my mother made him stop.

On the day of the birth Happy must have waited all day for my mother to get home, because as soon as she walked in the door Happy followed her around from room to room until she finally got noticed. Then my mother led her to the box in the kitchen beside the stove and sat down on the floor and just patted her and stroked her slowly. Long soothing strokes, murmuring soothing sounds. 'That's okay, baby. Just take it easy now. Okay now, you're okay now. Good girl, that's a good girl.'

Naturally we kids wanted to watch. My mother made us sit down on the other side of the room. 'You're so fidgety, you'll make her nervous.' Andy soon gave up and went outside, but I stayed close and watched the entire birthing, five puppies. Delivered nicely wrapped in translucent packaging that Mama-Happy licked off, cleaning up almost pure white fur on the pink skin. The skin looked two sizes too large for their bodies, waiting for them to grow into it. Floppy ears hanging down. Little sealed-shut eyes. Squeaky voices coming from gaping pink mouths. She'd just barely get one puppy cleaned up and the next one would come squeezing out and I could see her pushing and pushing, straining to get each puppy out.

Once three of them had been born, I was allowed to take my mother's place sitting on the floor beside the box, stroking Happy and making soothing noises, while my mother busied about the kitchen getting dinner started so it would be ready when my father came home.

My father always wanted dinner on the table just about as soon as he walked in the door. She'd say to me, 'Would you go and call your brother for dinner,' and I'd call Andy. 'Dinner's ready, Andy,' I'd say. 'In a minute,' he'd say. My father would sit in the living room looking at the newspaper and she'd call out to him, 'Lawrence, dinner's ready.' He'd say, 'Is it on the table?' She'd say, 'It will be on the table as soon as you sit down.' He'd say, 'I'll sit down when it's on the table.' And so on and so on. 'Where's Andy,' she'd say to me. 'Did you call him.' I told her that he said he'd be here in a minute, so she'd go to the back door and have to call out to him, 'Andy, would you come in here right now.' She never seemed to realize that Andy wouldn't pay any attention to anything I said, and he certainly wouldn't do anything I told him. I mean, he was my big brother, wasn't he? Since when do big brothers have to do what little sisters say?

Andy was obsessed with girls. He was desperate to know about female body parts. I had refused to play 'you show me yours and I'll show you mine' when I was six years old, so whatever made him think I'd play it now that I was twelve? And wrestling, pretending he was kidding. No, Andy, I don't want to wrestle. Once I caught him trying to look into the bathroom window. He had climbed up a tree and was leaning over onto the porch roof, peering, peeping in at me. He drove me crazy with his spying and snooping. If I'd known what would happen, I'd never have told my mother. But I did, and of course she told my father.

'You're going to have to talk to him, Lawrence. He's just at that age. All he ever thinks about is girls.'

So my father took Andy down to the basement to talk to him about it, and then came upstairs to have dinner. He sat in the living room waiting and didn't say a word. My mother told me to call Andy.

'Tell him to come up and wash his hands for dinner.'

I did and I heard him going upstairs to the bathroom, and then I finished setting the table. My mother was still in the kitchen and was just pushing bowls through the pass-through when Andy came into the room and I saw him. I heard my mouth, like a spirit in the room, *gasp*. The word gasp formed in my mind around the vision of his face all beaten. I started to say something to him, but he hissed at me between his teeth, mean and quiet, 'Shut up, you stupid. Just shut up. It's all your fault, a bunch of lies you told.'

'No, I didn't, Andy. I didn't. I just told Mama you were looking in the window.'

'I wasn't looking in the window. All I did was climb the tree. Who would want to look at you, anyway. You're just a scrawny stupid kid. You've got nothing to look at.'

I was practically ready to cry. My mother came in at just that moment and I saw her face too make a gasp. A small 'Oh' came from her mouth. 'Sit down, you two,' she said. Andy just glared at her and I knew he thought it was her fault too, that he got beaten up.

'Lawrence, dinner's on the table.'

He came in and sat at his place at the head of the table and we kids didn't say one word from 'Pass the potatoes, please' to 'May I be excused.' My father kept on talking about work and politics, and my mother nodded and hmmed. Nobody looked at anybody, especially at Andy. I just pushed my food around on the plate. 'Eat your dinner, Laurie,' my mother said to me.

'I'm not very hungry, Mama.'

'Eat your dinner, dammit,' my father said. So I did. I did what I was told.

Andy liked our new back yard. He'd always be wanting to camp out and build a fire and he'd put potatoes in the fire to roast. And sometimes my mother would give him a hot dog to put on a stick. He had a tent and a flashlight and that was his dream. To be out in his tent and read all night. Andy played out in the yard a lot, and went exploring around the neighbourhood with some other boys, and he was old enough to go downtown on the streetcar by himself. Sometimes he went to a movie. And he finally got a girlfriend, the kind of person I'd never have thought he would go for, or who would go for him. That just proved my own ignorance about what brought people together.

Jenny was a big buxom girl, all smiles and a great big way of laughing. She was open and direct, loved to have fun. She wore a flower in her hair sometimes, tucked into the blond curls. She was a bit like Gladys, the wife of my father's friend George. Andy was small for his age, short and sturdy, very smart. He was as sweet as pie with girls, kind and charming. He'd drape his arm over their shoulder and liked to be friends with them. And he'd steal money from my mother's purse to buy presents for them, chocolates and Evening in Paris cologne in a blue bottle. But with other boys he was aggressive and belligerent, always ready for a fight, always ready to take offence.

I wasn't even thinking about boyfriends yet. But I was really happy to have a girlfriend – Lorraine, the girl who lived across the street. She had red hair and freckles and was a bit shy, like me. We hung around together, did homework together, and she helped me when I went out collecting for the war effort.

Now that the Russians were in the war and Stalin was friendly and lovable Uncle Joe, my parents were no longer political outsiders. They were both busy in different ways helping in the war effort. My father, at the union, was helping to keep the shipyards working a seven-day week, building ships as quickly as possible. We sang songs like 'Rosie the Riveter'. My mother was involved with the Russian War Relief, raising money to send help to the Russians who were holding back Hitler's armies outside of Stalingrad.

I collected scrap around the neighbourhood, with a lot of other kids. We had meetings in my basement, and talked about the long list of all the things that were needed. We collected bottles and newspapers. Fat, too, cans of meat drippings and bacon fat, smelly and rancid. It nearly made me sick. But it was used to make bullets or something. Or soap. I don't know. And we collected cans. Any kind of cans, tunafish or beans, it didn't matter. Metal was what was needed most. And the silver paper from inside cigarette packages. Of course it wasn't silver, I don't know what kind of metal it was, but what we did was peel the thin layer of silver paper, it was called, from the paper wrapper. There'd be hardly any metal, but we could wad it all up together and it would soon amount to something. I made a wad as big as a baseball, all those cigarettes that people smoked. I'd even pick up an empty package thrown out on the street, just to get the silver paper. And I collected a lot of metal. I'd take a wagon and go around all the local streets every Saturday, knocking on doors asking for scrap. Once I got a whole iron bedstead, an old one painted white. It was pretty, but a bit wrecked. It took me three trips to get it all home on my wagon, and everyone had to move off the sidewalk to let me pass. All of this scrap I kept in a corner of the basement and then a truck would come by every month and take it away. I was the captain of my neighbourhood scrap team, about eight other kids, including my friend Lorraine. We won some kind of prize for the city, and I went on the radio once to tell about how we collected so much junk.

I was sure I would be a teacher, that was pretty certain. I didn't have much notion about wanting to be married and have a family. At school I was getting good marks now and enjoying everything except home ec. That class was frustrating, boring and useless, I thought, teaching me things I already knew how to do: sew an apron, cook potatoes, set the table, wash dishes. The dishwashing routine was new to me: wash the crystal first, then the silver, then the china, then the kitchenware, then the pots and pans. I wondered where the teachers ever got the idea that people lived their normal lives with crystal and silver. Unless they thought they were teaching the girls to be servants. I was used to washing the dishes at home; I'd been doing it for years. My mother thought that my brother should help; she thought it might be good if my father would too, of course, but he wasn't the type. She asked my father to tell Andy he had to help with the dishes, but my father said, 'Why should he wash dishes when there are two women in the house?' So that was the end of that.

The big topic of conversation at school that year was menstruating. Everyone talked about it. Who was, who wasn't. We were supposed to be learning about it in hygiene, but we learned more from each other because the teacher was afraid to talk about it straight out. Lorraine and I were in the same class and she said that the boys could tell when a girl was on her period. 'They can smell it,' she said. There was one girl in my class that had been getting her periods for almost a year already. She was strong and confident, bigger and taller than any of us. So tall that we could see right up her nostrils. It was disgusting. I tried to sniff at her to see if she was on her period, but I was afraid she'd get mad.

Becky was the one really beautiful girl at the school, beautiful as a movie star, with long golden hair that always seemed to slide over her face. She'd have to lift her hand and slowly ease the silken shawl of hair back over her shoulder. I think the movie actress that she learned it from was Veronica Lake. I used to stare at her; I couldn't imagine how her hair came to be so golden. And one day she invited me to come home with her and watch her wash her hair. Egg yolk and lemon juice and who knows what. What a rigmarole it was. After that I never wanted to be friends with her. I decided she was some kind of fool. Vain, with nothing in her mind but her looks. I mean, who would waste an egg just to put it in her hair?

One day when I got home from school I found a surprise from my mother on my bed: a blue box of Kotex and a sanitary belt. And a little booklet, 'Things you should know …' She never said a word to me though. The very next day I started menstruating, so I thought my mother must be psychic. Or else she could smell it coming on. I worried about that. About smelling, and about being old enough to have babies, and the boys knowing. I thought I'd die of embarrassment.

When the puppies were big enough, Lorraine and I spread a blanket over the front lawn and we carried the puppies outside to introduce them to the world. Five puppies and their mother, enjoying a summer day in front of the house. Up on the steps to the porch Andy was sitting with his arm around his girlfriend, just watching us playing with the pups. Happy was a bit nervous about her babies leaving their basement home for the first time, as any mother might be, but the pups were brave explorers, plodding across their lumpy brown plaid world. At the edge of the world we would pick them up and lift them back into the middle, where Happy lay enjoying her carefree holiday but keeping a watchful eye on all of us.

When my family decided to move to a new house I was terribly unhappy about leaving Lorraine, my first very special friend. We made a pact, vowing to meet each other at the post office on the corner of

Granville and Hastings at twelve noon on a certain day in the year 1951, when we would be twenty-one years old and would have jobs and money and be free to travel anywhere and do anything; when there would be nothing to stop us from really being ourselves. We would be adults then. Full of power and freedom.

18. MILK

Vancouver. It must have been Vancouver; it was raining. My mother had sent me three or four doors running through the rain, down the street to a neighbour. 'Ask her if she can spare a little milk,' my mother said. Now, carrying a jar with about a cup of milk in it, I was running down the path to the sidewalk. I stepped out to make the turn, sliding, slipping, my foot went out. I hung on to the milk jar with both hands to save it. Crashed to my knees on the pavement. I was crying, very wet, and blood was running down my leg. I limped, hobbled, homeward, in the back door to the kitchen and said, 'I didn't spill the milk.' My mother took me for stitches. She fainted when the doctor cleaned the cut, when I screamed. And I had to walk backwards for a week, dragging my sewn-up knee. At school, I went up the stairs backwards and was often late for class. But I learned a word: *patella*, kneecap.

This is my third scar, a puckered zipper on the bony kneecap. It has never left me. It is always the milk, the jar. It means: take care of things that matter. It means learning, new words.

19. A LITTLE SONG AND DANCE

I made my stage debut in one of my mother's productions, *The Shipyard Revue*, produced in Vancouver in 1943 or '44. At a time when theatre was celebrating the glory of the navy, the army, and the airforce with musicals, a little song and dance ... Ellen decided to produce a musical honouring the people who worked in the shipyards. Perhaps it was John Goss she worked with, I don't know. There must have been other musical 'comrades' but that is the only name I remember. She used classical music. 'It's out of copyright,' she told me, 'so we can use it for our show. We'll just write new words.' Little lessons she taught me – here, learning about copyright. You can't just steal the words that someone else has written. Not until they are long dead. Then it's okay.

There were songs about working the night shift: 'Go home at dawn today, the same tomorrow.' That was 'None But the Lonely Heart.' That one was about working overtime. One called 'After the Whistle Blows' acknowledging the lonely life of women whose husbands and boyfriends were away. The shipyards had hired a lot of women during the war. Here in the Revue they sang and danced. I couldn't sing, but I was one of the dancers. A chorus line of women wearing short red overalls, sewn by one of the volunteers.

Was it in the Ukrainian Labour Temple? What stage fright ... all of us crowded together in the stairwell waiting to go up on stage. Waiting for our musical cue. But once I was on stage under the lights it all swung into place, all the moves, all the bends and steps, all the music keeping us in time.

The Revue was a great success. I do remember that. My mother's pride. The ecstatic newspaper review. My father's jealousy. Someone actually had the nerve to introduce him as 'Ellen's husband'. Surely that was unfair. Surely she was *his wife.*

And I didn't know then that I would remember the tunes and the words forever.

I had never seen a moon like this. Huge and hanging orange against the horizon. My mother and I were walking home in the evening. We were tired and she ... what's this memory? ... she has taken her shoes off and is ruining her stockings on the sidewalk. But we were both excited. It was all about theatre, but I'm not sure how it connects. Ellen had always been involved with theatre, in the early Depression days it was 'agitprop' – agitation and propaganda, I know now. But at the time I thought it has something to do with having very few props, which one could move around easily.

It wasn't very late in the evening, it seems to me. Of course ... it must have been a matinee, to be bringing us home at this time in the evening in fall.

It was 1944. We had been to see *Othello* and were fizzy with excitement. This was a special tour into Vancouver, arranged by Ellen's friend John Goss. That's the name that is familiar to me. Paul Robeson, Uta Hagen, José Ferrer. I will remember those names forever. The dark theatre. Iago declaring his intentions, this glimpse of planned treachery. But when Robeson came in from the left he was calm and formal. The theatre was silent, soaking up the vision of that large man, black skin, firelit torches glinting off his tunic and robe. He was quiet and still, waiting for us to get over the shock of him, the bigness and blackness, so that he could speak to us. The tiny first line: ''Tis better as it is.' His voice moved effortlessly through the hall, open, deep, pushing all the air out of the room, pushing out any other sound that might have been there. We were all caught in his huge royal glory. And when that voice said 'the gentle Desdemona' we felt the love, and we loved her too. Oh Iago, how could you do this? I was shocked by the treachery, shocked at Desdemona's death, and I was crying quietly there in the dark. Forever, this would be the greatest treachery … to bring down this grand noble beautiful loving man.

We came home on the streetcar, my mother and I, and walked the few blocks to our house. What is a pair of stockings compared to that aching excitement?

On Sunday there was a reception for the city officials to meet Paul Robeson. There were tables with teacups and tiny sandwiches carefully arranged on platters. Some plates of cookies.

My mother wore a little suit that she made herself. Soft crepe the colour of cream, with a gored skirt, slightly flared. A bolero jacket and a pale pink blouse with a bow at the throat. She was thrilled to be there, invited by John Goss no doubt, who knew of her passion for theatre, her passion for this production of *Othello*. But the politics of the situation made her something of an outsider. Here, among the wives of city politicians, she felt like an outsider. But she introduced me to Paul Robeson and he shook my hand. My small white hand seemed weak and fluttery as a bird, meeting his big hand – his pink palm a great surprise to me. And he smiled at me, that beaming sunny smile, from way up there to way down here.

20. ANDY RUNS AWAY TO SEA

It was Andy's departure from our family life that started the breakup of our family. He had always had plans for a life of adventure. They got more and more specific, until finally he had his grand plan: 'I'm going to run away to sea and be a writer, like Jack London.' That was his hero, Jack London. *Call of the Wild* was the only book of his I knew. I read it because Andy raved about it so much, but it wasn't my kind of story, all adventure and no love except the wolves. But Andy liked it and I knew why he'd see that kind of life as his ideal. The hero was strong and independent, didn't need anyone. Completely free. He could live alone and do as he pleased.

So when Andy finally left home he called it 'the time I ran away to sea like Jack London.' But it wasn't like that, not running away. My mother signed him into a school in Halifax. A naval academy.

He says it was Christmas Eve when he left, but it really wasn't, it was Boxing Day. He just blanked out on that Christmas completely. It became one of the things he didn't remember, except my father saying, 'Smile, goddammit, it's Christmas.' Years later we'd laugh about that. But there's no way I was going to forget it, our last one all together, my god. My father was out all night Christmas Eve and I sat up sewing, finishing a dressing gown I was making for him. Dark red wool, with a shawl collar of navy blue with small white polka dots. It was about one in the morning when I finished, and he still wasn't home. My mother said I'd have time to wrap it up in the morning. I certainly did, all right, because he didn't come home until almost noon.

Even though it was Christmas morning she wouldn't let us open any presents without him there. 'He won't like it if we have Christmas without him,' she said, perhaps remembering a scene from years ago. So we had to wait and wait. When he got home Andy sassed him about something – hardly even that – and my father went for him. Dived at him across the room and threw him at the wall. I ran to hide. But I heard my mother calling, 'Lawrence, Lawrence, it's Christmas.' She managed to stop the beating before Andy got bashed up badly.

Later she made Andy apologize. 'Go and tell him you're sorry.' Andy was angry. 'What for? I didn't do anything wrong.' She insisted, 'I know you didn't, but if you apologize, then he'll settle down and we can get on with the day.' So Andy did, a lesson in appeasement. I don't think he would have done it if he hadn't known he would be leaving the next day. He knew it wouldn't get to be a habit.

My father said, 'Smile, goddammit, it's Christmas.' Andy said, 'Yeah, 'tis the season to be jolly,' and my mother held her breath. But my father didn't notice Andy. Or decided not to. The house smelled of Christmas chicken cooking, and we started to open presents. I gave my father the dressing gown I had made and gave my mother a pretty scarf. I have no idea what presents I got that year, how could I possibly remember? My mother gave Andy a duffle bag and I gave him a book to read on the train. Zane Grey? Who knows?

Boxing Day, about five o'clock in the afternoon we all went to Chinatown for a nice dinner before Andy left. Pork fried rice, egg foo yong, shrimp with lobster sauce, beef and green peppers. A real feast.

He was wearing his grey pants, the ones my mother bought him when school started – he was in grade ten – and a navy blue windbreaker. White shirt and tie, of course. He was faking eighteen, dressed up for the train. A pullover for warmth. He had the duffle bag with a few clothes in it, a couple of books too. The school in Halifax gave my mother a list of things he'd need.

I don't remember going to the train station. 'Why don't I remember that?' I asked Andy when we were grown up. He said, 'Well, they didn't take me to the station, that's why. They put me in a taxi outside the restaurant. Just as well. No use faking any fond farewells.' I'm sorry about that now. I'd like to have had a fond farewell, faked or otherwise, but Andy said my father hadn't finished his dinner yet when it was time to leave. Too busy arguing with the waiters about Chinese politics. Mao Tse-tung, the good guy, against Chang Kai-shek, the bad guy, still.

So he didn't really run away, not if my parents put him in a taxi. My mother's persistence had got him accepted into the school somehow. He was so wild, always in trouble. And my father – hardly a week went by without some kind of battle between them. Andy had just turned sixteen. The naval academy didn't take kids until they were eighteen.

Many years later Andy said, 'She was complicit in it.' That's his kind of word, *complicit*; partners in an evil action, the dictionary says.

An evil action? 'She lied about my age so they'd take me,' he said. 'I loved that train ride. All by myself, all the way to Halifax. Complete freedom.' An evil action? Was it an evil action? At least he was away from home. But he always wanted to blame her for something, all his life he blamed her.

He sent me a picture of himself wearing a cadet's cap with a gold medallion on it and I carried it around with my school stuff. I'd pretend he was my boyfriend. Oh, he was really handsome then, when he was a boy.

Later, when it was time for him to come home, there was no home to come to. My mother wrote and told him. She didn't say she had run away from home, just that she had left. Really this time. She'd send him an address when she had one. 'Oh well, oh well, tsk, tsk, such is life,' said Andy.

After the war he wrote me a postcard: *Thru Panama to Frisco, where some wonders began, and some ended. Still a young man, and still stupid, but still hoping. We have to have hope. Sayonara!*

21. SWEET TOOTH AND SOUR GRAPES

Once I darn near killed myself on a hill in Vancouver. I was riding a bike that belonged to my brother's friend, and it didn't have any brakes, at least not pedal brakes like I was used to. I was careening down that hill and I was scared to death, thinking I'd never be able to stop. I could see the traffic on the cross street at the bottom, just whipping by. I managed to turn into a side street and then stick my foot out to stop. But that hill nearly got me then. It was just like my brother's nightmare – he used to have nightmares about riding his bike down that hill. 'It's trying to kill me,' he said. 'It's going to throw me out into the traffic and bash me to death.'

From our back porch I could look out past the other houses all the way to the water, Burrard Inlet, and if there was no fog I could see over to the other side. Over the cargo ships, the flat barges loaded with logs, the oil tankers. My brother Andy wrote a poem about it that got published in the high school newspaper.

We lived up at the top of the steep hill. Even if I was just trying to walk down it, the slope was so steep that it pushed me along and I had to go fast even if I didn't want to. I wasn't strong enough to resist. It was out of my control, really, the way I was being rushed along that year.

My girlfriend Isabelle lived in a grocery store at the bottom of the hill. She already had her figure, but she was still surprised by it. She wore it like a big coat that belonged to someone else, her mother maybe, a padding that wrapped around her body, that filled up her skirts, expanded her sweaters. Her new body bumped into things, sometimes bumped into people. I was still skinny, waiting eagerly for my figure to arrive, like a package from the mailman, long overdue. 'Oh, when am I going to get my figure,' I'd moan to her.

Isabelle was Italian, exotic, with dark copper eyes and thick black hair curling wildly to her shoulders, escaping from the prison of rubber bands. We were in high school together, grade nine. I was sort of mousy and plain, but we were best friends anyway. I used to stare at her eyebrows; I think I was in love with that curve. The wings of a tiny bird hovering over her eyes. Her skin glowed from the kind of fire she carried around inside.

She was just about really rich, I thought. Her parents owned the grocery store, and her whole family lived in an apartment at the back, with bedrooms upstairs: mother, father, grandfather, Isabelle, and three little brothers. The room behind the store was busy, noisy: it was kitchen, dining room, living room, where everybody seemed to be talking at the same time.

It was 1944 and we were both in grade nine at General Brock High School. Once Isabelle invited me to come over after school and stay for supper – *dinner*, we said at my house, but I knew to say *supper* when I talked to her and *dinner* when I talked to my mother. I knew there were two languages, one that you talked with your friends and a different one for your parents. My mother said I could go. Isabelle had to work in the store for an hour so her mother could have a break. I stayed with her and watched how she took care of the customers, getting a can of stewed tomatoes from the shelf, a loaf of sliced white bread, weighing out three pounds of potatoes. And the big cash register – she had to press so hard on the keys. She rang up 57 cents and the drawer clanged open. Her mother could even hear it in the back room. 'You can't ever open the cash register without her hearing it,' Isabelle whispered.

She asked her mother if she could treat me to a bottle of pop. I had a lemon-lime and she had a Hire's. We sat on boxes in the store drinking from the bottles, kidding around, clanking the bottles against our teeth, blowing foghorns across the top – playing like little kids. We could do that together and not be embarrassed – it was one of the reasons we liked each other so much. She stuck her tongue down into the bottle and pretended she couldn't get it out. Her tongue was all purple underneath, with veins. I nearly gagged.

There was a busy time in the store between four-thirty and six o'clock, when everyone was buying something to make for their supper. Isabelle helped her mother with the customers, and the family didn't eat until nearly seven o'clock. Isabelle sometimes cooked supper while her mother worked in the store, but that night, 'since she had a guest,' she didn't have to help.

I forget what her mother made for supper. Hamburger and mashed potatoes maybe. But I remember she said to Isabelle: 'Bella, would you run into the store and get me a can of peas.' I went with her and she showed me. Was that ever wonderful! Just to pick it off the shelf and not pay. That was what it was like to be rich.

The store stayed open until nine o'clock. Bella wanted me to stay with her because her parents were going out to a movie after they put the boys to bed. She had to take care of the store and close up when it was time. They couldn't leave the grandfather on his own, she said. He was old and a bit crazy. But really, he was drunk, I could tell. I knew what drunk looked like, that's for sure, from my father. And so bossy to Isabelle, then saying 'You such a pretty girl, so pretty, Bella. Come give your poppie a kiss, Bella.' She hated him.

She was going to make knockout drops, she said, the way she'd heard about. You could put someone to sleep, just like *that* – she snapped her fingers. She wanted to do it to her grandfather so he wouldn't be mumbling there trying to get her to sit on his lap. Me even, he tried to. Not on your life. I knew about old guys like him from my uncles and also from my father's friend George. She told me, 'You put two aspirins into a bottle of Coca-Cola, and when they drink it that puts them right to sleep.' Oh boy, was I scared. 'It won't kill him, will it?' She told me don't be silly. And she called out to him from the store, real sweet: 'Poppie, you want a Coca-Cola?' But he didn't want one and she had to get him a beer instead.

I went home at eight o'clock, like my mother said. 'Can't you stay till my parents get home?' Isabelle asked me. But I knew I couldn't. And secretly I didn't want to, anyway. It was spooky there when the store was closed, dark, and the grandfather muttering in his chair.

I had to walk up the long hill to get home, past all the houses. When I got home from Isabelle's my mother was there. Not my father though. Sometimes he came home really late, usually drunk. Sometimes he'd throw up in the hall – I nearly did it myself too, from the smell. Then I'd hear them arguing.

My mother was always firm and quiet and reasonable, as if he could understand what she was saying. He did a lot of shouting, if he was sober enough. Otherwise he'd just start to lie down wherever he happened to be, oozing down the wall, and she'd have to lead him toward a bed or a couch so he wouldn't just pass out on the floor. If he did that there was nothing she'd be able to do then; she couldn't lift him, she was so little, and we'd have to walk around him. When my father was at the roaring-drunk stage, Andy and I used to practise being invisible. Andy had built a secret place in the basement where no one could find him. I usually hid around some corner; I wanted to see what was happening. To see and not be seen.

The war was still on but everyone said it would be over soon. The Russian army and the British and Americans were moving toward Berlin, looking for Hitler. My father was working for the union, but sometimes his salary was gone before he even got home. He'd spent it all in the bar. Business agent, he was. Shipwrights and Boilermakers' Union – and that was what he usually drank then, a boilermaker: rye in a shot glass, sunk in a glass of beer. He showed me how to do it, gave me a taste. My father's world was easy for me to know, all I had to do was laugh and have fun, try to look pretty in front of his friends, and never criticize him or anyone else.

My mother was working on a newspaper, a weekly political one. She'd bring home the galley proofs to read, long sheets of paper. Sometimes she'd go out to work in the evening. *We're putting the paper to bed*, she'd say. I loved that phrase. She said it as though she enjoyed doing it, as though the newspaper was her baby; I imagined soft blankets, a little pillow, tucking the blankets in. She learned to read upside down and backwards, because she'd check the metal type for last-minute changes that had been made. She showed me how to do it too.

If I wanted to be in my mother's world I was expected to think, to read, to have ideas and be able to accomplish things. Always something to measure up to.

We actually had new clothes for school that year, Andy and me both. My mother took me shopping, downtown to Hudson's Bay. I was growing up and we were almost the same size but she didn't want me to wear her clothes. I didn't want to either, of course, not for school. But she had a nice party dress that I was just dying to try on. Black with a little trim of gold braid, little gold stars all over the skirt. 'It's much too sophisticated for you,' she said. 'Don't be in such a hurry to grow up.'

At the store we looked at clothes for girls and I got two skirts and a jacket that went with both of them; one skirt was pleated, in green and blue plaid; the other was flared, dark blue. The jacket was blue like the skirt, with sleeves and patch pockets in plaid. I didn't like that patchy look, as though you didn't have enough cloth to make it all match. But it was the style that year. And I got a couple of blouses. My mother bought me a blue sweater to go with everything. That was a terrible mistake, but I couldn't tell her. She never understood why I wouldn't wear it. I always hunched my shoulders over, and she'd always say to me, *Why don't you stand up straight*. She just didn't know how embarrassing it was, although you'd think she would remember from when she was growing up. She had very big breasts even though she was thin; she had worn straight flapper dresses then, but you could tell in the old photographs. At high school you just couldn't wear a sweater. A couple of girls did. The boys called them 'sweater girls', after Lana Turner and went *wooo-wooo* at them. And wolf whistles. The other girls didn't talk to them much.

My mother bought Andy some grey trousers and two shirts and a windbreaker. That was before Christmas, before he went away. She must have known he was going away, but she hadn't told me yet. I'm not even sure that she had told my father, or even Andy.

Gladys, the wife of my father's friend George, came to clean the house, usually on Thursday. She'd get there before I left for school. My mother and Gladys liked each other, though they weren't exactly close friends. Too different. My mother always said, 'Boy, am I glad to see you, Glad.' And Gladys would laugh and say, 'Go on, Ellen, you just go off to your work. You've got better things to do than mess around in here.' She'd be tying on an apron while she talked, already starting to put dishes in the sink. Gladys liked to have that bit of extra money that she got from my mother, just hers alone. 'I don't have to ask George for it, and I can do whatever I want with it, and no explaining. Sometimes I think I wouldn't mind going out to work, maybe in an office or a store, but George says no. He says, No wife of mine is going to work. Like the whole world's going to think he doesn't make enough money to support a wife.'

But I would hear the women talk it out in the kitchen on Thursday mornings. Gladys told Ellen, 'It's no disgrace for gosh sakes, you going out to work. It's no disgrace you don't get a big thrill out of cleaning up after Lawrence and the kids. If I had kids I know it'd be hard for me. If I was you, I'd do the same. I always read what you write in the paper, just because it's you as wrote it. I don't read that much, but I love a good story. I don't know where you get your ideas.'

Gladys was proud of Ellen – said she felt as if she was actually helping Ellen at the newspaper, which she was, of course. She was probably more proud of Ellen than my father was. I think he couldn't make up his mind whether he was proud of Ellen for the stories she wrote or ashamed of her because she didn't want to stay home and take care of the house. A little of both, it seemed to me. I guess I sometimes felt the same way myself, when I'd really want her to be like other mothers, making cookies and chocolate cake, but at the same time I was proud that she was different. Working at the newspaper, writing things that were interesting.

I knew one thing though, George didn't mind that his wife Gladys came to clean house for us. He even gloated that she was a better housekeeper than Ellen. He really enjoyed rubbing Lawrence's nose in it, because usually Lawrence was such a big shot and know-it-all bully to George. But here Lawrence's wife would rather be out working on a newspaper than taking care of her own house and family. *Women*, he'd say, *you just can't fathom them.* I heard that often enough.

I liked to hear Ellen and Gladys in the morning, the way they just exchanged a couple of sentences and then they each went to their work and I went off to school. 'Bye, Mama. Bye, Gladys,' I'd say, and I'd zip out the back door at the very last possible minute.

This was a new place for us to live, a bungalow with a pretty living room and two bedrooms, and Andy had a bedroom closed in on the back porch. We'd only been there a few months. Gladys said she really liked taking care of the house, it was so different from her apartment. My mother didn't like housework. 'It's such a boring, repetitive job. You no sooner get it finished than you have to do it all over again.'

My mother got bored very easily. Gladys didn't. She would bake a cake too, while she was there, or a pie. Lemon meringue. I had a sweet tooth then. I used to love the days that Gladys came; I'd get home from school and walk into the kitchen and see that pie, oh I just about fainted just from the look of it, the smell of lemony sugar.

My father never really cared about the pie. He didn't have a sweet tooth, just a liquor tooth. He just wanted to go out drinking before he came home. Out with the boys. I never heard of the word alcoholic when I was a kid. And we didn't say he was a drunk, of course. I guess he wasn't really, because he was sober enough to go to work every day. But he'd start on Friday afternoon and drink until Sunday night. When I was young my mother used to say that he drank because there were no jobs, just to cheer himself up and be able to get along better with people. But then there was no money even for food, let alone drink, and I guess that kept him under control.

It was all about power, it seemed to me. I thought he was even worse now that he was a success in Vancouver. Maybe the Party in BC liked thumbing its nose at the Alberta branch. Maybe *drunken hooliganism* wasn't so bad here. Who knows. Anyway, now with the war on the really important thing was to keep the shipyards moving. Part of my father's job was to bring more members into the union, so I guess he spent a lot of time being friendly with strangers. But I thought that being a boss at the union brought out all the meanness in him, the way he loved the power, the importance. Oh, did my brother get it before he left. Seemed like he couldn't do anything right and my father was always whipping him for something. Since I started to become a woman, he didn't whip me any more. He would never hit a *woman*, he said. Well, not unless his temper ran away with him, I guess.

When Andy finally left home to go to school in Halifax, my mother hoped it might 'straighten him out'. No matter how much my father whipped him, Andy just never seemed to straighten out. And now he was gone.

Then I was alone. I'd hear my parents arguing, after my father came home very late at night. Or maybe he'd come home in the morning. Sunday morning, Monday sometimes, after being out all night, or a couple of nights. He'd come in about noon. This latest 'carrying on' was with someone named Betsy. All my father's girlfriends – his 'women', my mother called them, like it was a dirty word – had names like that: Betsy, Maisie, Daisy, Patsy, Queenie.

My mother said she'd had enough. She was going to leave him. She meant it. She sold our house – she just made him sign the paper to sell it the same way she'd made him sign to buy it. She was a great one for burning her bridges before she even got safely across – just so she'd have to keep moving. 'I'm leaving,' she told me. 'Do you want to come?' Said we'd go away somewhere. To Toronto maybe. To New York. She started selling all the furniture so we'd have money for the train. I thought it would be a good idea to get away from my father and his buddies, the parties, the fear. It would be an adventure, she said, we could do it together. I knew that was the direction my life would have to take, into my mother's world and out of his. He didn't believe she'd do it, not till she sold his easy chair right out from under him. When she sold the record player she forgot to take the records out of the cabinet, so her favourite music was gone too – songs of the Spanish Civil War, some Fats Waller, Mozart flute and harp, Duke Ellington playing 'Sophisticated Lady'. That was her theme song, I thought.

For a couple of weeks, while the furniture was being sold, I slept with my mother in the big bedroom. My father was sleeping in my little bedroom. One night I woke up and she wasn't in the bed with me. I walked down the hall to the bathroom half-asleep and when I passed the door of my room, there, hanging on the doorknob, was her underwear – brassiere, panties, slip. Like hanging out a white flag. Surrender.

Morning corn flakes. She told me we weren't leaving. She'd find a nice furnished apartment where we could all stay together. Things would be better, she said, a lot nicer, Lawrence had promised. Toronto probably wasn't a very good city to move to anyway. It was a lot colder than Vancouver, and I'd have to change schools again, and I'd miss my friend Isabelle.

But I was miserable; betrayed. I wanted to confront her with what I knew: *You let him persuade you. How could you do that? How could you let him do that?* But I couldn't. I didn't ever argue with her, I didn't ever tell her what I was really thinking any more than she told me. So I agreed it wasn't such a good idea – going. As if I had a choice. But he didn't beat me any more, so I didn't really need to be scared. It's not as if there was anything to be scared of, really, in his sort of life. He had a lot of fun.

But I was afraid then of the power of love or whatever it was. The way it could warp the will, override the desperate escape plans of someone like my mother. The power of men, the power of sex. I thought about Tony, a guy I had a crush on. He shined shoes after school at a place downtown. Sometimes I'd go down there and stand across the street and watch him, yearning. Hoping he wouldn't see me, but kind of hoping he might. My longing flowed out through the traffic, drifting to the other side of the street, under the arcade to the shoeshine parlour outside the barbershop; the high padded chairs, the metal foot racks, the smell of shoe polish – I loved that smell. And I loved the way Tony's hair would fall, dark, over his forehead. And he'd spit on his hand and slick it back. Once he kissed me in the back alley behind Isabelle's grocery store and I cried. I don't even know why I cried. It was so sweet, so tender. Was that love?

I walked down the hill to see Isabelle, to tell her I wouldn't be going away. But I couldn't tell her about my mother's underwear. I wanted to warn her about love, but I was ashamed of what I had learned. I just said my parents had made up again.

She told me, 'Come out back and you can help make candy. We're going to make sour balls for the store.' She was really glad I wasn't going; we were the only friends either of us had, I think. I don't know why.

Behind the store was a big shed, maybe it used to be a garage, now a divided room with a kind of kitchen – huge pots and a stove and in front two long tables and some shelves. It wasn't a store, just a place for making different kinds of candy; the candy shed.

From the hot kitchen Isabelle's mother gave us a slab of warm candy, clear, like pink glass, but soft and droopy. We rubbed butter on our hands and stretched the slab out. Warm and smooth, oh I loved the way it felt, like silky skin. I lumped it up into my two hands, holding it out in front of me like big breasts, sticking out my chest. 'Hey Isabelle, I got my figure. Wooo-wooo,' laughing. Isabelle turned red as a cherry, but she laughed anyway. Even her mother laughed. All of us, women, laughing together. Me dancing around. Oh, it did me good that day.

'Come on girls, stop fooling around.' Isabelle's mother had to get us back to work, of course, but Isabelle grinned at me when she took the slab of candy and pushed it into the candyball machine. I tried to turn the crank, but it was really hard work; I was surprised. 'Here, let me do it. We have to do it fast, before the candy gets cool.' So we changed places and I fed the pink slab into the machine and she turned the crank. Out the other side popped round cherry balls.

She spread them out with her buttery fingers onto a big metal sheet, so they wouldn't touch, wouldn't stick together while they cooled. All afternoon: cherry balls, lemon sours, then orange and grape. Shiny bright colours, sweet jewels glittering. The smell of sugar filling the room, spreading through my mind. All that sweetness, stickiness.

Isabelle's mother gave us a sieve filled with powdered sugar. 'You can be the Snow Queen,' Isabelle told me. Above the candy jewels I jiggled the sieve, sprinkling sweet white powder over everything. Isabelle's hands darted in and out under the snow, rolling the balls about, getting powdered sugar on the back of her hands. Licking it off with her pointy pink tongue.

We put the sour balls in a big glass jar for the store, and Isabelle's mother gave me a little bag to take home. Of course I said thank you and told her it was fun, which it was. But my sweet tooth was gone. Gone forever. I hated the way the stickiness got into my mind, the way it covered up everything else, rushed at me till I couldn't even think straight, it seemed to me. So I just walked up the hill, wondering when we would have to leave the house, and where we would live.

22. YOU BELONG TO MY HEART

My mother's hand reached out to rest on the white newel post and she swayed slightly toward the banister. Her other hand held the letter out in front of her. I stood in the front hallway, awed by her poise, that controlled calm. Her chin came up and she smiled ruefully at Mrs Spenser, 'I'm afraid it's bad news.' She must have read it aloud then: I remember hearing the words, *You always said I would.*

This was the first letter from my father since we had left him in Vancouver, since my parents had separated in the spring of 1944, just after the war in Europe ended. She expected a cheque for $50. He had agreed to send her that much every month until she got a job, or until I became sixteen, or until she came to her senses. Whichever came first, he said.

I can't send the money because I smashed up the car, he wrote. *You always said I would.*

Yes, she always said he would. As my father bumped through the doorway of some place we lived, my mother said: 'I don't know how you can drive. You're so drunk you can barely walk. You'll smash up the car one of these days, Lawrence. And you'll be lucky if you don't kill yourself. Or someone else.' Constantly, over most of the years of my childhood. Over and over.

I wondered how my mother could have expected him to send the money. How could she have believed him? He had always lied to her, so why should she expect him to keep his word this time? It was probably not so much expectation as living on her wishes, as usual. Living on her dreams. Perhaps she couldn't tell the difference between expecting and dreaming. Waiting and hoping, as though she had been born speaking Spanish, where the same word serves for both ideas.

'Oh, Ellen. I'm so terribly sorry,' Mrs Spenser told her. 'Don't worry, my dear, everything will be all right.'

Marion Spenser lived on Toronto's west side, near the lake. I think it was the prettiest house I had ever been in, and Mrs Spenser was a truly elegant lady, I thought. In the dining room was a walnut sideboard with a clock under a glass dome; three golden balls swung round and round to measure out eight days at a time. We stayed with Mrs Spenser while Ellen looked for a job and an apartment that spring.

From Vancouver to Toronto my mother and I had travelled by train, 'tourist class'. I can't compare the accommodations and facilities with those in first class, since I didn't ever see them, but in tourist the seats were dark red plush, scratchy on bare skin. We slept in bunks in the sleeping car, made up each night by the porter, who transformed seats to beds and opened the upper berths, making rows of curtained uppers and lowers on each side of the aisle. In the ladies' room Ellen changed from her day clothes into her nightgown, robe and slippers; a towel was provided for each sleeping car passenger, and a small cake of soap wrapped in paper. In the top bunk I twisted my body in the small space to put on my pyjamas.

I was just fourteen, lurching with one foot in the world of childhood and a toe reaching into adulthood. My childish self liked the adventure of climbing up into the top bunk, but once up there I felt imprisoned in the dark and airless womb with no vision of the passing country night. My adult self couldn't complain or be afraid. My mother and I had already had our share of fear, now was the time for bravery.

In 1944 the trip took four nights and three days. Overnight to Calgary first, for a visit at the train station with Ellen's mother, the grandmother I barely knew, didn't remember after five years in Vancouver. Just passing through, a stopover of half an hour while the train discharged and took on passengers, that's what Ellen had planned.

To the beautiful marble train station Grandma wore the standard old lady's uniform – a navy blue dress with tiny flowers and a crisp white collar, detachable so you could starch it by hand. It was only the end of May, so she needed the straight black coat she wore over it; black gloves, a little hat, and the husband she had married in her widowhood standing mutely behind her. It was after Queen Victoria's birthday, so she had left the glass-eyed fox at home. That fox draped around her neck was one of the things I remembered about her. And the trunk in which she used to keep the tea towels she received as gifts from her children, and handkerchiefs boxed in sets of four, embroidered tablecloths, glass jars of pink bathsalts, and innumerable boxes of chocolates. Once when I was eight she gave me a whole box of Laura Secord chocolates all for myself. The chocolates were dried out and white with age. I ate them anyway. Maybe I shared them with my brother Andy.

'My, how you've grown,' she told me there in the train station, seeing me as tall as my mother, looking very grown up.

'What did you expect, Mother, that she'd shrink?'

I was startled that my mother was rude, I'd never known her to talk that way to anyone, not even my father. I didn't know where to look.

'I don't expect to come back this way, so I don't know when I'll ever see you again.' Ellen tried to burn the bridge with her mother on it, I could hear her lighting the match. 'I'll write when we get settled.'

'Goodbye, Grandma.' I didn't know what else to say. Years later I wished that I had said I would write to her, I wished that I had written to her, wished I had her address. When she died, eight or ten years later, no one even told me.

Then we were back on the train, bound for Toronto. Ellen told me, 'She's an old lady with old-lady ideas. She'll never change. Every time I left your father she always told me to go back to him. A woman's place, she said.' This taking leave of her mother, this dismissal, seemed to be another necessary step in Ellen's separation from my father.

The train became our little home. At the front end of the tourist car was a small kitchen with a two-burner gas stove, a pot and a frying pan, a few dishes, a sink, and two tea towels that were changed every day. Ellen heated vegetable soup, Aylmer's probably, from a can, unwrapped the bacon sandwiches she had made on our last day in the apartment in Vancouver. All her life she would make bacon sandwiches in every country she ever lived in – the United States, England, Mexico, Canada, France. The one constant reliable thing was a bacon sandwich. Good for travelling, she said. It would keep without refrigeration for two or three days, provided good nourishment, packed into a small space, wasn't messy.

My parents' separation marked the beginning of a new life not only for them but for me. What kind of life would it be, a life of bravery? I didn't have my mother's knack for inventing stories about the future; I didn't trust this scary world, so I looked everywhere for signs, for reassurance. I tried to read tea leaves, I imagined crystal balls, I longed for the wisdom of a fortune teller. For years I looked at ads in the windows of tearooms: 'Fortunes told'.

I had a book about palmistry that came with garish purple ink and a roller to paint palms and make prints for careful study. Or to send to the author for a 'detailed personal reading at a cost of only $1.00'. I was sure that failure lurked in the lines of my palm for anyone to read. I wanted to know about my future – would I be safe? would I be loved? would I be happy and rich? I studied the islands and stars, the pattern of the lines; heart, head, and destiny, which one would rule? Compare left and right, potential and actual. How long is life, how many loves, how many children, how much success, when and where and how? Who was I, really?

When we arrived in Toronto we walked from Union Station up Yonge Street enjoying our freedom, the sense that we had arrived here at this city where our new lives would start. Ellen was a wearing a little woollen suit and a raincoat – B.C. clothes suitable for mild summers in Vancouver. I was in my school clothes, the pleated skirt, white blouse, blue and green plaid jacket. It was June and hot in Toronto. Suddenly it seemed urgent to shed our Vancouver characters, to transform ourselves into the new women we would become. Ellen herded me into a clothing store, desperate in the heat. She bought me a cotton skirt in a pretty print and for herself a shirtwaist dress with a flared skirt. We stuffed our well-travelled clothes into our suitcases, wore our new clothes out of the store, feeling self-conscious, newly created.

My father had written a letter to the Communist Party Central Committee, to Tim Buck, so they'd know that he had given his wife permission to leave him. This was our first destination, the Party office where Ellen knew she could get help. That kind of visit became as constant as the bacon sandwiches – the first thing to do in a new city was check in with the Party. It was there that we found out about Mrs Spenser.

On the Queen streetcar Ellen and I travelled out past the Exhibition grounds. Past the Seaman's Institute that made me think of my brother Andy sailing out of Halifax in his merchant seaman's uniform. Now that the war in Europe was ended he was safer, we thought, taking supplies through the Panama Canal to the Pacific, where the war would surely be over soon. To be ended by the bomb we had never heard of, which ever after became 'the Bomb'.

A couple of blocks north, away from the lake, was Marion Spenser. Our refuge. Our first home in Toronto.

Ellen answered ads in the paper, looking for an apartment, in short supply in Toronto then. She didn't like imposing on Mrs Spenser, sharing the little room on the second floor with me. She hated taking favours, being beholden. The Party arranged a temporary job for her, writing a report on a labour conference, and they paid her for it, which was certainly not usual. It helped though, when my father didn't send support money that first month.

Finally I went with her to look at a flat on Euclid Street. On a small porch outside the front door, two wooden chairs were occupied by a man and woman in their early fifties. They seemed puffed out with layers of clothing, topped with matching brown cardigans buttoned up to their chins.

'I'm renting out the second floor flat,' the landlord said. 'There's a living room at the front, a bedroom off the hall, and a kitchen at the back. We'll all share the bathroom.' Ellen would have liked something more private, but beggars can't be choosers she said to me while we looked around upstairs.

'Our son Paulo lives here also, the three of us. He's sixteen,' the landlord told Ellen. Hmm, I thought. Sixteen and male. Italian like the boy I had had a crush on back in Vancouver. Romance?

My mother and I rode crowded together with the driver in the front of a small pickup truck early Saturday morning. In the back, a bookcase and chest of drawers given to us by Mrs Spenser, with our suitcases and a box of odds and ends, also contributed by Mrs Spenser and her friends. In the yard, contained behind a low wooden fence, the boy. Paulo. He was about as tall as Ellen, five feet or so. He had very broad shoulders and a big chest. And a neck so short that his head seemed to swivel right on his shoulders. Face pudgy and pale, eyes soft as a puppy, with long lashes.

The driver carried our things upstairs, Ellen walking ahead, me trailing behind, already discarding Paulo into the wastebasket of love. Ellen and I walked through the empty rooms – she had negotiated the use of a small table and two chairs for the kitchen – and began thumbtacking newspaper curtains at the windows. I washed out the cupboards and set out our dishes. Two plates, two bowls, two cups and saucers, two knives, forks, spoons. A kettle, a pot, and a frying pan. Like playing house. Waiting for new beds to be delivered from Simpson's

I put my hair up in pincurls because Ellen said we'd go out to dinner to celebrate. We'd walk up to Bloor Street to one of the little Hungarian restaurants and eat goulash and dumplings. With my head tied up in a turban, I stood on the front porch waiting for the delivery truck. Paulo's mother sat on one of the chairs and the boy, Paulo, stood in the back corner, watching me. Paulo looked at me with his brown puppy eyes and smiled a chewing sort of smile, wet and tonguey.

I tried to talk politely without saying anything. Nothing about myself, about my mother, about our past or our plans for the future. In my turban I felt like a gypsy. Impulsively, showing off about what I thought I knew of palmistry, I asked Paulo,

'Would you like me to read your palm?'

As the words fell from my mouth I realized with horror that I'd have to hold his hand to do it. But there was no backing down. His wet mouth smiled and he stepped forward and stuck his hand right under my chin. I reached out but my palm leapt away from the hot current in his thick hand. I tried to remember the diagrams in my book. My eyes scanned instantly and a small puff of terror burst into my mind.

His palm was blank as a newborn baby's, a rubber doll's. Nothing there but the elementary tracing of the trio of head, heart and destiny. And a plain curve of life. Nothing would ever happen to him. There was no future, no past.

'Other hand,' I instructed briskly. I held his warm baby hand in my cold rejecting palm, hoping for a salvation I couldn't find, desperate with what I thought I saw. No hopes, no dreams; no little stars of talent, islands of misadventure.

'You have a strong heart, your life will be very happy. I have to go now.'

I fled inside, upstairs to my mother, frantically pulling at my turban and curls.

The twin beds – box springs and mattresses – that Ellen bought from Simpson's arrived and went one into the bedroom for me and one into the living room for her.

'It will be very pretty,' she said. 'I'll put some bright pillows against the wall and we'll use it for a couch in the daytime.'

Ellen sent me out to the grocery store for bread, milk, butter, eggs, tea. Just to get us started, she said. Paulo followed me down the front walk out toward the street. 'You beee-long to my heart,' he sang, a thick monotone. 'Now annnd forever.' He stood against the fence in the front yard and watched me go up the street. When I returned he was sitting on the front porch. As soon as he saw me he came down the walk and opened the gate.

'Thank you, Paulo,' I told him, trying to be polite but not really friendly. 'Don't encourage him,' my mother had told me. Easier said than done. I was probably the first girl who had ever held his hand.

'You beee-long to my heart.' Up the pathway. 'Now annnd for-ever.' Up the steps and into the house.

'Stop it, Paulo, leave me alone.'

'You beee-long to my heart.' Up the stairway to the second floor.

'Mom,' I called out, nearly in tears.

'That's enough now, Paulo. Go away.' I guess you had to have a mother's voice to get through to him. He stopped singing and then walked away, back downstairs.

Ellen made a cup of tea and we sat on the linoleum floor in the living room getting used to our new home. We unpacked the clothes from our suitcases and put them away. In the closet, written in ink: 'This landlord is a cheat!'

The worst thing about the flat was that we would have to share the bathroom. It meant that the whole stairway and upstairs hall would be shared with three other people and you could encounter a total stranger there anytime. I complained to my mother that they'd be able to see me if I was sitting in the kitchen in the morning. She knew what I meant – with my young embarrassing body in pyjamas.

'You'll have to get a better bathrobe or else get dressed in your room before breakfast.'

When I went to bed that night I hated it all. Sharing a bedroom with Ellen at Mrs Spenser's was better. Nothing had really prepared me for the fear, the sense that Paulo could be right outside my door, could be upstairs here. And in the middle of the night my worst fears were in the dark room with me when I opened my eyes to the pale dusting of moonlight spread onto the linoleum from the window. The door opened slowly. I was stiff and paralyzed, holding my breath, afraid to move or shout. A figure moved forward silently into the room. It held something in its hand, up about shoulder height. Was it a knife? Was Paulo in my room?

But it was my mother – with a rolled up newspaper. She flipped on the light and started hitting the walls and crying. I thought she had gone mad. Hitting and crying.

'Bedbugs,' she wailed. 'The place is full of bedbugs.'

I was out of bed already, scared to death of all of them – Paulo, the bedbugs, my mother.

'Let's have some tea,' I gurgled, heading out to the kitchen – away from the madwoman.

We sat in the kitchen and she jabbered at me, 'I'm bitten all over. Did you get any bites? I woke up burning all over, I'm very sensitive to them, like an allergy, my body starts burning at the first bite.' Trying to calm herself. 'Look here, on my leg. What about you, are you okay?'

'I think I might have two or three bites.' I inspected my legs.

'They suck your blood, you know. It's not really a bite. They suck. They live on blood.'

'I was really scared when you came in the room, I thought it was Paulo.'

'I'm sorry I frightened you. I had to see them to make sure that was what it was. When you turn on the light they all run, you can see them running on the walls.'

We sat up in the kitchen for the rest of the night and made plans. We'd go back to Mrs Spenser's right away and find something else, even if it cost more.

'They lay eggs in the mattresses. Maybe they didn't have time to infect the beds, but we can't take any chances. We'll have to send them to be fumigated. Brand new beds.'

Ellen challenged the landlord in the morning, demanded her money back, 'Why didn't you say there were bedbugs?'

'You didn't ask me,' he said.

Before we left she added to the message in the closet, a warning to other tenants. 'Bedbugs!' she wrote.

The little truck came to pick up our things and carry us back to our fairy godmother, to Mrs Spenser's predictable calm, Ellen with half of the rent money, me with my lap full of groceries in the brown paper bag. Paulo stood on the porch and watched us get into the truck, and as it began to move he rushed to the fence and called out, 'You beee-long to my heart. You beee-long to my heart.'

23. NONE BUT THE LONELY HEART

There was a huge street party in Toronto when the war finally ended in the summer of 1945. I stood on the back of a flatbed truck in the raucous parade across Queen Street, unrolling toilet paper into the breeze, deliriously happy to feel part of the celebration. My family had still been living in Vancouver when Germany surrendered in May, and I'd been in that parade too, down Granville Street, sitting on the edge of a float next to Lorraine, swinging my legs – bare knees and bobby socks – and cheering. Here in Toronto everything was bigger, bolder, noisier.

Soon after my mother and I arrived in Toronto she was sent to a conference out in the countryside. A perk arranged by Tim Buck, the Communist Party leader, to give Ellen a bit of holiday after everything she had been through with my father. She told Tim they had to allow me to go too. 'I can't leave her alone in Toronto, she's only fourteen.' So they gave her a voucher for both of us. For Ellen it was a writing assignment and a week in the country, away from the heat of Toronto. For me it would be a holiday, because I wasn't expected to do any work or go to the meetings. There was nothing to do – no other kids there, so the only thing was to sit around and listen to people talk, talk, talk. Or go for walks by myself. I did that too, but it was a bit scary being out in the country, in a new place where I didn't know my way around. It was better to sit on the hard chairs at a meeting. I had become very much a city girl, I think.

The conference was about time and motion study, a new strategy that management was using to exploit the workers. The delegates discussed it so they could take information back to their union members. The delegates were the usual kind of vigorous political activists that I had seen in Vancouver, the only difference being more Jewish people and fewer Ukrainians.

After the week was up, Ellen went back to Toronto to write up the story for the *Tribune*, the Party newspaper. She worked out something with the organizers so that I could stay for another week and help out in the kitchen. After Ellen was gone I wasn't allowed to attend any more meetings, so between kitchen times I could wander around or

Toronto, 1945.
I am fifteen years old, or perhaps about-to-be-fifteen.

else stay in the dorm. I went for long walks down the gravel roads, marking my trail with piles of rocks so that I'd be able to find my way back.

During one of those walks I met a boy. About seventeen, a healthy-looking country boy from one of the nearby farms. We walked a bit together along the road and then stood on the bridge over the river and looked down at the water, talking about ourselves, making it all up. Looking down at the flowing water, dreaming. The trees hanging over the stream, the glittering ripples, like some movie scene. We kissed a couple of times and I let him feel my breasts. I promised to meet him there again the next day. 'I'll meet you in the middle of the bridge,' I said. But I didn't go. He was pretty boring compared to the grown-ups I was used to, the Party people and union people. It wasn't worth the effort, just to get a bit of a thrill on the bridge.

At the end of the conference there was a banquet and I helped out in the kitchen in the afternoon. Everyone was supposed to wear a costume that they had made from materials around the camp. So I took an enormous supply of paper napkins from the kitchen and sewed them together into a bridal gown. I got a big round of applause for the costume, but I couldn't sit down because it would tear, so I had to stand up all evening until finally I spilled a glass of lemonade all over myself and I could go to my room and get changed.

In the car going back to Toronto there were four of us. Two men in front. Another in the back seat with me. I hadn't had enough sleep the night before, so I was pretty dozy, sprawled under a blanket in the darkness. He lectured me on becoming an adult, 'You'll have to learn to make your own decisions, comrade, to do what it is that you want to do,' all the time groping me under the blanket, fumbling at my breasts. 'In this time of women's emancipation, you won't have to conform to bourgeois conventions. You'll be able to do as you like, decide things for yourself.' I decided he was old and stank of cigarettes. They dropped me off at Mrs Spenser's where my mother was waiting.

Ellen started work at the Seaman's Institute as a typist – another favour arranged for her by Tim Buck. And we moved into a new apartment on Lippincott Street just north of College. All clean and modern and private. No bugs. A bit too expensive, Ellen said, but we'd have to manage somehow. I found a summer job through an ad in the newspaper – I was a mail girl at Abitibi Power and Paper Company, downtown on University Avenue I think, delivering mail around the huge building. All the mailgirls worked on roller skates, whizzing through the long corridors. I wasn't a very good skater, but I could manage. And I loved the shush of the skates on the dark green Congoleum floors. My first *real* job.

Ellen hated her typing job. 'All they want is my flying fingers,' she said. 'They don't care whether I have a brain in my head.' She told me then, 'Don't ever learn to type, or you'll be doing it for the rest of your life.' Important career advice: avoid the secretarial pool. Rows on rows of women, typewriters clattering. It's a wonder they didn't all go deaf. Or lose their minds. Or both. Maybe they did.

At the end of the summer I had a birthday and finally turned fifteen. My father sent a present – I couldn't believe it. I think it was probably the first present he ever got for me, except for a wounded pigeon he brought home in his lunch pail once. He made a good choice. He sent me a book called *Mathematics for the Million*, a socialist book by Lancelot Hogben, about using math as an instrument for the people, to help the working class. I was really impressed, because I didn't know that he was even aware that I loved math and was very good at it. It wasn't a kid's book, it was for adults, a big thick one, and I think that I read most of it. My mother didn't say anything about it, and I could tell that she didn't want to know that I liked it. I think she gave me a skirt. I needed new clothes for school. I was sorry to have to quit my job to go back to school, but since I was only fifteen there wasn't any choice in the matter.

The high school just up the street from where we lived was Central Tech. I registered there to start tenth grade. We had just come from B.C. and didn't know about the Ontario system of two kinds of high schools, one for kids who were planning to go to university and one for the rest of us. Going to the school just up the street seemed a logical thing to do, so I did it. At Central Tech one of the choices I had was between shop and home ec. I'd already had home ec in Vancouver at General Brock High School so I signed up for shop. I was the only girl in the class and even the teacher seemed bewildered to see me. I felt like an *alien*, some creature from another planet, there among all the boys, but I loved it. Not because of the boys, but because of subjects – a lot more interesting than learning how to wash dishes and sew, which

I'd been doing since I was just a little kid. I learned about building a house, about laths and joists, sills and tie beams. I learned how to repair a toaster and rewire a lamp. To take out the old wiring and put in a new light socket and a new on/off switch and a plug. But apart from the shop class, the rest of the school was very boring for me.

Ellen's Party group in Toronto was very different from anything she was involved in during her life with my father. For the first time she was a person, just another person in the group, not Lawrence's wife. And she could say what she thought without being glared at by him. The group seemed to be made up of artists – a photographer, a musician, a painter, and Ellen, a writer. But I never met any of them, because they didn't come to our apartment for meetings. Ellen went out to wherever they were. Now that she was away from my father she began to extend her separate identity. It must have been sometime around then that Ellen met David, her first boyfriend since she left my father. It occurs to me now that she might have met David at the conference, and gone back to Toronto with him. He started coming to our flat to visit.

David was a gentle man, small and dark haired, brown eyes so new to her. He had a good sense of humour, liked to joke and laugh. 'He walks like Groucho Marx,' I complained. But I liked him. He was twenty-five years old, halfway between Ellen's age and mine. David and Ellen went to political meetings together, and sometimes a movie. Occasionally all three of us went out for dinner or to a movie. Sometimes she'd invite him for dinner at our apartment.

He'd sit on Ellen's bed in the living room, leaning back against the pillows along the back wall. A cloth over the trunk transformed it into a coffee table. David lounged comfortably across the bed; Ellen sat next to him with her feet curled up. We'd just sit and talk, joke about things. They'd talk about books and politics, I'd mostly just listen.

Ellen and I had our first Christmas on our own, without Andy or my father. It was strange being just the two of us. Ellen bought a small tree and a package of ornaments, and I made paper chains like I used to when I was just a kid. Ellen made shortbread with her special recipe and it was wonderful. She pricked the top of it with a fork before she baked it, and it had to cook at a very low temperature so that it wouldn't burn – or even get brown.

My father sent a package to us for Christmas – I can't remember what he sent Ellen. Maybe a scarf, something like that. He sent me a boxy kind of purse made of orange pigskin. It was hard and stiff and looked rather like a football. I hated the colour and the shape and especially the pigskin – you could see the spots where the hairs had been. I didn't ever use it. But I had to send a note to say thanks. I'm sure I didn't send him a present, maybe a card, but I don't think so.

On New Year's Eve Ellen was sick with a cold, so she said I should go out by myself to a movie. I didn't exactly want to go alone, but I wanted *something*. So I walked up to Bloor Street and went to a movie to celebrate the beginning of 1946. I think the movie was *Notorious* – Ingrid Bergman and Cary Grant, love and spies, clinging evening gowns, and the men in tuxedos. Champagne. When I got home it was almost eleven, and Ellen had been dozing in bed all evening. This was an important occasion for us, this beginning of a new year on our own, so we had a little party then. And she didn't even have to get up, since her bed was the living room couch. I read to her for a bit from her new Dorothy Parker book, where I encountered the word *whore* for the first time and didn't know quite how to pronounce it. 'Whoar,' I said. But she didn't laugh at me, that was good. We turned on the radio and listened for the new year to come in. *Guy Lombardo and His Royal Canadians coming to you from the Make Believe Ballroom high atop the Astor Hotel in New York City.* At the time, and for years afterwards, I thought it was the Maple Leaf Ballroom, not Make Believe.

We talked about trying to listen all the way across the country, as each time zone caught the year, but Ellen was sick and sleepy so all we managed to hear was the countdown in New York. We wished each other a happy new year almost formally. 'Happy New Year, Laurie,' 'Happy New Year, Mama,' with some sense that this occasion marked a change in our lives. Looking ahead to some adventure mixed in with our troubles.

I moved the radio into my bedroom and stayed awake to hear 1946 arrive in Chicago, but by then it was one in the morning and I had to give up on the rest of the night. I was coasting along with whatever was going to happen, just muddling through. I hadn't learned to make decisions, or even to know that every action I took was a decision of some sort. Everything seemed to happened without any volition on my part.

Sometimes I'd do my homework in the kitchen while Ellen and David talked. And pretty soon I'd get into my pyjamas and say goodnight. I usually tried to stay up late, until he went home, but he always outwaited me. And Ellen didn't say, 'David, you'd better go now because it's getting late.' They both waited me out, I guess.

I'd lie in bed and read for a while and eventually I'd turn out my light and go to sleep, feeling very lonely and shut out. Then David took to coming into my room to talk for a few minutes after I went to bed, to say goodnight. And then to kiss me goodnight. He was a good kisser. Better than Tony, the boy I had a crush on in Vancouver, the first boy who ever kissed me, and better than that friend of my father's who mashed me up against the wall one time, and better than the country boy I kissed on the bridge. I began to get a lot of practice. But he couldn't stay too long in my room. My mother was waiting for him.

Oh, David, what a situation. Rampant teenage sexuality from me, and Ellen a newly emancipated woman thoughtful trying out another man for the first time after nearly twenty years with my father.

Shall I confess? If not now, when? And David dead for thirty years. I'd barely turned fifteen, still feeling gawky. A pocket Venus, my mother called me, but not till later. Meantime I was just a kid. Sweetening my lips with lemon drops before David came in to say goodnight. Isn't that the meaning of *sweet kisses*? So when he asked me if I'd like to come to his room some day after school, I was pleased to be able to explore this love thing just a little more. We decided on Thursday afternoon. I took some money I had saved to the 5 & 10 and bought new underwear. A pair of dainty white panties, a brassiere, and a petticoat embroidered with pink flowers. Cheap and shiny. A kind of trousseau. I put them on after school before my mother got home from work. I peeked at myself and preened in front of the mirror on my dresser. I thought I looked like a magazine model, and I loved the slinky smooth satin.

David lived nearby, in one room of a large house that might have been converted from a small apartment building into this neat rooming house. The long hallway was a clean and shiny brown, with polished linoleum and a row of wooden doors with brass numbers on them. Down the right side they went neatly, 2, 4, 6.

I don't know what it was I expected, maybe an afternoon of cuddling and kisses, of lovey talk, of slow exploration while he tried to persuade me and I tried to resist, while he told me how beautiful I was, how irresistible. I didn't actually think anything would happen. It would just be a movie scene. And I hoped for a bit of that tingling I felt when he was kissing me. But with all the kissing, David talked not of love but, like the smelly old groper in the car, about emancipation from bourgeois ideology, about my freedom to make this kind of decision. There were only two choices: yes, or capitalism. Not yes or no. It was an intelligent political decision that I was making, not a romantic one, even with the warm buzzy feelings. The politics sort of took the edge off my schoolgirl movie notions. And David's condom turned the afternoon into an anatomy lesson. I had never actually seen one of those before. That was a relief, really, because I hadn't even thought about getting pregnant, although I should have been scared to death. It had just never crossed my mind that anything *real* would happen. Where was my mind, anyway? So it was an afternoon of great disappointment – politics and anatomy. Not a romantic love scene.

But it was definitely interesting. There was some potential there, I could tell. But I didn't want to do any more exploring. I hid my new dainties from my mother. And it was the end of the lemon kisses with David. Neither of us said anything, he just stopped coming into my room.

My mother thought I was happy, and I probably was. I behaved like a happy girl, cheerful at school, not moody. But I always felt alone, didn't seem to have any friends, always felt that I was somehow different and would never be able to be like ordinary people. I used to wear my mother's clothes to school because we were about the same size. Little cotton suits that she made. I remember one that was red and white checked gingham, with a black belt and a bouncy peplum over my hips. I thought I looked very grown up, of course. But grade ten isn't a place for grown-ups. Nobody liked me, I thought.

I was not very happy after my little afternoon with David. I suppose I had hoped that he'd turn into my boyfriend. But he didn't. He couldn't, really. Even I knew that he was too old. I didn't even think that he might be my mother's boyfriend; I never gave it a thought.

At the end of term there was a dance at the school – a prom – and I wanted so much to go. I'd never been to a school dance and I couldn't bear to miss it. So I asked David if he'd go with me, if he'd take me to the dance. There he was, twenty-five years old, and he had to take me to a high school dance for grade tens. He couldn't very well refuse me, could he? I knew he'd be embarrassed to be there, and I knew I would be too, although I convinced myself that since I was so much more grown up than the kids at the school it would be okay for me to have a date with a grown-up adult man. David and my mother tried to talk me out of it. But I had no one else to go with. I was desperate. I wore Ellen's black crepe dress with the flared skirt and tiny gold stars painted all over it. David and I danced together a couple of times, round and round the gym in front of the teachers and all the kids. Nobody talked to us. And then I asked him to take me home. Maybe I even cried, walking down Lippincott Street holding hands.

After mid-term exams at Central Tech the guidance counsellor suggested that I change to an academic high school. He said I had the highest marks of anyone in that school for over twenty years, maybe forever, at least that's what my mother told me. I hadn't given any thought to going to university, perhaps Ellen hadn't either. I didn't know anyone who had gone to university, and I don't think she did. We were a working-class family, politically, economically and socially. University was beyond even dreaming about. We talked about it. I thought I might as well stay at Central Tech for awhile; I could walk to school and walk home at lunchtime if I wanted. To get to the nearest collegiate school I'd have to take a bus and carry my lunch every day. All that nuisance and extra money, why bother? And we might not even stay in Toronto, who knew? But in the end I made the switch to Jarvis Collegiate. A new school again. New people. Starting over.

I had a kind of melancholy, a deep loneliness. Some afternoons I'd walk along College Street feeling bereft, disconnected. At a drug store near Spadina Avenue I'd sit on the stool at a long marble counter – like my father sitting at a bar – and I'd order a Bromo-Seltzer. I don't know why. A Coke was a childish treat. For pleasure. A Bromo was an adult indulgence, a sign of trouble. Perhaps a headache like Ellen's migraines, which sent her to bed with a scarf over her eyes, the blinds pulled down, the house quiet. .... There was something appealing to me about unwrapping a Bromo, taking the blue paper off and dropping the big white tablet into the glass of water, watching it sink to the bottom and send a geyser of bubbles rising to the top, drinking it while it fizzed. Champagne maybe.

David and a lot of the Party members in Toronto were Jewish, and Ellen and I had our first experience with the great kosher delis of Spadina Avenue. Nothing like that out in Vancouver. Oh, the steaming chunks of corned beef and pastrami sliced wafer thin and piled high on good rye bread. Green tomato pickles and kosher dills.

Ellen, on her old red portable Smith-Corona, wrote a play about anti-Semitism that was accepted by CBC. She had always been in love with radio drama, and we listened to our favourite programs regularly. Mercury Playhouse, Stage One. Ellen thought she could see a future for herself in writing for radio. She wrote to Norman Corwin, who was a big-time radio writer in New York. He invited her to visit a rehearsal 'if she was ever in New York'. So that decided her. As soon as spring began, she made the trip.

I have no idea how long she was away. Two or three weeks? I don't know. Long enough to make friends and make plans. Long enough to write a letter to me and tell me some of the exciting things she was doing. *I've seen Norman Corwin producing a play! I went to CBS and gave them my name. Oh yes, they said, I was expected, and then someone came to escort me up to the studio. He came in and held out his hand. So you came, he said to me. Welcome to New York.*

Ellen had arranged for me to stay with some neighbours while she was away. The house was quiet, no kids, and after I'd finished my homework there was nothing to do. But I found a little dark formal room that I loved, with a small upright piano. In that calm room the blinds were drawn to keep the world out, to prevent the afternoon sunshine from damaging the carpet and the dark stuffed chesterfield with its fat floral cushions. No one in the family played the piano, and I couldn't play it either. In fact, music was my worst subject in school. But I spent hours in that room, trying to pick out tunes on the piano, trying to write them down the way I was studying at school. The tune I kept working on was one I had learned a couple of years earlier in Vancouver, from a musical play that Ellen and her theatre group had put on. All afternoon I twisted on the piano stool in that dark room, picking out the mournful tune. I drew staffs on paper and wrote the notes while I struggled through the melody, humming it, listening, writing. I'd sing it quietly while I picked out the syllables: 'None But the Lonely Heart Can Know My Sorrow'. The dark room suited my melancholy mood perfectly.

But Ellen brought her happiness back from New York and began planning to move there. 'Everyone I met was encouraging, welcoming. Oh, Laurie, you'll love it!'

And I caught excitement from her, turning toward joy in just that moment, delighted to leave my melancholy days behind.

PART TWO
RUNNING AWAY FOR GOOD

A typical row of tenements on the Lower East Side.
The first apartment we looked at on Monroe Street was
in a building just like this, although I don't remember
restaurants, bakeries and delicatessens.
(Photo: Brian Merlis)

24. WAITING FOR JOHN GARFIELD

We took the overnighter from Toronto and arrived at Grand Central Station early in the morning, each of us carrying our clothes in the kind of boxy suitcases of the time. Brown plaid, I think. I loved sleeping in a tiny room on the train, like a little dolls' house – I had the upper berth. My mother the lower. Oh, how we laughed trying to get dressed in the morning, bumping into each other.

When we moved to New York in 1946 it was part of my mother's search for independence, for a new life. She would be a writer in the land of opportunity, she thought, where her talent would be recognized. It was a very simple plan. Her typewriter, a sleek Smith-Corona portable, was in a red leather case.

The spy trial of Fred Rose, the Communist MP, opened in Ottawa in the spring of 1946 – the day after we took the train out of Toronto. But it was only coincidence that we left Canada then, on that particular day, I'm sure it was. Ellen didn't seem to be paying attention to political activity then, only to her creative push and her ambition. When she separated from my father she was able to separate from the hubbub of politics too. But she must have told Tim Buck she was leaving. The Old Man, they called him. He was the one who had recruited her back in 1933 in Calgary. She was always proud of that: 'Recruited by Tim Buck himself,' she'd say. Only not right then, not when we were crossing the U.S. border, she didn't say it.

For months she had been writing to people, begging for help to find a cheap place to live. A friend had taken an apartment for us. *It's not much, Ellen,* she wrote, *but you know how scarce apartments are here right now.* It was just post-war. Returning servicemen had priority for everything. Jobs, housing. Yes, we knew. Or really, *Ellen* knew. I was such a muddle of post-pubescent hormones that I barely knew my own name, it seems to me.

My mother rushed through the splendour of Grand Central in the morning, the dome of the ceiling – a brilliant soft blue, the blue I remembered from back home in Vancouver, clear sizzling summer sky blue. Here that summer sky twinkled with thousands of painted stars and lights. The hard shining floor, swirling pink marble, crowds of people hurrying. But I couldn't stop to gawk – at the big clock in the centre, the shining brass – I had to rush along after Ellen and concentrate on not letting a redcap take my suitcase away. 'We can't afford to tip him,' she said. 'And we can carry them ourselves. They're not heavy anyway.'

She gave the taxi driver the address. Monroe Street, the heart of the Lower East Side. We knew about that from books and radio, and from American movies: *Golden Boy* with John Garfield, Burgess Meredith in *Winterset*, under the Brooklyn Bridge. Poetic poverty, that was Hollywood's message then: the people were poor but respectable, facing life's hardships with courage and pride. We could do that. With dignity and honour. I was sure of it. Ellen, thin and eager, leaned back against the worn fabric of the rattling taxi, sighing into our future. We jiggled and jostled against each other on the bumpy ride through unfamiliar exciting streets – tall buildings, people rushing, traffic, noise.

We got out of the taxi in front of a brick building – four storeys. The fare was 85 cents and my mum gave the driver a dollar and said *keep the change.* She had been watching too many movies; that was the grand lady scene. She always did everything with such style.

(Later it turned out that what she gave him wasn't a one, it was a ten. It was our first experience that all American money looked the same. We learned to be careful about it, and look at the numbers, not just the colour. She said the cabbie was 'a crook. He just took advantage of us. He knew I didn't mean that. He ought to be ashamed of himself.')

Up three steps to a heavy wooden door. Into the vestibule. Pressed tin in decorative squares, painted brown, brown woodwork. Everything brown. A row of metal mailboxes set into the wall above a hot water radiator. Discarded envelopes, newspapers and advertising lay scattered on top of the radiator and wafted to the floor in the air currents when the door opened. Cigarette butts on the tiled floor. The inner glass door showed a hallway ahead; on the left it went back to darkness, and on the right a flight of stairs going up. A dim lightbulb hung in the centre of the hall.

Ellen had keys, sent to her by Betty, the friend who had found the apartment for us. Into the hallway and the smell of cabbage. In 1946 these halls weren't the needle parlours and toilets of the druggies, merely the homes of the poor. Dusty, dirty, dark. Slums. A musty airless smell.

We started up the stairs, and I noticed that my mother didn't really touch the wooden stair rail. Her fingertips just grazed the top. Too elegant for this slum, I thought, and grabbed the railing tightly. Dried gum was stuck underneath, all the way up. I adopted her elegant style a bit clumsily.

'Come on, Laurie, we're almost there.'

We were wearing tailored suits. Mine was navy blue. I had on a white blouse and my hair was turned under in what was called a pageboy. There is a picture of me from that time – I looked fifteen going on forty, so serious. I was wearing penny loafers and white ankle socks turned over once at the cuff – bobby socks. At almost sixteen, I was very grown up, but I felt clumsy next to my dainty mother. Ellen was wearing a grey wool suit with a faint white stripe. She made it herself, using fabric from a man's suit. That's what women did then, after the war. At her throat was a frilly pink jabot; she was very feminine, very graceful. She was five feet tall and weighed eighty-seven pounds, a fluff of brown hair around the delicate face. Eyes hazel, it said on her immigration form. She thought it sounded more interesting than blue.

We were wearing gloves and carrying handbags. Over Ellen's arm she carried a fur coat. Top-of-the-line muskrat. It represented all her worldly goods – a purchase she made in Toronto with an inheritance, almost eight hundred dollars, from a never-known uncle. She had been skinny and cold all her life and so, through a comrade in the furrier's union, she got a really good deal on something she had always wanted. The rest of the money paid for the train to New York, some advance rent on the apartment, and a bit left over to keep us for a week, maybe two.

As we reached each landing we put the suitcases down for a minute and changed hands. Ellen's shoulders were straight as she went up the last flight, her back firmly upright. We were on our way to 3A. Third floor, right side, the door set at a slight angle to steal some space from the hall for the rooms within. The Yale key turned and Ellen pushed the door open. Kitchen.

Two paces from the sink a tall sashed window, its tattered brown shade pulled partway down, let in the soft morning light from the airshaft. A black telephone was on the windowsill. Crushed cigarette packages and old envelopes, mostly bills, littered the floor. Linoleum with trodden flowers, worn to grey in front of the sink. Cabinet doors swinging open to display the dirty wooden shelves, a saucer left behind, the top of a jar. A mirror over the sink picked up a wavering reflection as we stepped into the room.

A cockroach, brown and shiny, lifted his head, waved antennae, tasted our alien Canadian smell, and slowly inserted himself into the crack between the sink and the wall.

We watched silently, assessing the scope of this danger, this measure of our personal disaster.

'Let's go, Laurie,' she said, as she turned me around and pulled the door shut with a thud.

I don't remember her talking to me, but I read her mind a lot in those days, the way you do with your mother when you're tagging along. So I think she didn't say much when we left the apartment. We certainly couldn't live there, that was all that mattered. She may have said that. She may have said, *We couldn't possibly live there.* It was as obvious to me as it was to her. Worse than any Depression apartments we'd had in Calgary or Vancouver, and we'd lived in a whole lot of cheap places. Furnished rooms, empty offices with the bathroom in the hall, apartments in Chinatown, over a laundry. Maybe she said that. *It's worse than any place we ever lived in during the Depression.*

Out the door, suitcases bumping down the stairs, out to the street where all the buildings looked the same. Then we walked a few blocks. Ellen was very quiet. I tried to get my bearings, to learn the language of New York: uptown, downtown, East Side, West Side. We walked to the Bowery, the street of pawnshops. Perhaps her old dream, the fur coat, would help to finance the next stage of this new dream.

'You wait here with the suitcases. I'll be right back.'

I started to panic, to call out, *No, don't leave me here, don't leave me.* But she was gone, already gone, and I heard the clang of the bell over a door as she pushed through. Well, she knew what she was doing. There was no need for me to panic, we'd be all right. Stand up straight. Learn to laugh about it. I stood there by the entrance, looking in the window at wristwatches, cameras, a saxophone. A large china dog looked back at me with haughty brown eyes. I stuck out my tongue.

Coming out, Ellen wore her stormy lady face, angry and righteous.

'Thirty dollars! Thirty dollars is all they'll give me for this coat! It's worth eight hundred at least. Sid Belker told me that when I bought it. *It's worth eight hundred dollars, Ellen, and I'll let you have it for only six.* I'm not going to give it to them for thirty dollars, the crooks. They ought to be ashamed of themselves!'

Her anger was always cold and clean. How could she do that? Mine got hot and messy, all rumpled and red and out of control, like my father's. So I had to be careful of it.

We put the suitcases down on the broad sidewalk, in the shadow of the El, dark and gloomy there on the Bowery. Bars and flophouses and cheap coffee shops lined the sidewalk. Ellen sat down on her suitcase and I did the same. If she had liked Stan and Ollie movies, I could have said, *Here's another fine mess you've gotten me into.* But maybe she wouldn't have thought it was a funny line. She was pretty excited about what we were doing, just running off from Canada that way. Was she scared too? Well, if she was, she certainly didn't show it. A train rattled overhead and I looked up at the rush of sound, thinking it would surely fall on us. Finally I decided that I had to do something. I was getting nervous sitting there listening to my mother think. But what could I do? The only thing was to talk.

'What will we do?' I asked. 'We don't have a place to live. We don't have any money.'

People passed by, ignoring us. Not bothering to ask us for a handout. Ladies – sitting there with gloves on. Sitting on the suitcases in the shadow of the Third Avenue El on a cloudy morning in May. We were not really contemplating our future, no, not that; we already knew it would be better than what had gone before. I might be scared, but my mother wasn't. I was sure of that. We were just taking a breather, working things out.

'What do people do in this kind of situation?' asking her as if she knew the answer.

In the movies, we'd have been discovered by John Garfield, a handsome working-class hero, who'd have taken us home to his mother in Brooklyn, to eat spaghetti at the kitchen table and feel loved and safe.

'We're doing it,' Ellen told me. 'We're doing what people do.'

Oh. What people do.

And I laughed then to see us in a new movie, two brave young women, doing what people do. We'd pick up our suitcases and walk off down the street to start a new story by ourselves, without John Garfield. The camera would watch us passing through poetic light and shadow under the El. Barbara Stanwyck could play Ellen – people said there was a resemblance. But there was no one in Hollywood to play me – the girls were too childish or too trite. Adolescent caricatures. Judy Garland, tremulous and syrupy, conventional, middle-class. Googie Withers, spunky but charmless. And what a name – I couldn't stand her.

I might have to do it myself. Ah, an actress. I could do that. I was sure of it.

25. HERALD SQUARE

In the shadow of the Third Avenue El we sat on our suitcases. My mother's suitcase was a little bigger than mine. She stood up. No luck at the pawnshop. New York, 1946. 'There's no help for it,' she said. 'We'll have to try to get into a hotel.'

Ellen knew her way around a bit. She had been in New York on a scouting trip a month earlier. And for years, dreaming of her escape from my father, she had been reading street maps and guides. She knew where every subway station was, and Macy's and Lord & Taylor and Saks Fifth Avenue. In the library in Vancouver, she had read *The New Yorker* from cover to cover every week. After we moved to Toronto she'd shown me the listings of movies, of Broadway shows. So she already had a hotel in mind from reading ads. The Aberdeen Hotel was in midtown Manhattan. Just a few streets away from the Algonquin, where Dorothy Parker and the witty writers Ellen talked of constantly had been said to drink, at a big round table in the lobby bar.

We got off the subway at Herald Square, right in front of Macy's department store. Down the street from the Aberdeen we passed a Schrafft's restaurant; its frilly curtains and brass door handle beckoned us in to tea, but we declined the invitation.

Of course the Aberdeen had no vacancies. I listened while my mother talked to the desk clerk. She told him the truth: she had just

Under the Third Avenue El, where we sat on our suitcases and considered our future. I have no memory of pushcarts or of other people, but I think I can see the pawnshop across the street. (Photo: Brian Merlis)

arrived by train from Toronto with her daughter, a nod in my direction. On cue I made a shy smile at the clerk. *Maybe I'll be an actress*, I thought again. She had arranged to rent an apartment, but it had been 'entirely unsuitable', and now we needed a day or two to make other arrangements. Of course it was the truth, just not the whole truth. We looked like such ladies, standing there in our neat little Canadian suits. Wartime suits still, skimpy and close fitting.

I used to marvel, in later years, at the effect Ellen had on landlords. They seemed to want her to live in their apartments, to go out of their way to have her as a tenant. Perhaps it was her careful manners, the precise voice articulating each word. At that moment I wasn't aware that I was seeing a process that would be repeated over and over, with minor variations, for most of Ellen's life: trying to find a home that was better than the last one.

Here on our first day in New York, Ellen did it. She got a room for us – single beds. There was a three-day limit. Returning servicemen had priority in everything: in jobs, in apartments, in hotel accommodations. So we would have to find something else before then. In three days we would have to move out – have to pay the bill. There in the dark and dignified hotel with its shiny brass and its red velvet curtains, watching Ellen, listening to her, I became not entirely sure that she didn't have money for the room. She convinced even me, and I certainly should have known better. We looked so reputable, standing there in the pretty lobby with our suitcases.

The room was a small one on the fifth floor, usually kept for staff emergencies. We sat at the little table by the window. Pale yellow walls, an iron radiator under the window, painted white. Little white curtains and blue bedspreads. I loved the uncluttered room, the two small beds, the reading lamps with frilly shades. I felt like a princess. It was so peaceful, so calm. Wasn't this a scene from a Shirley Temple movie?

'Now we need some money.'

Ellen phoned a friend in Toronto, David probably, to beg for a loan. If he could mail it right away it would be here in three days, when we would have to leave the hotel. He promised.

One of the great advantages of left-wing politics is that you can always find friends anywhere in the world. It's a family sort of attachment. We went to the office of the communist newspaper, the *Daily Worker*. Ellen introduced herself to Mike Gold and told him her story. Not all of it, but a lot. She said some important names that he knew, and she borrowed twenty-five dollars. He probably didn't expect to see it again, but somehow she always paid back whatever she borrowed.

Perhaps in the excitement of the day Ellen didn't even think about the FBI. Was the office under surveillance? Probably. Who in that office was the stoolie? Money had been passed to someone from Canada. Perhaps that information earned someone a few dollars. Perhaps it went into a file somewhere. Ellen wasn't an important communist, she was just what they called *rank and file*. Ordinary.

It must have been Mike Gold who told Ellen about the little Spanish restaurant with the great food. It was a bit early for dinner, but our breakfast on the train had been pretty spare and we hadn't had any lunch. On West Twenty-third Street, up on the second floor, La

Bilbaina. Five courses for $1.75. Posters on the wall – bullfighters and señoritas. We had a huge meal, appetizers that we chose from a tray, spicy vegetables, some soup and bread, hot sausages and white beans, rice pudding. I even tried a cup of coffee. Not Ellen – she had some pale tea. I wrapped up two buns in a paper napkin and squashed them into my purse for later – breakfast, maybe.

We took the subway back to the hotel. On the small table by the window Ellen spread a map of Manhattan.

'Here's where we are right now,' she showed me. 'And there is the apartment on Monroe Street. Here is the *Worker* office, and this is the restaurant.' On the pink map everything seemed logical, a simple grid. The streets went across from side to side, the avenues went up and down, and Broadway ran diagonally through it. Bright tangles of subway lines, the stations strung like coloured beads. I thought I'd never be able to get to sleep that night, but I went right out. Like a princess in my little bed.

In the morning Ellen phoned Betty to tell her the bad news about the apartment – 'entirely unsuitable' – and she came to visit us at the hotel. Gilbert, her name was. Betty Gilbert. She was the cousin of the wife of the brother of an important leftie novelist. I liked her because she was so lively and breezy. Dark hair, big lipsticky mouth, laughing. Bright coloured clothes. Flamboyant, there's a word. But she couldn't get Ellen's rent money back for the apartment.

'Tough luck, Ellen. It's money down the drain. Look, I'm sorry, what can I say? I thought it would be okay.'

'It can't be helped,' Ellen said. But I could hear her thinking, *What kind of person would think that slum would be okay?*

'Listen, we gotta have lunch at the Automat.' Betty laughed. 'You'll like it. There's one just over on Broadway. You hafta know about this place. The food is so good and it's cheap.'

I loved it. Horn & Hardart Automat, the name said. There were two walls lined with compartments like glass mailboxes, full of food. You could get casseroles of baked beans or macaroni and cheese. Things like that. Or sandwiches or pie, whatever you wanted. What you did was, you turned a crank until you saw what you wanted in a compartment. Then you put a dime or a quarter or something in the slot and the glass door unlocked. So then you could open it and take what you wanted. There was a cafeteria counter with all sorts of vegetables – more than I had seen in one place in all my life: mashed potatoes and baked, green beans, corn niblets, creamed cauliflower, cabbage, Harvard beets, baked squash, creamed spinach, succotash, sweet potatoes. On and on. You could get a vegetable plate for about thirty-five cents, with your choice of four. That was the cheapest meal. And a slice of bread, too, came with it.

In the middle of the table there was a round metal stand, raised up, with salt and pepper shakers, a huge jar of ketchup and a bottle of Worcestershire sauce, a jar of sugar with a chrome top, and a cruet with vinegar; everything right there, convenient.

Betty never stopped talking.

'I'm in here the other day with Stevie, my new boyfriend, and we're sitting here – the place is a little crowded, like always in the evening – and this guy comes in from the street. He's a bit bummy-looking, you know? scruffy? He goes over to the tea and coffee machine, and he just picks up an empty cup from the rack and fills it with hot water. That's free, you see. Only the teabag costs money, and coffee. He comes over to our table. *Okay if I sit here?* he says. *Sure*, we tell him. So he sits down and he takes the ketchup bottle and pours a bunch of it in his cup. He sits there, stirring and stirring. Tastes it. Adds salt and pepper. *Soup*, he says. *Not bad*. We all laugh our faces off.'

I laughed my face off too, and my mother smiled at the thought of it.

When Betty walked over to get coffee, Ellen rolled her eyes at me. So I know I'm not supposed to like Betty a lot. The eye-rolling means she's not our kind of person. She's a little like the kinds of girlfriends my father used to have, all the Dollys and Maisies and Queenies.

The Automat was a great place to know about, a cheap place to eat. Ellen's budget allowed seven dollars a day for the two of us. Times three days until the money comes equals twenty-one dollars and she has twenty-five, so we're okay. Transportation is okay too: the subway costs a nickel. She might even buy a copy of the *New Yorker*, but not till the third day. We could manage on two meals a day, she said. 'It will be better when we have our own place and don't have to eat in restaurants.'

Early in the morning we started looking in the *Times* at the listings of apartments for rent, me dancing around the room in my pyjamas. There certainly weren't many. Seven-thirty, Betty phoned. An apartment. Grand Street, near her place. 'Honest, I couldn't believe it, I was just on my way out the door and I saw they were putting up a sign in the window.' Gave us the address.

Ellen was annoyed. 'She's pushy,' she said. 'Trying to take over our lives. As if she'd know what we want.' Ellen was still angry about losing all that rent money on the Monroe Street apartment, two months' rent. 'I suppose we'd better go and look at it anyway.'

We found Grand Street on the map. Right there in lower Manhattan on the West Side, near Canal Street where the Holland Tunnel connects Manhattan to New Jersey. There was a subway station just a block away.

We took the IRT subway down to Canal Street and walked to the address Betty had given us. Big windows of a paint store and a blue doorway. A long wooden counter ran the length of the store; two hanging bulbs provided some dim light. Cans of paint in all sizes and colours and brands filled dark shelves on both sides. The clerk told us, 'It's the side door. Upstairs. Youse'll hafta go see Rosie.'

The door beside the shop was nearly invisible behind layers of brown paint. Inside, in the small vestibule, another door was windowed and curtained. A bell handle. I twirled it. It responded with a grating jangle. We waited. Footsteps above, and a woman's voice calling out words we didn't know. And there was Rosie at the door in floppy slippers. Round, smiling Rosie in her black dress covered by a printed smock-apron in small red and white checks. It was her uniform, and later we would see her in the street, in the grocery store across the way, at the greengrocer's, always wearing the same kind of apron.

Ellen talked in her polite Canadian way.

'Good morning. We've come about the apartment.'

'Si, si,' said Rosie. Or 'See, see.' Who could tell?

'Yes, we'd like to see it. Could we see it?'

'You see,' said Rosie, waving us into the hallway. 'Second floor. You go. I slow.'

I hung back a bit, smiling at Rosie, while my mother went ahead. Perhaps this is when I began to search for a grandmother, never knowing that I was doing it, never realizing that I had left behind two perfectly good ones in Canada.

On the second floor my mother and I waited in the hallway by the door. Rosie's floppy slippers shushed their way up the stairs. She caught her breath and pressed her hand to her bosom in the general vicinity of her heart. Then jiggled the keys out of a pocket in her apron. As she unlocked the door, she shoved it open. Sunlight burst all over us and drew us in from the dark hall.

Rosie began her grand inquisition. She would always be full of questions.

'You mama, daughter? I got daughter too. She work.'

I watched my mother catch enchantment from the sunshine, as she would all her life. Ellen hummed yes, almost dancing in the sun in the big front room.

'You got husbun? I widow.'

The Italian widow's black dress had registered with me too, and the small gold cross. Respectable. Divorce was uncommon in 1946 – a stigma, someone guilty of something nasty. And Ellen wasn't divorced anyway – she had just walked out. Walked away. No divorce. No alimony. No child support. Nothing but a suitcase, and me. I knew the reasons she walked away: the drinking, the fists, the women. I listened carefully to the words my mother said, preparing my own part in the script, should it be necessary.

'No. I don't have a husband now. Not any more.'

Rosie seemed to sympathize. She told us about the death of her husband. An accident at work.

'Twel year ago. How old you.' Ellen looked startled, but Rosie had directed her question at me.

Sixteen, I told her, even though my birthday was still a couple of months away.

The three of us walked through the apartment. It was bright and sunny, a bedroom and living room at the front, with windows looking out onto Grand Street. In the middle there was a room off the hall, on the airshaft. Beyond, in the back, another large room with a stove, a sink, and an icebox. Two windows that opened onto the roof of the paint store below. Ellen was ecstatic. She opened one of the windows and leaned out.

'Look, Laurie. We could have a roof garden. We could eat outside in the nice weather.' Ellen the romantic, I was beginning to see that. I looked out at the roof, the rusty cans, some weathered old chairs, hunks of wood, little pebbles, and tar in lumps. My brother Andy used to chew that black gooey tar when he was a kid.

Rosie tried to show us the pantry, although Ellen seemed more interested in the potential of the barren rooftop than in the reality of the kitchen facilities.

'Lotsa shelves. Big space.' In the bathroom Rosie pulled a chain hanging down from the water cabinet high up on the wall over the toilet, to assure us that it flushed. It never seemed to stop. She turned on the taps in the sink and when the pipes clanged she turned them off quickly.

'Make noise sometime,' she shrugged. 'Where you from? You no New York.'

Ellen said that we had just arrived from Canada and needed a place to live, but we didn't have any furniture. She hadn't yet said we didn't have any money – first things first. The apartment would need furniture, she told Rosie, it would need painting. 'He got furnitch,' Rosie gestured at the floor. 'He got paint, he got ever-tink.'

Ellen talked enthusiastically about how much she liked the apartment. She asked the important money question – how much was the rent?

'He want forty dollar, but you get for thirty-fi dollar month. I tell him. You pay two month first.'

Seventy dollars. Ellen agreed that the rent was certainly reasonable and that yes, she would like to have the apartment. The only little problem that remained was that just at the moment she didn't really have any money for the rent, but she did think she would have some money in a day or two. I watched her hold her chin up and smile at Rosie all the time she talked. Look straight into her eyes. This was important. This was the future, this very instant. She took a breath. Everything depended on it. She held up her chin and didn't look the least little bit frightened.

Rosie looked at her shrewdly.

'You got job?' she asked. Ah, the moment had come. Well, no. Not really just yet, Ellen explained. Not a job, exactly.

'What kind work you do?'

'I'm a writer. I write radio plays.'

Rosie just looked and waited. Ellen began talking again. 'I write stories – for radio and for magazines. I have a letter from an important producer here. He says he'll help me get a job in radio.'

Rosie still waited. What was going on in her mind, looking at the two of us? Canadian waifs.

'I will have money on Thursday. Not enough for two months, but for one month. Could you hold the apartment for us?'

Rosie's head moved very slightly, very slowly, waiting.

'We are very good tenants. Very clean and quiet. We could move in right away. Tomorrow morning. And I could give you thirty dollars then. And I'll have the rest in a couple of days.'

Rosie made up her mind. 'Okay. Okay, I tell him.'

She changed our lives right then. Rosie, who had never seen us before, had become the classic immigrant mother from every movie about the slums of New York, the mother of John Garfield, an inspiration to the needy. We were all movie stars there, standing in the sunshine.

26. LITTLE ITALY/GREENWICH VILLAGE

Ellen and I were painting four weathered kitchen chairs we had found on the roof of the paint shop. My mother had thinned the paint with turpentine for the first coat because the wood was dry as a desert; she had chosen the colours downstairs in the store, bright colours.

'You give her paint. Whatever she want,' Rosie told Mr Amadeo, our landlord. She made him supply a big kitchen table, too. And paint for the floors. At the used furniture store around the corner, 'She need stove. You give her and she pay you later.' We would have liked a refrigerator, but Ellen said no, we couldn't afford it yet. Rosie agreed with her. 'Ice box okay. You get ice, twenny-fi cent for week.' Besides being our upstairs neighbour and caretaker, Rosie was clearly the boss of the whole street, if not all of Little Italy.

Ellen bought a teapot and Rosie lent us some dishes. Life began again. Toast and tea for breakfast. Ellen made potato soup on the new stove. As long as we had a couple of potatoes and an onion we could survive anything, we thought. Add a can of corn and call it chowder. That was old Depression training, always showing up whenever we needed it.

From the front windows of our apartment we could look across Grand Street into the windows of the tenements across the street, amazed to see refrigerators. How could they afford that, we wondered, until we saw how many people lived in one apartment. The father, the uncle, the adolescent boys, all out working. The women at home, mostly, raising young kids. Buying groceries, cooking, doing laundry in the bathtub, carting it up to the roof in baskets, hanging it on the lines up there. Cleaning all day. They all wore the same kind of smock-aprons that Rosie wore. Bright colours over dark respectable dresses.

Out our back windows we had our own private roof, practically a penthouse. The old chairs had been lying out there for years, probably. Just a bit broken. Rosie said, 'Sure, you take,' so Ellen got some glue and repaired the stringers before we started painting.

'These patterns are copied from hand-carved chairbacks, like the ones my parents had at home when I was a child,' Ellen told me. 'Oh, Laurie, we had such a pretty dining room when I was young.' The backs of the chairs were embossed with swirling patterns and sensuous floral shapes. The word 'pressback' had never yet been uttered, and these chairs weren't sought-after antiques yet – only leftovers from someone's Depression home.

Two years before, when we first left Vancouver, my father had said he'd send Ellen some money every month. Sometimes money came, sometimes not, mostly not. Now that we were in New York he wrote to Ellen, *This has gone on long enough. I've given you all this time to come to your senses, now I wash my hands of you. Don't expect any more help from me in this foolishness of yours.* Ellen just said, 'Help, Ha!'

We carefully picked out the flowers in red and yellows and blues against a black background. 'The kitchen will be so cheerful,' Ellen said. 'Like a cottage in Italy, near the ocean. Should we paint the linoleum blue, do you think? Dappled like waves?' Our new life in Manhattan was going to be happy and sunny. We were free. We could make our own decisions.

Ellen was indignant. 'Arthur Godfrey! That's what they offered me. Assistant producer on the Arthur Godfrey Show. I didn't come to New York to do that kind of radio. Big freckled oaf.' My mother had high standards, left over from Depression-era politics.

She had been to see the radio writer – the one who had sponsored her immigration because he thought she had talent. He'd set up an interview for her at CBS; she didn't seem know that he might have had to pull some strings to do it. And he was probably startled when she turned down the job. Years and years later, he married an actress and Ellen had some romantic regrets. They might have suited each other, she thought.

I started looking for a job for the summer. I learned to read the Help Wanted Female ads in the *New York Times* and the *Tribune*. If you wanted a good job, you had to look there. The junky jobs were listed in the *Daily News*. And the lefty organizations advertised in *PM*.

The first job Ellen got was with the Committee for Émigré Writers and Artists, working for Mrs Canby – Mrs Henry Seidel Canby – her friends called her Lady. The group helped writers who had emigrated from Europe, displaced by the war, Ellen explained to me. They spoke mostly Russian, or German, or Yiddish, or Polish, or Hungarian. A bit of Greek and Italian, not much. Ellen said, 'I help them to English-up their manuscripts – I'm learning how to edit.'

From Ellen's point of view one of the great advantages of the job was that she could borrow a typewriter, since her pretty Smith-Corona resisted intense work. So she had something to use at home until she could afford the Olivetti portable she had her heart set on. She began to get on with her own writing, some short stories that she hoped *The New Yorker* might take.

Rosie helped us with everything. After she saw Ellen making potato soup again she decided it was time we knew something about Italian food, so every day she brought dinner to us. All of it simple, basic, delicious. Three courses, *pastina in brodo, ensalata, e-spaghetti*, she said. My first Italian words. I thought, *Maybe I can learn to speak Italian and go to Italy, when I'm an actress.* 'Thank you,' we told her, 'it's delicious, but it's too much food, we can't eat it all.' She told us, 'You no like, you no eat.' And that was that. At first we'd save what we didn't eat until the next day, but the next day there'd be more. She was like the sorcerer's apprentice, unstoppable. Bowls of stale pasta began to pile up in the icebox. We thought of putting the leftovers in the garbage, but Rosie was the one who emptied our garbage pails, so she'd surely find it no matter how carefully we might bundle it up. Flushing the extra spaghetti down the toilet occurred to us, but we didn't think the plumbing could handle it, and then Rosie would be sure to find out. We finally took to wrapping it in newspaper, into a tight little bundle that I would carry away with me when I went out. I'd drop it into a big trash barrel in the subway station or on the street corner.

Rosie liked to walk into the apartment anytime – was deeply offended if we locked the door. 'You no want, I no come,' she'd say, and we'd have to apologize.

That kind of intrusion was really hard on Ellen. She'd be sitting at the typewriter working on a story. In would walk Rosie. The iceman was right behind her, a little skinny man carrying a huge block of ice on his back, over a leather pad to keep his shirt dry and his back protected from the cold, supporting it by a leather thong across his forehead, the ice hook in his hand keeping it steady. She'd take him to the kitchen, supervise the placement of the block in the top compartment of the icebox, then stop on the way out. 'Twenny-fi cent,' she'd say. And Ellen would have to go and find her purse and give Rosie the money. Sometimes she just came for a visit maybe. But Ellen didn't want to visit. 'Good morning, Rosie. I can't talk to you now. I'm writing,' she'd say, 'I'm working.' Rosie would stand and stare at her. 'You work. I no trouble.' She'd look at Ellen's empty page. 'Go ahead. You write. I watch.'

Every morning she came into the apartment, through the hall to the kitchen; she drew the big flat pan from under the icebox and carried it carefully to the bathroom, poured it into the sink, and replaced the pan. 'I can do that, Rosie,' I suggested, the first time I saw her doing it. 'No. I do.' She was right, I would probably have forgotten it one morning, and there'd be water everywhere, dripping down into the paint store probably. Now she came in early every morning. Ellen and I were usually still asleep, but sometimes I'd be in the kitchen – sleepy in my pyjamas. She'd be wearing her black dress with the apron. 'Good morning, Rosie, buon giorno,' I'd say, practising, smiling stupidly. We had to leave the door unlocked, even at night. We got used to it.

I got a job ushering at one of the movie theatres in Greenwich Village.

On Eighth Street, right off Avenue of the Americas, which was the name for what was once simply Sixth Avenue. 'Usherette for Art Cinema' the ad said. The theatre showed 'foreign' movies. Sometimes British, sometimes European, with sub-titles, so you'd know what people were saying. I had to wear a uniform, sort of grey-blue, with silver buttons. And on weekends between shows I served 'demi-tasse' to the patrons in the waiting area. I carried a silver tray and learned to say 'ess-presso,' not 'ex-presso.' It felt like a very sophisticated life. A long way from Toronto or Vancouver. A long way from my grandparents' farm. I liked serving coffee and helping people to their seats. I had a flashlight and felt very important, really.

It was a pretty good job. The last show of the evening started at 9:20, so I could go home soon after that. Not too late. I'd be home by ten, usually, ten-thirty. I made enough money for subway fare and a few treats – a whole wheat doughnut and an orange drink at Nedick's for only fifteen cents. I loved that. I had it almost every day for lunch. I could help with the grocery money, save for some new clothes now that I was growing up. I'd need clothes for high school.

I saw *The Seventh Veil* at least a dozen times in the week that it ran. Ann Todd and James Mason. But the scene where James Mason cracks his cane over the keyboard while Ann is playing the piano was very scary. It reminded me of my father, except he never used a cane. I guess he would have if he'd had one. He used a belt, or a broom handle. And he didn't aim to miss, like James Mason. And we didn't have a piano.

I looked a lot like Ann Todd, I thought – sort of plain. Straight blond hair. Well, mine was light brown, mousy. If only my hair had been curly, or blond – or both curly and blond would be the very best – I'd look a lot better. When I complained to my mother about my hair, about the way I looked – so dull – she said, 'But Laurie, you have a classic face, and such nice eyes.' I didn't want nice eyes. I wanted to be pretty.

The summer went quickly, working, helping fix up the apartment. It was bright and shiny so Ellen was willing to face the relatively small problems with the other inhabitants: the mice and cockroaches. Mice in the pantry, leaping out of the cornflakes in the morning. Cockroaches in the kitchen. We poisoned them with Rosie's 'blue powder from the drug store.' Darn near poisoned ourselves too. They had lived for generations in the walls of the old building – in every Manhattan building, actually – and now found our groceries very tasty.

When I was young I used to think mice were cute. *They nibble things they shouldn't touch / and no one seems to like them much / but I think mice / are nice.* Now it was different. Now it was my breakfast they were nibbling. I always kicked the pantry door before I opened it. Scaring them away, I hoped.

Our things arrived from Toronto: two beds, two chests of drawers, a bookcase, a sewing machine, three boxes of books and some winter clothes. Everything we had acquired during the year we spent there while Ellen was sorting out American immigration procedures and getting used to being independent. Now here was our home, come by truck. I tell you, it felt like Christmas, unpacking that shipment. The brown tweed coat, Harris tweed, given to me by Mrs Spenser, the lady who lived out Queen Street West, a long streetcar ride. It was a very good coat, good British wool. I hated it.

I turned sixteen and then it was Labour Day and the summer was over. I started high school, grade eleven. Every day I took the subway. Washington Irving High School. Imagine, a high school named after a writer. In Canada they seemed to be named for the royal family, mostly – King George, Queen Elizabeth – and generals and politicians; General Brock was the one I went to in Vancouver. I kept the movie job, working two nights a week and on Saturday. That was terrific.

I was really smart at school, except for spelling, they said. I had to learn American spelling because they marked all my Canadian spellings wrong – that was really humiliating. I hardly ever *really* spelled things wrong. The teachers didn't even know that words like 'labour' and 'colour,' for example, were correct spellings in Canada and England and Australia and India and lots of other places. They didn't know there were different ways to spell things in different countries; some of them didn't even seem to know there were other countries. I was angry. I didn't like to be marked wrong. Too proud, I guess.

I had some great blanks in my education that I had to fill in unobtrusively, just so I wouldn't seem totally ignorant: the American Revolution, the Civil War, the forty-eight states of the union then. The

President was Harry Truman, that I already knew. The Congress. The House Un-american Activities Committee would come later, out of the paranoia of these years.

I propped a stack of books on my left hip, hitching it up with my arm, sticking my hip out to hold the stack. You had to alternate, left and right, so you wouldn't get too lopsided. I felt smart and important carrying my books, with trigonometry on top, to impress the boys in the neighbourhood. But no one seemed to care. Who would be interested in me when the streets of Little Italy were full of dark-eyed Italian girls, all breasts and bums?

27. EAST 18TH STREET

Ellen's job as an editor paid our rent and put food on the table, but finding a writers' group lifted her spirits. She came home glowing: 'I've found my friends! Wonderful friends!' Contemporary Writers, they called themselves: Eve Merriam, Martin Michel, Bobbi and Julie Fast, others. All of them working at becoming writers. It frightens me just to put these names on the page. These are names I've never said before, even to the FBI when they wanted to know. Even now I hesitate to say their names, though they're surely all dead. I know Eve is.

Ellen and Eve took to each other right away. Eve was already published, acclaimed as one of the important younger poets, published by Yale. She was smart, sophisticated, everything Ellen admired. Her real name was Evelyn Markowitz but she had changed it for a name that didn't sound Jewish. She worked at *Vogue* magazine and dressed like Ellen's dream woman, in practical clothes with a kind of androgyny that was not fashionable at the time, except for a few movie stars like Katharine Hepburn. 'Fashion is spinach,' Eve said. 'Use it for the power and strength it gives you. You can't dress like a piece of candy-floss without getting eaten up.' She raged at the designers of women's clothing. 'Pockets. Women need pockets in their clothes, just like men do.' Trying to promote fashion revolution while working at *Vogue*. 'I'm boring from within,' she'd say.

The group rented a studio on East 18th Street, over a florist shop. There was a tiny elevator, unusual in those smaller New York buildings. The owner lived on the third floor. They organized readings by prominent authors. Ellen would ask writers, and they would agree to come and read. Or speak. She'd put ads in *PM* – 'Contemporary Writers presents A Studio Party.' People came. There was always food and usually some drinks, coffee at least. Sometimes there'd be a little table where people could buy drinks. Mostly American whisky and rum, things like that, with ginger ale or Coke. Rum and Coke was big then, I remember, because of the American sailors coming home from their base in Cuba, singing 'Rum and Coca-Cola'. The group made some money selling drinks – cheaper than a bar, and classier, and entertainment too.

'So who at the studio last night?'

'Dorothy Parker. She's so shy; isn't that surprising? She's an alcoholic, of course. Very timid about going out in public; Beth had to go and pick her up and coax her and get her to the studio at the right time. But she came. And then she was absolutely wonderful.'

'I don't think I know her, do I?'

'Yes, of course you do. Remember that piece about waiting for the telephone to ring? You read it to me on New Year's Eve in Toronto, when I was sick.'

I usually felt like a complete fool when Ellen talked about books and writers, but I did remember 'A Telephone Call'. 'Oh, yes. She sits at the phone waiting for him to call and you hear everything that goes through her mind. I remember. *Oh please God let him telephone me now. I'll never ask you for anything else.'*

'She read another of her stories about women, men and women, I guess. And she talked a bit about herself. A self-deprecating kind of humour.'

I knew what self-deprecating was. A way of insulting yourself before someone else did. Another way of trying to protect yourself. The way I might say, *I'm such a lunkhead. I guess my brains are down the drain.* And that's really better than hearing someone else say, *Oh, Laurie, can't you pay attention? For heaven's sake stop mooning around.*

My mother said she didn't remember this as a characteristic of me. 'You were always concentrated – not dreamy and mooning around.' Hmmm. Were we in the same world, I wonder?

Ellen's writers' workshop met about every two weeks. In the

beginning they met at each other's apartments, sometimes at our place, once we got some chairs for the living room.

I got used to the people, seeing them come in. Eve, the poet, was a really interesting woman, I thought. Such lively eyes; she took in everything. Ellen and I went to her apartment once for dinner. Her husband, Martin, did the cooking. A kind of beef stew with wine in it. *Boeuf Bourguignon* and noodles. He was a really good cook. Years later, but not until after two sons were born, the marriage broke up. Painfully for both of them. He had finally decided to come out of the closet he had been in for all those years. He moved in with Tony.

Claire Donner had been writing for years and years, she said, in between children and whenever she could find the time. Her husband was a high school teacher – geography, something like that. They'd lived out in the country up near Syracuse, but when the kids were in their teens, Dan got a job in New York and it seemed like a good chance to move up in the world. Claire used to say, 'I don't want to be a hick all my life.' But her stories were about growing up in the country, raising kids, about making jam and feeding the pigs. Full of her love of country life. She had already had one story accepted in *Harper's Monthly*. Claire still dressed like someone's picture of a country woman, wearing full skirts in pretty florals, and a white off-the-shoulder blouse. Ellen let me read some of her stories and they reminded me of my grandmother's farm.

One of the women in the group wrote 'romantic bedroom drivel', Ellen said. 'But when anyone tries to criticize her, "*I've* been published," she says.' One story she read referred to someone as 'a horsey Canadian divorcee', then she turned to Ellen and whispered, 'I'm sorry.' 'Doesn't bother me,' Ellen told her. 'I may be Canadian, and I may be divorced – actually, I wish I were that lucky – but I know I'm not horsey.' She was such a little thing, Ellen. More like a frisky colt than a horse.

Julie and Bobbi were both writers – such a noisy, busy couple. I was fascinated by them. I thought it was so funny that *she* had a boy's name – Bobbi, and *he* had a girl's name, Julie. Bobbi was beautiful. I thought she was one of the most beautiful women I had ever seen. 'Well, she's flamboyant, I grant you,' Ellen said. A great mass of curly black hair, long earrings swinging, her breasts bobbing about in blouses that were always sliding off one shoulder or the other. She was writing for *True Confessions*. She made it sound so easy, 'I say to myself, *This is for the rent money*; and I just tap it out.' Julie was a social worker, wrote non-fiction. Articles about ways of helping people. Sociology. That sort of thing. Pop-psych, Ellen called it.

They lived in a tenement building on the east side – a big apartment, it seemed to me. The door to the apartment was in the kitchen, it was the first time I had ever seen that. And it was a big kitchen, with a table for eating, and an easy chair with cushions, a bookcase, in the corner. A window on the airshaft. Plaster walls, chalky with white paint. A Mexican poster in the kitchen, people crushed together, a peasant army, vibrant with orange and red. Orozco, Ellen said, *The Zapatistas*. Rooms trailing out in both directions, off to the front of the building, off to the back. Bedrooms, living room. That was where Bobbi worked. A typewriter on the table. Books everywhere, and woven things hanging on the walls, wooden figurines from other countries, pillow covers embroidered by women in Mexico.

Julie said that his brother Howard was furious with them for living on the Lower East Side. He paced the floor in the living room and did an imitation of successful Howard: *Our parents worked all their lives to move out of the slums, to get us an education, and just look at you, you bum. Right back here because you think it's more working class. You're a schmuck, you know that? A schmuck.*

Sometimes Ellen and I went to their apartment for dinner, or on Sunday afternoon. There were usually a couple of other people, too. Bobbi was so busy telling stories that she could never seem to get dinner organized. All the women helped out, setting the table, making salad, while the men talked in the living room, drank. 'The woman question', which Ellen said was so earnestly considered in the Party, hadn't become a personal issue yet. Equality in the workplace, in the voting booth, in education, yes. But at home, the traditional division of labour wasn't even noticed. We were all so used to it we took it for granted. If anyone mentioned that Martin cooked meals and took care of his apartment with Eve, the men would look at each other and say, 'That's different.' Nobody talked about that.

We sure had a lot of fun, folksongs on the record player, Pete Seeger and the Weavers singing 'Goodnight Irene'. Wine in bottles covered with straw. Chianti. Italian. I drank ginger ale – they usually got some for me. Now and then Betty Gilbert came too, usually with a guy. She didn't like to be alone. She was Bobbi's cousin and looked a lot like her, only Bobbi seemed more serious, even with her wildness. 'It's because she's a writer,' Ellen said. 'It makes you see everything twice.'

They were really nice to me. I was used to being the kid in a room full of grownups. It had always been that way except for a year or so when we last lived in Vancouver, when I was friends with Lorraine. (Our pact to meet each other on her twenty-first birthday at the post office in Vancouver was to go unfulfilled.) Here in New York I didn't know anyone my own age at all, except the kids I was meeting at high school. But Ellen's friends were interesting.

And always, writers talking about writers.

'What a night, last night,' Ellen told them. 'You know it was supposed to be E.M. Forster? I wrote to him in England as soon as I knew he was coming to New York. And he said yes, he'd do it. We built the whole program around him. Three other speakers. Ads.'

'So what happened?' Bobbi asked.

'At the last minute, almost, he decided he couldn't make it. Oh, he sent a lovely message: *It is with great regret that I find I am unable to appear. I entreat the audience to give the other fine speakers the same courteous attention they would have given me.* Ha! People lining up to get in – and we had to tell them our main speaker wasn't going to be present.'

'That's awful. Why didn't he come?'

'Well, he was staying with the Trillings, I hear. So probably they told him *oh, that's a left-wing group, a bunch of commies, you don't want to get involved with them.*'

I didn't know who the Trillings were, but everyone else did.

I was supposed to know who they were, Lionel and Diana. So I didn't ask. I don't know why she always expected me to know all those names. I could say, 'Who's he?' And then she'd say, 'You know, he's the book review editor for *The New Yorker*,' or 'You know, he wrote that book on Forster a couple of years ago,' or 'You know, he's the literary critic for such and such.' I *didn't* know, that was the trouble. Any more than Ellen knew my high school principal was Mr Hendrickson, or my math teacher was Mrs Felder. I figured out that I had two different ways to be ignorant. One was to fake it and pretend I knew, the other was to ask her and feel like a fool. I usually chose option A.

I sometimes went with my mother to parties in those days, if I wasn't working at the movie theatre, or doing my homework. I was a very serious sort of girl, and I looked older than sixteen. Everyone said I was very grown up.

At the studio. Big casement windows overlooking the street. It was those windows that got me into trouble, really.

One night there was a reading and a party at the studio and I stood leaning out, watching city life on the sidewalk below. Windows like a movie set, opening onto the New York night. Feeling glamorous. A New York party – just think of it. Ellen had stayed at home because she was feeling a bit sick – cold and bronchitis, her usual. She told me to go by myself if I wanted. 'Here, wear my fur coat. It will be cold out.'

'Can I wear your black dress too, Mama?'

Standing there, leaning out the window, I felt the chill of the October night and draped the coat over my shoulders.

'You look so lovely standing here by the window.' Was I blind or something? I hadn't even noticed him before. 'I brought you a drink,' he said. He was like a movie star, a bit like John Garfield, Tyrone Power, maybe. The cheekbones of a Greek fisherman, black hair curling – lazy against a broad forehead. Dark eyes, a smile wild and Hollywood. *Lovely*. He said I was lovely.

He was an actor, just finished a three-week run at the Playhouse down on Christopher Street. His friend came over to where we were talking. The friend wasn't handsome, just plain, blond and skinny. The friend was used to being ignored, you could tell. They lived in the same building, he said. I guess my eyes told him to go away, because he did, and I went back to staring at Mr Handsome Actor.

You'd think I'd know something about alcohol, my father was such a lush. But I never even thought about it, that drink. The one time my father gave me a glass of gin and 7-Up, when I was twelve, maybe thirteen, I danced and generally made a fool of myself. If I remember correctly, which I probably don't, my father was quite proud of me. 'Isn't she getting to be something?' he said. I think I had a good time; I loved the music and the whirling dances and the laughter. My mother was furious. She didn't speak to either of us for two days. I must have I decided I needed my mother's approval more than my father's. So if my father offered me a drink again – and really, I don't think he did, my mother must have given him such hell – even if he did, I knew better than to take it.

Now, Mr Actor brought me a drink. Rye and ginger, I think. It seems to me that rum and Coke was politically incorrect, now that I think about it.

I know I went home with him, although I can't tell you how or why. I woke up in a dark room, the street lamp shining in through the crack in the curtains. I got out of bed and got my clothes on. Searching through the pile on the floor. Garter belt, brassiere, panties, slip. My mother's dress. God, it was all rumpled; she would have a fit. I couldn't bear to sit down and put my stockings on. I shoved them into my purse and pushed my bare feet into the black shoes. *Oh, please don't let him wake up. I have to get out of here.* I walked out of the apartment, with not the slightest idea of where I was or how I got there, or how to get home. Nothing but a spinning head and the rather vague memory of being naked in his bed with the fur coat over us. The fur against my skin. The animal smell.

I was on East Twenty-eighth Street. At least I wasn't in the Bronx. I could get the Lexington subway and change at Union Square. I was moving in a daze, but at least I was moving. I tried hard to think. Where was my mind? Nothing there. I couldn't seem to focus; I was sort of dizzy. What time was it anyway? About two – not too bad. On the subway I looked out the dark windows, seeing the reflection of the inside of the car. The ads. The empty seats. Looked at myself in the darkness. Just a girl. Nothing else. Cover my tracks – make a story for my mother. Got to clean up before I get home – fix my hair, put the stockings on, who knows what. I wanted desperately to wash my face. Betty. I'd stop at Betty's on the way home. She'd help.

Knocked on the door. And again. Muffled sleepy 'Who is it?' Quietly in the hall, 'Betty, it's Laurie. Please? I need help.' I could hear mumbling. There was a man in there. Betty in a blue dressing gown. 'Can I come in and use your bathroom for a minute?' Betty had a man in her apartment. Undershirt. Rumpled brown hair.

I shut myself in the small cluttered bathroom, stood at the little porcelain sink and looked at my face in the mirror of the medicine cabinet. Would my mother know? The dirty shower curtain beside me smelled of mould. God, I was thirsty. I washed the glass before I drank from it. Two glasses of water, tepid. *I look okay*, I thought, *it's not too bad.* I washed my face, combed my hair. Folded the seat down and sat on the toilet to put my stockings on. Tried to pay attention. Whoever invented garter belts and suspenders? – the way the rubber button presses into the edge of the stocking and the metal tab ring slides over it on top. Some medieval torture device, it looked like. I didn't usually wear stockings – these were Ellen's, precious. At least I hadn't put a run in them. That would have been a disaster. Ellen would have killed me for that.

When I left the bathroom I felt better – cleaner anyway. More normal. More in control.

'Are you okay, kid?'

'I'm okay. Thanks a lot. I'm sorry to get you up in the middle of the night.'

'Don't worry about it. You sure you're okay?'

'Betty, if my mother asks, could you just say I was here tonight? Visiting with you. If she asks. Please?'

It was only three blocks to walk. Cold this morning. The streets dark and empty. Every step I took reverberated up through my skull. I was so thirsty.

At home, I went in quietly. What good luck. Ellen was asleep. I took off the fur coat and hung it on its hanger, then turned off the light Ellen had left on for me and went into my bedroom.

In the morning Ellen was still pretty sick. I could hear her coughing.

'How are you feeling, Mama?'

'Pretty awful, I'm afraid. I went to sleep right after you left. What time did you get in last night?'

'I think it must have been about one-thirty or two. Sorry to be so late. I stopped by at Betty's on my way home. Did you know she's got a new boyfriend?' A diversionary tactic.

'She has? She does go through them. What's this one like?'

'It's hard to tell really. Okay, I guess. He looked just like the last one. She did most of the talking. Would you like me to bring you some tea and toast?' Another diversion.

'Oh, if you would. That would be very nice. I think I'll just stay in bed this morning.'

I had done it, got away with it. What I felt was some combination of triumph and shame. She hadn't noticed anything. Was that because she was sick? Luckily I could keep out of her way while she was ill, just let her sleep, so she wouldn't ask me a lot of questions about last night. In my dressing gown and nightie I went through the hall to the kitchen. On the way, I stopped in my bedroom and reached for the crumpled black dress. After breakfast I could press it a bit and put it back in the closet.

Lots of tea would help the headache. Tea and toast for Ellen. I wasn't hungry – just tea. Toast maybe later. The metal breadbox held nearly a whole loaf of bread safe from the mice.

On Monday morning I went to school and it became just another one of those things I forgot about – like my mother's friend David, or my Uncle Davey, out at my grandparents' farm, pawing me when I was a kid. Even in my bed once. Or twice. Life went back to normal, or so it seemed.

28. GRAND STREET AT NIGHT

The writers' group met every other Wednesday, and Ellen's Party group met once a month. When you mean Communist Party, you always capitalize the P, even when you speak. People came to the apartment sometimes and sat in the living room talking about important political things.

I was mostly in my room reading, doing homework, studying, things like that. I didn't pay much attention. I wasn't supposed to anyway, I guess. Ellen's group was 'closed', secret. I didn't really know their names, except for the one man. I knew his name because it was easy to remember – Christmas. Walter Christmas. And I paid attention to him also because he was black – Negro, we said then. He was only the second Negro I'd ever met. The first one was Paul Robeson. I always remembered him, when he was in Vancouver, on tour playing Othello with Uta Hagen and I got to shake hands with him. He was beautiful. So big, smooth black skin, a smile like a sunny day.

Now, in New York, there were a lot of Negroes, but I didn't really meet any of them, except sometimes to give them coffee at the movie where I worked. But here was Mr Walter Christmas. A serious political man, very handsome, and very nice, very polite and so neatly dressed. Dapper, I thought. In spite of all that, Rosie was alarmed about us having a black man visiting us.

The major topic of the time was 'the Position of the Negro in the United States'. I heard them talking about it. The Party was working on a proclamation that the Negroes within the United States constituted a separate nation and should be given the powers of nationhood and self-government.

Ellen argued, 'But surely they're Americans, like everyone else.'

'Yes, of course they are Americans. But they have no voice in the administration of the country. Not federally, nor in the States or municipalities.'

'But isn't it the Party's role to work for full enfranchisement of the Negroes throughout the country?'

The chairman, Irving, got up and walked to the front window. He stood there for a minute looking down at the street. Maybe he saw the two men in the doorway of the shoe repair shop down the street, probably not. Maybe they saw him. Probably. He sighed and turned around. His rubber-soled shoes squeaked on the wooden floor.

'Comrade, the Negroes fulfil all the recognized criteria of nationhood: one, a distinct history and culture; two, a distinct language; and three, a territorial integrity.'

'I understand the distinct history and culture.' Ellen sounded so much like a teacher when she spoke, just like Irving. 'And to some extent a distinct language – certainly a usage differing from standard English. But you can say that about the Scots, about the Irish, about the cockneys. So I can't agree that theirs is a different language. And I don't feel that the claim of territorial integrity is justified. The Negroes share territory with the white population of the United States.'

I heard her reasonable voice trying to make them understand.

'In many of the southern states they represent an overwhelming majority.'

When the vote was taken, Ellen voted her definite *no*. She was the only one. The chairman spoke and the discussion went around again. They would have to vote again. Ellen offered to abstain.

'That's all I can do,' she said. 'I simply can't accept this resolution.

But I am willing to abstain from the vote, if you wish.'

But no, they were required to deliver a unanimous resolution apparently.

Irving walked across the room – a big man wearing brown corduroy pants, a rumpled tweed jacket, a wool knit tie – and stood looking down at Ellen's unhappy face.

'Comrade Ellen. You're new to this country and you don't fully understand the situation under discussion. It would be best if you accepted the experience of those of us who are more familiar with the American situation.'

That made Ellen angry. Her voice sounded icy. 'You've heard of Quebec, I suppose? There there's a common culture and history, a common territory, a common language. But I don't see the same pattern applying to the American Negro. I simply don't see it.'

But it's hard to persist when you're being bullied. Finally she had to give in, just as she had given in to my father. Until at last she hadn't any more.

'Maybe they're right,' Ellen told me later. 'Maybe I don't know enough about the United States. It was humiliating, though, being told I was a foreigner. Back home people had some respect for what I said. People listened to my point of view. Here, they just want to lay down the law. And I can't accept that. I've been a part of the Movement so long – through the Depression. And the war ...'

Ellen had always been crazy about theatre. Wherever she went, she started a drama group. Left-wing stuff, of course. *Waiting for Lefty*. *Bury the Dead*. Before we came to New York, she'd had a group in Toronto. She had no hesitation about asking people to help. Important people. Paul Robeson, for example: she wrote asking if he'd be the narrator for Norman Corwin's *Set Your Clock at U235*. (He agreed, although it all fell through at the Toronto end.) And because no dream was impossible in her eyes she made some of her dreams come true. I guess no one had ever bothered to tell her she was a dreamer.

After we lived in New York, friends from Toronto came, to binge on plays. Friends of friends came too: 'Pearl said to look you up.' Sure. Why not? *Bloomer Girl*. *Brigadoon*. *Oklahoma!* They stayed with us, sleeping on the floor. They'd hang around a theatre, wait under the marquee. They'd mingle with the crowds at intermission, go back into the theatre when they returned. Spy out unoccupied seats.

George Hislop was one of Ellen's protegés. A thin, gangly kid, he had a comic sense of dance. Ellen thought he was going places – especially with a little help from her. When Yip Harburg was casting for *Finian's Rainbow* she wrote to him: 'You said you were looking for fresh faces. Well, here's one....' Got an appointment and talked up young George. Got him an audition.

'Get yourself down here, George. This is it....'

He obediently presented himself. My mother and I went with him to the audition. We sat with Yip Harburg in the auditorium, and there he was, our very own George, up there on the stage. Looking fine. Someone gave him the script and cued him. He read his lines. Did very well, too: Ellen nudged me: she thought Harburg was impressed too. 'Okay,' he called out. 'All right, George. Now will you please dance for us.' Music cue. George just standing there. 'Dance, you fool,' I heard Ellen whisper under her breath. But George didn't dance. He looked out across the auditorium, and said, apologetically it seemed to me, 'I can only dance when I feel like it.'

Now there's a theatrical moment for you.

I don't remember what happened after that: where we went for coffee, I mean, whether Ellen berated him immediately, or waited till we were sitting there drinking coffee. I can't even remember what she said. Or perhaps she just said nothing, just let him see that she was furious with him. And her feelings for George never quite recovered from that catastrophic loss of faith.

When he got back to Toronto he wrote, abjectly apologizing for letting her down. 'Letting me down?' It was his life, she replied, and who was she that he should ask her forgiveness. Just as long as he could forgive himself.... Had he any idea what he'd done? and so forth. He pursued the matter 'like a lover', Ellen said indignantly. He wrote: 'I know you've lost faith in me. I know I deserve it. But please write to me. Please....'

One day, after school, I took the subway up to East Twenty-eighth Street and walked around, looking for the place where he lived. Mr Handsome Actor. I found the building and looked at it carefully, worrying all the time that he might catch me. Maybe I even hoped he would. I needed to be sure that I knew what his real name was, so I went into the hall and searched the doorbell tags until I found it. Memorized it so that I'd never forget it. I went back outside. When the door behind me opened, I jumped. But it wasn't *him*. A plain young man, pale and blond, watery eyes. 'Hi. You're Laurie, aren't you? Didn't I meet you a few weeks ago at a party? I was there with a friend.' He nodded back toward the building. 'Yes, I remember you,' I lied, and then remembered him. 'Umm, I was just passing by. Have to go. Sorry.' I left him standing there looking puzzled.

29. CATHERINE STREET/ KNICKERBOCKER VILLAGE

Louise worked in the same office as Ellen, at the Committee for Émigré Writers and Scholars. They became friends, ate lunch together. Louise was pleasant, in a middle-class conservative sort of way. Not at all lively, like Betty. Ellen told me that she was appalled that we were living in a slum down in Little Italy. She had a nice apartment with two bedrooms. Why didn't we move in with her? Ellen could pay half the rent and other expenses. She'd been hoping to find someone to share her apartment, she said. And think how much better it would be financially.

At Rosie's we had to say goodbye. I hated that. I promised to visit her. Another grandmother bites the dust.

One of the people in Ellen's Party group was happy to take over the apartment on Grand Street, buy the furniture we couldn't take to Louise's; we could only fit in our beds, a chest of drawers, a bookcase, an easy chair. Ellen and I would share a bedroom, and we would have full use of the rest of the apartment. A decent bathroom. A modern kitchen. No mice.

But it turned out that Louise was on a perpetual diet, so we didn't share food costs, or have meals together. 'You just cook for yourselves, leave me out of it.' Ellen cooked our usual: macaroni and cheese, meat loaf, omelettes, Depression soups.

From the first night we were there we realized there would be problems. Louise seemed to stay up all night, restlessly prowling through the apartment. Ellen had trouble sleeping – she was always a light sleeper.

Louise wasn't what I'd call man-crazy, not eager and full of passion like Betty; she was marriage-crazy, determined to be a wife before her next birthday – the last one before her thirtieth. Louise was such a puzzle to me; I used to stare at the girdled tree-trunk of her body, listen to the convoluted proprieties of her marriage plan. She tried to teach me the rules of dating: make him come to the door to pick you up, never meet him anywhere; never accept a Saturday night date later than Wednesday; never kiss on the first date.

Too late, Louise, I wanted to tell her.

The apartment development was one of New York's early slum clearance projects. Knickerbocker Village, it was called. For the old Dutch settlements in that area of Manhattan. The city had cleared out two square blocks of the worst slums – the old village streets, village shops – and replaced them each with a low apartment building built around a garden square. Every apartment unit had light and air; windows facing either out to the street or in to the garden. The buildings were good, well-made brick, with hardwood floors, casement windows. Compact and charming.

Louise stood at the window on Sunday afternoon and watched the people in the garden. Couples. She always wanted to talk about the couples. 'See that Chinese couple,' sitting on the bench at the south side. Both of them in dark brown padded coats. 'They are on that same bench almost every day. I think they used to live here in the old buildings. The people who lived here had the first call on the new apartments when they were built. It's a good idea – kept the neighbourhood feeling.'

It's unlikely that Ellen ever met Julius and Ethel Rosenberg. Just because they were both communists and they lived in the same apartment project is no reason to believe that they knew each other. Ellen's was a 'closed' group – the members were not visibly active as known communists. So they weren't known to other communists, only to each other, and only the chairman connected with other levels. And it was an arts group: that set it apart a bit too. Julius might not have been in a group at all; he might have been solo. They might have passed on the street, in the garden, in a corridor, an elevator. They wouldn't even have noticed each other, wouldn't have nodded or smiled even if they had known of each other's existence. Still, looking back on it later, I can see that it might have looked suspicious. Ellen living next to Julius and Ethel Rosenberg.

Poor Louise. She was in love with a man from her office; she talked about him endlessly. He was her ideal husband material, educated and handsome *and* she loved him. The perfect combination. And he finally took notice of her, asked her for a Saturday night date. But alas, it was Thursday so she had to refuse him, lest she seem dateless, too available. He didn't say, *Next Saturday, then?* like he should have. Maybe he didn't know the rules. She kept hoping he'd ask her again, on a Monday maybe, or Tuesday. Wednesday, even. He never did.

Our food began to disappear from Louise's cupboards: 'Whatever happened to that leftover meat loaf? I thought we'd have it for supper tonight?' I always had to explain – it wasn't me. I didn't eat it. 'I was going to make a corn chowder for supper, but I can't find that can of corn. I was sure we had one.' We searched all the cupboards. Could Louise have used it? 'Oh no. She wouldn't. She's not interested in food. She's dieting.'

'Well, *somebody* took it,' I pointed out. 'And it wasn't me. And it wasn't mice. It has to be Louise.'

'Well – I suppose I could ask her ...'

Louise was indignant. 'Why would you think *I'd* take your food? You know I'm on a diet....'

Emptying the garbage, I found the answer: 'Mom, look: here's the can. Empty. She's a sleep walker, a sleep eater. She gets up in the night and eats!' Nuts, she must be.

'That's an interesting diet,' Ellen said. 'No wonder she has trouble losing weight.'

Somewhere in here we had Christmas. My grandmother sent a wonderful fruit cake that she had made herself. It vanished immediately. 'That whole big fruit cake!' Ellen confronted Louise: 'Louise? Do you know what happened to our fruit cake?' Louise said she was sorry, but she had to flush it down the toilet. 'Down the toilet? A big fruit cake?' Because it attracted ants, Louise explained.

'She looked straight at me,' Ellen told me, 'looked me straight in the eye and told me a bare-faced lie.' It was Ellen's turn to be indignant.

Ellen began to make plans to move again. We'd only been there three weeks, I complained.

'Well, I'm not going to pay her another month's rent. I won't do it.'

Could we go back to Rosie's, I wondered?

'Oh, no. Irving and Henrietta are all settled in.'

Ellen wasn't good at confrontations; she couldn't talk to Louise. And yet they had to work together all day at the office.

Ellen's bronchitis flared up again; she was terribly ill and off she went to the hospital. The Grosvenor, I think it was. It was free – one of the few public hospitals, built by the city to treat the poor. There were too many of them, though. Too many poor, too many sick. More than the city had expected.

After school I visited her. At night I stayed home with Louise, or worked at the movie. One night I visited Rosie to cheer myself up. She fed me spaghetti.

Ellen fretted at being stuck there at the hospital. Her bed was in the corridor – the place was very crowded.

'Could you bring me some orange juice next time you come? And bring me something to read, would you? Any of the books by my bed.'

'Okay, Mama.'

'And could you bring me a clean nightgown. I can't bear this hospital thing. I must be a sight,' she fretted.

'Sure. How much longer do they think you'll be here?'

'I don't know. A few days, a week at most. But don't let anyone come to see me. I don't want visitors. This place is so horrid.'

I was afraid, in this neighbourhood around Catherine Street, in a way I had never been on Grand Street. Walking home in the winter evening after work I was frightened. The wide sidewalk, a high wall at the inside. A bridge embankment, perhaps. Walking in the dark. Men leaning against the wall. Two or three of them. Things written on the wall in chalk. I'd walk quickly, firmly, eyes straight ahead. A brown wool hat pulled down over my ears, my heavy tweed coat. My legs freezing. Uneasy. Moving quickly, not looking at the men.

When Ellen was about to be discharged from the hospital her boss, Mrs Canby – 'Lady' – was very concerned about poor Ellen's health and insisted that she needed a holiday away from the city, a week or so with some friends on Long Island who would pamper Ellen and take care of her.

I could stay with crazy Louise, it was decided. They all worked in the same office and together they decided that I'd be all right with Louise.

'Why can't I go with you?' I complained. I'd have liked to be spoiled and pampered too.

'Oh, don't be silly. You'll be fine with Louise, and you'll be in school all day.'

'But I don't want to stay with her. She's crazy.'

'Yes, I know. Well, we'll have to get out of Louise's when I get back. Tell Louise … No – I'll write a note and send it to her. Tomorrow you can bring in the papers and we can look at them – look through the ads. You can go and look for an apartment while I'm away. Okay? Could you do that?'

Sure. I could do that. I'd looked for apartments with my mother often enough, so there was nothing to stop me from doing it on my own. I just hoped Louise wouldn't be too nasty to me after she got the news that we were going to move.

Money matters were starting to get desperate now that Ellen wasn't working. Ellen said we had to hold on to enough money to pay a month's rent in a new place, so once she set that aside, there was only a few dollars left. I asked for an advance on my pay at the movie theatre, but they wouldn't give it to me and they seemed kind of mad at me for even asking. And they didn't seem to trust me any more. They looked at me differently. And so I learned: if you let people know you are poor, they think you might steal from them. Well, I decided I'd have to do something, even if I did think it was stupid. It certainly wouldn't be the first stupid thing I had done. I wrote to my father. Mum was sick, I told him, we were having a really rough time. Could he send us any money? Sure he could. He sent ten dollars. 'Thanks for the ten dollars,' I wrote. 'I ate it.'

Ellen marked the newspaper ads and went off to Long Island for her rest cure. I walked around after school and looked at apartments. Betty helped a lot, telling me how to get places, explaining things: 'Cold-water flat, that doesn't mean there's no hot water, it means there's no heat; Walk-up, that means there's no elevator. Share facilities, that means the toilet is out in the hall.' It made for a lot of walking. From the Lower West Side to the Lower East Side. From Italian to Jewish.

On the first weekend Ellen was away I wandered around on East Fourteenth Street, not knowing what to do with myself, not wanting to stay home with Louise. I was still a stranger at my school, hadn't made friends with anyone yet; I really didn't know anyone except Ellen's friends and I felt awkward about visiting them on my own. I knew that I wasn't a real friend, just an extension of Ellen. I should have gone to visit Rosie or something.

But without even knowing that I was looking for it, I found the studio where Mr Actor rehearsed. The long narrow wooden stairway led up to the second-floor rehearsal space, the entire floor was just one room with a few pillars, and one small enclosed office at the back. I wasn't really looking for him, I told myself, I just wanted to see what it looked like. There were three people there – two men and a woman.

'Are you looking for someone? Can I help you?'

'No thanks, I'm just looking around.'

Posters on the walls, ads for plays, notices of classes and rehearsals.

'I'm afraid I can't let you stay. We'll be starting a rehearsal in about ten minutes.'

I was about halfway down the stairs when he came in the door from the street. When he saw me his face lit up with a big smile.

'Where did *you* disappear to? I didn't know how to find you.' Oh god, he still looked gorgeous to me.

He asked me to come back later and I did. Stupid. I saw him a lot while Ellen was away. Once I invited him to Louise's apartment for lunch. I thought I could do that, make a simple lunch like Ellen talked about. An omelette and a salad, it sounded so sophisticated. But in my nervousness I over-prepared, so the omelette was ready almost an hour before he got there and was egg-leather by the time I put it on a plate. He wasn't really interested in food anyway, as it turned out.

I went to his apartment sometimes, but my memory of all this is very hazy. He had a camera on a tripod. I certainly was a stupid girl.

The apartment I found was bright and clean, newly painted. It was a cold-water flat, a fifth floor walk-up. The big windows in the living room and the kitchen gave us a close-up view of the Williamsburg Bridge. The trucks rushing back and forth between Manhattan and Brooklyn rattled the windows. Cheap though. The door from the hallway opened into the kitchen, where a small four-burner gas stove faced a white bathtub. In the corner, a diagonal wall closed off a small toilet. This was a special feature of the apartment – part of the modernization of the building. Most cold-water walk-ups had a toilet in the hall, shared by all the tenants on each floor. We were lucky to get the apartment without having to pay key money.

As soon as Ellen came home, we moved in. Full of hope. We could heat it with the kitchen stove and a small electric heater for the living room. But we found that we couldn't heat both of the bedrooms, so we used the coldest room for a refrigerator. Ellen's bed was in the living room. As always, she put the pillows along the back and put a cover over them and it looked like a living room couch. I had the other bedroom. It was small, and it could get some warmth from the living room. And the best news was that we got a telephone at last, after being on a waiting list for a year.

'Those people weren't much to my taste.' Ellen may have been spoiled and pampered, she may have been well fed, but she wasn't suited to the Long Island holiday crowd. 'They weren't leftists, they were anarchists. Full of philosophical nonsense. We used to sit around and have discussions like *where do the lines on your hands go when you die?* Your left hand is your past and your right hand is your future, and when you're dead you have neither past nor future. So what happens to the lines? Someone actually called the *New York Times* and asked, but now I can't remember what the answer was.'

Ellen got a letter from Lady – a lovely letter, really, Ellen said. Lady explained sadly that obviously Ellen wasn't physically strong enough to cope with the strain of a full-time job. And Ellen must not be angry with Louise, but Louise was going to take over her job with Lady. Ellen was not to worry, though: Lady would send manuscripts for her to edit at home. And she was to take very good care of herself, and above all she must not worry.

Ellen laughed, a funny kind of laugh that didn't sound real. 'Oh God! Louise gets my job, and I mustn't worry!' She didn't blame Lady, though: 'She's really a very sweet person. But she's never been poor herself, so she just doesn't know. *Above all, don't worry.* How can I take care of myself – and you – without a job. How can I not worry?'

So the next problem to solve was a job for Ellen. Riding to the rescue, Contemporary Writers. They really appreciated all the work Ellen had been doing for them, and now that she was free, and in need of a job, they created one for her. She'd be administrative secretary. She'd manage the Studio, schedule the various workshops, arrange for speakers, write ads about readings and lectures and so forth. A half-time job, with half-time pay, but for Ellen it was the right thing at the right time. With that, and small amounts from the émigré writers Lady sent her way, we could get by. And my little fifteen dollars a week from ushering helped a bit. Ellen was thrilled. 'I'll be working at something I really *love* doing – and getting paid for it!'

Her idea of heaven, I guess – or as close to it as she ever expected she'd get.

'And Laurie – another thing: I'm even learning something, working on those manuscripts,' she said happily. 'Imagine, me editing an essay about Goethe's *Elective Affinities.* Can you beat that? I'm an editor!'

We cooked mostly in the oven – casseroles and baked potatoes. We could make dinner and heat the apartment at the same time. It wasn't bad. I usually put dinner in the oven before Ellen came home from work. In the little black stove with the five white handles. In the oven with the white enamel panel on the door – swirling letters that said *Prestige.*

A bathtub in the kitchen seemed funny to us, but people in New York seemed to be used to it. A big slab of wood went across the top, usually an old door; you could use it for a table. Ellen said she'd make a skirt for it, to hide the tub, but she never did. It was hard to clean under the bathtub, around the feet – like big bear paws. One of the jobs I hated.

I loved the apartment, all except the kitchen, I loved the high ceilings, the light and the air. The long view of the river, up past the bridge arcing over to Brooklyn. The coal barges and cargo boats, heading downriver to the big docks, the big ships. The garbage scows heading out to the bay to dump their loads. Across the river, the factories near the shore. I could open the window and the sunny wind would come swishing into the room; I'd lean out and look down, watch people on the street. 'Close the window, Laurie, do you want us to freeze to death? Come away from there.'

We still had hardly any furniture. Beds, of course. Some dishes and a couple of pots. Everything else had been left behind at Grand Street, even those pretty chairs that we had put so much work into.

Ellen found a small round coffee table at a secondhand store. We sat on cushions on the floor. Very 'Bohemian', one of our Canadian friends said, sitting on the floor, drinking jasmine tea from one of our matched set of jelly jars. Tiny flowers floated in the jar.

'What does that mean? Bohemian?' I asked later.

'It comes from the name of a country. Bohemia. It's where Gypsies came from. So it means Gypsy-like. Unconventional. Or exotic, maybe. Now, I'd say Betty is Bohemian.'

'Is it a compliment?'

She laughed. 'That depends on who says it and who hears it.'

I decided to take it as a compliment, anyway. Because I thought it was just fine for the way we were.

In the middle of March I was doing my Regent's Exams at school. Every high school student in New York State had to take the same test on the same day. It established a standard for the schools, they said. During the math exam I had to ask to be excused. A monitor went with me to the girls' room, where I threw up my breakfast. When my marks came in a week later I was pleased that they were all in the 90s, including a 98 in math. Too bad I'd missed 100; I wondered which question I had done wrong. Or maybe I just got distracted. I seemed to throw up a lot. And my breasts were bigger, heavier. I didn't want to think about it.

30. SHERIDAN SQUARE/
THE WILLIAMSBURG BRIDGE

'Pregnant and Scared? Call us.' I was and I did. They gave me an appointment, an easy address in Greenwich Village, after school. I was really scared. I needed to talk about it.

Dr B's office was in his apartment. A dark green carpet, nice maple furniture, sort of country style. Green drapes over the windows to the street – a pattern of bamboo leaves dappled by thin sunshine. He looked like a worried teddy bear, rumpled and brown, circles under his eyes matched his brown corduroy pants.

'Come in, come in, my dear. Now you sit down right here on the couch. Are you comfortable there? You can tell me about it.'

I sat there on his couch in my schoolgirl pleated skirt, I was so relieved to be able to talk about it – I cried and cried.

'What am I going to do?' I asked, over and over. He was very reasonable, very helpful. Kind.

'I'm sure we can help you. There's a place out on Long Island – a big house – especially for pregnant young girls. It's a place where the girls can go and be taken care of until their babies are born. And it's all free. No cost at all. Then they can either decide to keep the babies or put them up for adoption.'

'I don't *want* a baby. No. I'm not going to have a baby.'

'But you are, my dear. You are pregnant and you are going to have a baby. You have to face facts. We can help you, make it easy for you. No one will have to know about the baby.'

'You don't understand. Please don't keep saying *the baby*. It's not like that. It was an *accident*. A terrible accident. I'm sick. And I don't want to have a baby.'

When I began to cry again, he sat beside me on the couch and put his arm around me. Comforting me.

'Poor girl. Don't you worry now.'

'I won't have a baby, I won't.'

His mouth tightened up then, but he leaned toward me and stroked my cheek. Great pores on his nose, up close. Bumpy brown bags under his eyes.

I don't know where my mind was. I just let it all happen. I let him put my legs up on the couch, lift up my skirt. As if I had no choice. I didn't scream or make a fuss. As if I didn't even know what was happening. If I had screamed he'd have let me go, I'm sure. He wouldn't want a fuss, there in his office. So why didn't I? I don't know. As if I wasn't even there.

Later, when he opened the door and let me leave, 'If you change your mind and decide to have the baby, come back to see me. We're here to help you.'

I walked around the corner quickly, rushing out onto Sixth Avenue, afraid people were looking at me. Everyone could see that I was just no good, just a tramp. That's why he did it. That's what my mother would say if she knew, she'd say he did it because he knew I had done it before, he knew I was just a tramp, like my father's girlfriends. Tramps, every one of them. I pulled my coat closer around me, wrapping myself in it, hiding deep inside the coat. *Why did I let him do that?* I walked the long blocks home. *Why? I don't know what's happening to me. I just won't think about it.*

And while I wasn't thinking about it, I turned on all the white handles of the little gas stove – four burners and the oven. I should lie down on the kitchen floor, I knew, but it was so hard and, truthfully, it was not very clean. But just a step away I curled up in the easy chair in the living room and went to sleep.

When I woke I was in a small white bed at the hospital with my mother standing beside me. And everybody seemed to know everything. But everyone agreed it was an accident.

Ellen and I went back to the apartment, back to the big windows and the Williamsburg Bridge, back to the toilet and the bathtub and the stove. I sat on the bed and tried to drink tea. I didn't talk. I read the trucks, Nathan's Hardware, Fresh Chickens, Building Supplies, Manischevitz Matzohs.

I can see it all. I'm sitting up on my mother's bed in the living room. I'm drinking jasmine tea from a glass, looking carefully at the walls. At the window, at the trucks on the bridge moving so slowly. At the corner of the wooden window frame, a square, raised circles inside it, round and round. You can get trapped in that square, going round and round in the wooden grooves, sliding off the smooth white paint on the sides, so you can't climb out, wondering how, when, the circle got inside the square and how it changes all the time: circle, square, circle, square. But you can jump. You can get outside the circle-square and there are more grooves you will slide down. Down the long window to the bottom, crash, the bottom is the sill and you can rest for a minute there before you start to go up the grooves up the ridges be careful to the top again but the square will catch you be careful go down slowly again and rest on the sill. But you can fall. You can fall to the floor all wood full of lines to follow so you know just where you are going if you are going you just follow the lines.

'Does he know?' Ellen asked me. I nodded. I had called him, spoken to him very briefly.

Ellen said, 'I'd rather he hadn't known. But since he does.... Are you thinking you'd like to get married?'

'No.' Definitely. 'I made a mistake. I don't think I should have to pay for it for the rest of my life.'

I could almost hear Ellen say, *Good girl!* Just the expression on her face.

'Do you want to have the baby?'

I just shook my head. 'It's not a *baby*, it doesn't feel to me like it's a baby. It's like an illness, like I'm sick, and I just need to get better.'

So she asked me the next question: what did I really want?

'An abortion,' in a very small voice. 'That's why I called him. I wanted to ask him to help me get an abortion. I know we can't afford it. He said he could give me five dollars. But that's ridiculous.'

'Yes, that's ridiculous,' she said. 'We can't afford it, but we will. So don't worry. I just want you to be sure about what you want.'

If Ellen told me then about making arrangements, it didn't really sink in. I just couldn't seem to keep anything in my mind. I seemed to have turned it over to her, made it her problem instead of mine, and I didn't even know the details until years later. Ellen talked to her friend Eve. She knew an excellent doctor; a husband-and-wife team, in fact. Reliable and conscientious. It would all be done in a hospital. Expensive, yes, 'But don't worry. I can let you have the money.' Ellen talked to the doctor. Cards on the table: it would cost $500. 'That will include everything. The hospital. The surgery. The affidavits from specialists: we'll need those.'

A small fortune in those days, $500. Over a year's rent on our apartment. And on the spur of the moment. But Ellen knew it had to be done carefully, medically. She has seen too many back-street abortions, 'coat hanger abortions' too, back during the Depression. Too many women dying.

Ellen reported back to Eve. She nodded, unsurprised. Not so bad, she said. 'And he said I have to give them the money before it happens....' She knew that too, she said. She wrote out a cheque to Ellen. 'Eve, you know I have no idea how long it will be before I can pay it back.'

'You'll pay me when you can. I know that. Now stop worrying.'

Ellen took me to La Bilbaina for dinner. To celebrate an end to our problems, she said. But I didn't feel like eating, or like celebrating. I was scared to death. At least for now, a breathing space, I guess Ellen thought. Why did she always think we should celebrate by eating out somewhere? I guess it was left over from the Depression, when dinner at least marked the end of that day's troubles. No matter how bad things were during the day, there was always dinner.

31. CENTRAL PARK WEST/ SEVENTY-SECOND STREET

The doctor's office was on the West Side – Seventy-second Street just off Central Park. It was a ground floor office in a small grey building set back a bit from the street.

I kept myself very quiet, but I wanted to cry. I did what I was told.

'Take all your clothes off,' the nurse said. 'Wrap this sheet around you.'

It was as though I could watch myself doing what I was told. I watched the girl wrap herself in the sheet as she undressed, holding it around her breasts while she took off her panties. With one hand she folded her clothes neatly on the chair. 'Just sit down on the chair.' The girl sat in the chair. Her eyes roamed around the room looking at everything. They settled on a sign on the wall. She couldn't read it, except the doctor's name in black spiky letters. The doctor didn't look at her. *Maybe I'm invisible. Yes. I'm invisible.* 'Sit up there on the table. That's right. Now lie down and put your feet in here.' *I can just keep very still. Invisible is good.* She did what she was told. She let him poke around. *I don't even have to think about it. I don't even have to feel what he's doing.* The girl tried again to read the sign on the wall.

In the office, a bit later, I sat reading the certificates on the wall. *There are a lot more in here. Everything has his name on it.* Ellen was in the chair across from the doctor. She was wearing her good black suit, looking very respectable.

'Well, there is no doubt about the pregnancy, as I'm sure you know. She's in good physical health. However, I have the records here of her suicide attempt, which does indicate that she is in a rather fragile mental state.'

He looked at me, but I was busy reading the walls. Ellen turned to look at me too, then turned back to listen to him.

'So I'll sign the agreement to allow the termination of pregnancy, to proceed immediately. However, you must know that there is a potential problem here. Your daughter looks very young. I have to warn you that I can't have anything to do with a termination for an underage girl. Nor can any other doctor. In New York State, having intercourse with a girl under eighteen is statutory rape. It is a very serious matter that would result in criminal charges against the man involved. That would, of course, delay any medical proceedings to terminate the pregnancy.' He paused. 'Do you understand me?'

He looked at Ellen carefully. Measuring her understanding. Ellen turned again to look at me, but I was still reading the walls. Not looking at them. Blank.

'I understand,' Ellen said firmly, smiling at him. 'Yes, I understand you.'

He opened the file on his desk, took out a medical form, and picked up his pen.

'Now, perhaps we can just complete this application form. I have most of the information. All I need now is your daughter's place of birth and date of birth.'

'She was born in 1928, in Vancouver,' Ellen said.

I listened, and watched the two of them on the edge of my vision. It was as though they were in a play, a play that had nothing to do with me. But I couldn't understand the words. Somehow I just couldn't take it in. As if I weren't paying attention. As if I were off somewhere else. I knew I'd become two years older now. What happened to those two years?

At the hospital I was put in the maternity ward of all places. Therapeutic D & C. All the staff knew why I was there; I knew they knew. But no one said anything about that. After it was all over, I came alive again, seemed to understand.

One of the nurses said, 'You are so young-looking, Laurie.'

I made my voice older, 'Yes, it runs in the family. They call me Baby Face.'

Somewhere in the muddled haze of the past two weeks the school Easter holidays had come and gone.

After the break I was back at school, without missing even a day. In my English class I thought, *At least she didn't ask us to write an essay on what we did on our spring break. I could have shocked the pants off her.*

Since we had moved to New York a year ago I had been taking extra courses, so I suddenly found myself promoted an extra half grade. I was at the end of grade twelve. By January I'd be out of high school. I was ready now to begin thinking about the future. The worst of the past was gone, I knew.

Mr Beautiful Actor. Years later a handsome new face appeared in Hollywood movies. That same face with the high Greek cheekbones, the dark eyes, artfully dishevelled black hair. His name? Yes, it could be a good anglicization of the one I remembered but never spoke. Was it? Was it?

Is that him? How can I remember after so many years? Yes, I think it is. Look at those sexy eyes. Of course it's him. It must be. It probably is. Hollywood changed his name, that's all. His name was too *ethnic* for them. There's never been anyone so handsome. Could it be? I wouldn't go to a movie if I knew he was in it. But sometimes he would just turn up, there on the screen. He was never a big star, just a second-stringer. Never the hero, always the buddy. Never the villain. Not in the movies. Became a director and married a '10'.

32. EAST ELEVENTH STREET

Just before my school term ended Ellen found another apartment. She said, 'I really want to get us out of this neighbourhood, away from the tenements. I can't stand it. And this place will be really hot in the summer.' But I think it was to get away from the bad memories of that apartment near the bridge. From the heights to the depths. The new apartment was in the basement of a brownstone on East Eleventh Street.

'The location is excellent,' she said, 'close to Lexington Avenue. We were lucky to get it without key money.' The rent was reasonable because it needed some work; there was a bit of a problem in the kitchen, some water damage that needed repairing. The kitchen was at the back, where water dripped slowly from some mysterious source upstairs. The other two rooms were fine (as fine as they could be considering that they were in the basement, next to the furnace room and the two barking dogs and the trash cans). But in the kitchen, green mould grew on the back wall.

Ellen hung a bamboo blind over the front windows, to block out the view of the feet walking by on the sidewalk. You can tell a lot about people by their feet. The women in dresses, wearing high heels, the trousered gentlemen in polished brogues, more often just the scruffy loafers on anyone; children in sneakers. Workmen in boots. Families out in their Sunday best.

Years later we laughed at the Rosalind Russell movie, *My Sister Eileen*. 'That was us!'

The bamboo blind didn't block the view going in the other direction. Anyone walking by could see us at our elegant best there in the room, could look down through the cracks in the blind. It took us several weeks before we realized that. When our lights were on in the living room, anyone passing by on the street could tell a lot about the people who lived in that basement. The books, an easy chair, someone sitting in a robe, reading with her feet up; someone at the table writing, studying; two women sitting at the table eating dinner. Ellen was mortified. She put curtains over the blind.

What I hated most were the dogs, great brown monsters. When I walked down the outside steps from the sidewalk, they heard me – an intruder. By the time I had my key in the door they were barking furiously. When I stumbled on the garbage pails in the hallway, they started leaping against the furnace room door, throwing their heavy bodies toward me. I was terrified that they'd get out.

A couple of months later I brought a boyfriend home from a date, so that he could meet my mother. And we went in through the basement door and the dogs started barking and we bumped against the garbage cans. I think I must have turned into the Little Match Girl or something right before his eyes. He never let on to me then how shocked he was, but he told me years later that he'd never seen anyone live that way.

One Sunday afternoon Ellen and I went to a party at Pete Seeger's apartment in the Village, his wife's parents' place. I had a secret crush on Pete, as did half the women who had ever heard him sing. One of the jobs I had now and then was collecting tickets at the folk concerts where he sang with a group of other people. The concert was called a hootenanny, and people would stomp their feet and clap their hands and sometimes sing along. The office where Ellen worked, People's Artists, was right next door to the organization that arranged the concerts, People's Songs, so we got in free, and sometimes I made a couple of dollars taking tickets at the door.

There was a 'stoolie' in those offices, of course. The FBI could be expected to be everywhere. Theoretically, this was still the period of left-over good relationship between Russia and the United States, but the spy stories were beginning to build up, and the paranoia about atomic secrets. After the United States had dropped the bombs on Japan, maybe they couldn't stop worrying that someday some country would drop bombs on *them*.

My mother told me she thought the stoolie was probably the man who came in every week to service the typewriters. 'He never charged us anything, and I thought he was a comrade. I never really thought about it before,' she said. 'But he saw everything in the offices. Oh, we were all so innocent. We should have been as paranoid as they were.'

The Seegers' apartment was thrilling. I'd never seen anything like it in my life. Oh, how I hoped I could live somewhere like that some day. The ceiling was as high as two storeys and around three walls there was a gallery that overlooked the living room. There were little bedrooms upstairs – downstairs was the kitchen and living room and a space for eating. I was drawn to the fireplace – smooth and white, with a strange painting over it – full of bright slashes of red and orange. I sat in front of the fireplace, on a long wooden bench with a padded top in red leather. People stood around and talked and drank beer or wine.

I couldn't keep my eyes off Pete's wife. She was a tiny woman, Japanese, neat and precise, with her black hair tied back, wearing a silken kimono. Toshi, her name was. 'I'm all dressed up for the party,' she told me. 'I don't usually do this. I usually dress like everyone else.' I looked around at *everyone else* as though I'd never seen them before. Maybe I hadn't. They certainly didn't look like the kind of *everyone else* that I saw on the street. They didn't look like my teachers either, or like my relatives back in Canada. The women all seemed to be in costumes, long skirts, baggy pants, dangling beads, brown leather sandals. Like Gypsies. *Bohemian*, I thought. *Like a tribe from another country.*

33. FIFTH AVENUE/SEVENTY-FIFTH STREET

On the first of May, almost all over the world, there was a celebration of working people. A parade in the big cities. All the labour unions and the leftist organizations would be there in the parade, with music and floats.

We were on a bus going to join the May Day parade. Crowds lining the sidewalks. Banners being hoisted. Flags and streamers. It looked like a carnival.

A man sitting across the aisle looked increasingly angry. Finally he couldn't contain his rage any longer. 'Commies! Look at 'em! Goddam commies, right here in our own country.'

Someone else: 'Put the bunch of them in jail. Where they belong.'

Ellen, in the interests of justice, of course had to put in her two cents' worth. 'Well, they have rights, too. This is a democratic country.'

'Too goddam democratic. Those guys don't deserve any rights.'

'Damn Reds're everywhere. Look at 'em. Bunch of Russkis, Polacks, Jews – you name it.'

Ellen again: 'They're not all foreigners. Those people out there carrying those banners are Americans!'

'Why the hell don't they go to live in Russia if they think it's such a good place.'

'Yeah, look at them all out there. Commie bastards.'

'It's not all communists, you know. There are socialists and trade union people, a lot of working people, just like you. You should be out there too.'

'You calling me a Red? What the hell you talking about, lady?'

'You know so much, why don't you just go out there and join them?' someone called out from farther back in the bus.

'That's what I intend to do.' Ellen stood up. I did too. 'As a matter of fact we were just getting off.'

The man across the aisle inspected us suspiciously. 'Are youse Amurricans?'

'We're Canadian.'

'Canadian!' he snorted. 'You're probably a commie yourself. Why don't you admit it?'

Ellen smiled and I held my breath because I knew exactly what she was going to say next. I was glad we were standing close to the door, so that we could get off as soon as the bus came to a stop. 'Of course I am,' Ellen said, with one of her nicest smiles.

Back in Canada, in the days of political activity during the Depression, Ellen was the one who would always be sent out for fund-raising among the good middle class, or out to talk to city officials. She seemed like one of them – well mannered, articulate; relatively well dressed at the beginning of the Depression, thanks to the cast-off clothes of the wife of a doctor. Often, her voice of sweet reason would defuse hostility. She got used to that reaction: *This really nice lady is a Communist? Well, I guess they're not all a bunch of no-good bums.*

This time it was different. The hostility erupted in a torrent of abuse. The suggestion that she go back where she came from was the mildest sentiment voiced. I was glad we were getting off: I was pretty scared.

'Did you hear that? Did you hear what she said? She's a Red! A Bolshie!' He was over a foot taller than Ellen. Big and beefy.

The bus driver was worried about the shouting. 'Settle down back there. Settle down now or I'll have to put you off the bus.'

'That's right. Put her off the bus. Stop the bus and put her off.'

I was getting really scared. Ellen just tipped up her head and looked up at him and his anger. She spoke clearly, strongly to the bus driver. 'Yes, would you please let us off here.' She pushed me toward the front ahead of her, 'Go ahead, Laurie. Go on. I'm right behind you.'

Some very angry men glared at us through the windows of the bus as we waited to cross the street to join the demonstration.

Ellen was shaken too. 'Never in my entire life have I seen hatred like that before. Sheer mindless hatred.' I think she was shocked mostly because she was used to being able to reason with people. This time reason hadn't worked.

Along the parade route, there were more surprises: *Kill a Commie for Christ.* That's what the signs said. A whole bunch of people crowding along the sidewalk, shouting at the marchers as they went by.

It was getting scary now, being in the U.S.A., home of the brave, where *liberal* was a dirty word and *communist* defined the devil. Where you had to watch what you said and who you said it to.

When I was a kid May Day was really exciting. Once – I guess I was about ten – my brother and I rode on the back of a big flatbed truck with a lot of other kids. It was in Calgary, I think. We all wore red bandanas around our necks, tied in a knot in the front. On the side of the wagon the sign said Young Pioneers. We were the children of communists, on show. It was then a happy celebration and the parade went to a fairground and we all had a picnic, a party, and ate borscht and spare ribs that the Ukrainian ladies made. Downtown there was a building called the Ukrainian Labour Temple. Imagine that: Temple. What a powerful word. Imagine almost worshipping labour – worshipping working people. I had a hard time fitting those memories into this day, the jeering and twisted mouths: 'Kill a Commie for Christ.'

I think that was the last time the New York City administration issued a permit for May Day. That was the last lefty parade; 1947. The FBI filmed it all, I suppose. There's Ellen, smiling and waving, with me right next to her.

And so we celebrated our first anniversary in Manhattan.

34. UP THE HUDSON RIVER

Ellen came home one day with news. 'Guess what? Someone told me about a job you might like. At a summer resort. Waiting on table. You can do that. It's for the whole summer. You get paid, and you get room and board, too. It might even be fun!' I know she thought it would be good for me to have a little fun in my life, after our troubles.

'Sounds pretty good. It's not too fancy, is it? Where do I have to go, what to I do to ask about it?'

'The resort is run by a sort of left-wing group, so it's probably not too fancy. Shall I call tomorrow and arrange an interview for you?'

'Okay. I can try, anyway.'

'You know, it's not going to be *all* work. When you finish your work you can swim, probably.'

I began to think there might be a life, after all.

An interview. That sounds so important, so official. But it was easy. They asked a couple of questions. Trying to find out if I was reliable, I thought. And I had good references. Ellen got a letter from one of her writer friends to say that I'd worked at the studio after school. And I told them about ushering at the movie. I'd served coffee, so I could wait on table, couldn't I?

It was probably the happiest time of my life, starting work at the resort. It wasn't a big place, and not fancy, but it had a swimming pool and a lake with a big wooden dock, and a few canoes. I was the youngest, but there I was, with a dozen other people at least close to my own age – the rest of the dining-room staff. We all hung around together, roomed in staff cottages – four in a cottage, two upper bunks, two lower. We'd stay up late at night, talking, kibbitzing. That was another new word I learned. A wonderful New York word.

Waiters and waitresses, tied together by meal schedules. If we wanted coffee or anything before we started work we had to figure out how to get it without bothering anyone in the kitchen. We had to be on duty for serving breakfast starting at seven, but we were all through by nine-thirty. We staggered our own shifts to have some early servers and some late servers, to match the schedules of the guests, some early risers and some late. But usually by nine o'clock most of us were sitting at the staff table in the back, starting our own breakfast. And we rotated two people to serve at staff meals. You'd have office staff and counsellors and maintenance staff – a couple of tables of them. Eight at a table, the staff tables. I couldn't believe the amount of food we ate, and how much milk we drank. The dining-room manager finally put a limit on us of three quarts of milk per meal for the eight of us.

After we had breakfast we set up the guest tables for lunch, eight at a table, then we were free until a quarter to twelve, when we had to be back in the dining room, cleaned up, wearing white shirts and navy blue shorts, all ready to serve the guests again.

It was at Camp Beacon that I began to learn about Jewish food and what was kosher, what wasn't. There were things I'd never eaten before. Blintzes is what I remember mostly, with sour cream. Oh, that was wonderful food. The camp served some meals, lunch usually, with no meat. That was when they had blintzes, and salads with cottage cheese. For dinner sometimes it was chicken fricassee or flank steak or beef tongue, oh god I hated seeing that tongue. And I never once ate it, I don't think.

In the evenings there'd be entertainment in the big lounge. The staff could always go to these things too, we just had to make sure that we didn't take up all the chairs – the paying guests had first preference for anything, of course, and we were expected to pay attention to that. Sometimes we all sat around on the floor. I think the managers of the camp liked having the young staff around, being bright and cheerful. We were all so much younger than the paying guests and we made the evenings a bit livelier. It was as though we were part of the entertainment. So there were no real barriers between guests and staff, like there would be at a more *bourgeois* resort.

It was a lefty sort of camp, so one of the main activities was talking. In the evening there might be about a dozen or so people in one of the small clubrooms off the lounge – the entertainment would be something like a folksinger or a comedian. One of the waiters, Alex Cohen, played guitar and we would all sing: 'Good Night, Irene', or 'Foggy, Foggy Dew', old Burl Ives tunes, Pete Seeger songs.

One day I was sitting on the couch with a coffee table in front of me. I always liked to have some sort of barrier between me and the rest of the world, so that's where you'd usually find me, behind a table. My back protected by the wall. There was always coffee perking somewhere in the main cabin. Some mugs on the table. Some ashtrays. And a man on the other side of the room kept staring at me and smiling. And smiling. Lifting up one eyebrow to say hello. What is it about black turtleneck sweaters? I don't know. The colour didn't really even suit him, brown tumbly hair, brown eyes. I was used to thin people like my mother and all her family, so he looked a bit on the plump side to me, but it was one of the things that made him really cuddly, I found out later. Oh, I knew he was older, but I was used to older people. And he was very attentive, sweet as can be. He looked at me and listened to me as though I was a strange creature from another world. Me with my shy Canadian ways, my small accent. Maybe it was the accent that made him stare at me, lean toward me to listen, watch my mouth while I talked. 'I do *not* say hoose. It's *you* who have an accent. You say hayouse.'

When I was off shift Sol and I walked around the camp. We lingered in the sun at waterside – although staff weren't allowed to use the pool during prime afternoon hours. He went back home after two weeks, but I promised to call him when I got into Manhattan on my next day off.

Some weeks on my day off I didn't go home, saving the train fare. Sometimes I stayed at the camp and just loafed around with the rest of the staff, taunting them that they had to work. But the next Tuesday I took the train down to Manhattan right after serving dinner. That's what the staff did, take the night train into the city. I'd have that night and a whole day off, and the next night too, really. I usually took the night train back the next evening after Ellen and I had dinner on Wednesday.

Ellen was glad I was home for a day off. I think she really missed me. It was the first time we had lived apart for more than a week or so, the times she went off somewhere when I was just a kid. She was awfully depressed about the apartment. The water leaking into the kitchen seemed to continue and the plumber couldn't find the source of the leak. Green mould was growing on one of the kitchen walls, moss, really. We went out for dinner in the Village. She wanted me to go with her to look at a new place on Mulberry Street the next day. I phoned Sol as I had promised and agreed to meet him for coffee in the afternoon.

I certainly hadn't learned anything about dating from Ellen's friend Louise, thank goodness. I couldn't imagine asking him to come and pick me up at home. How horribly bourgeois. I was my mother's daughter, capable of doing things on my own, being independent. Besides, the basement entrance was disgusting, and I didn't want him to know how really poor we were.

Sol and I had agreed to meet at Times Square. Our first date. I thought it was a real date, my first. I thought he might take me to a nice restaurant or something like that, and was terribly disappointed when I saw that he was wearing a T-shirt under his jacket. I had dressed up, wearing a straight shift of shimmery blue knit fabric. Tube knit, we called it then. I had bought enough fabric to cover me from shoulder to knee, and a few inches extra for hems, and made the dress that morning in about half an hour. Cut a few inches down each side for arm holes. Sew the top together, leaving room for my head to get through, turn up the hem. A new white plastic belt and newly cleaned white shoes and I was elegant. I was almost seventeen, slim, blond, how could I not be lovely? So I was disappointed that I wasn't being actually taken out anywhere. I can't remember that date, only the disappointment. I think we walked across 42nd Street and took the subway to visit friends of his on the Upper East Side.

I had to be back at camp in time to serve breakfast so I took the early morning train – the milk run we called it – leaving Grand Central at four in the morning and stopping at every little town up the Hudson River.

At the resort, when we first met, I had told Sol I was seventeen. It was innocent enough, really. I always changed my age a couple of months before my birthday. So anxious to grow up. So naturally, when my birthday came along a month or so later, he thought I was turning eighteen. Available. No longer jailbait. His family had taught him wariness. He had no intention of getting involved with an underage girl, but I was turning eighteen, he thought. He was twenty-seven, teaching in Manhattan at a small private college for girls from well-to-do families, going to NYU for his master's in sociology.

In my own world, my previous Canadian world, I was part of the dominant culture, the British culture, even though for a lot of political reasons I was an outsider. But here in New York the dominant culture was the turbulent melting pot, full of energy and potential, full of European vigour. Here this introspective girl with the manners and voice of a calmer country was unusual, exotic.

Sol had come home from the war and taken advantage of the GI Bill to get himself the education his family had always wanted for him, had saved and skimped for. He was the darling baby boy of the family, the one they adored and had put all their hopes into.

The family lived in the Bronx, 'Brother Al, Brother Jack, Sister Helen, and Mama Gussie.' When he spoke of them he always gave them the family titles. The father, Sam, had died when Brother Jack was fourteen. Al was older, but odd in his ways, a grown-up infant. Jack had gone to work immediately to support the family.

Sol told me about working the beach at Far Rockaway, selling ice cream on summer weekends. The three of them, racing across the sand, calling out. *Ice cream, ice cream, gettcha ice cream.* Brother Jack, running with the heavy cooler slapping against his back, calling out; watching for the raised hand, the wave, the buyer's signal. Running. How many popsicles at seven cents' profit on each one. Run, run. Jack was a born salesman, the family said. Brother Al carrying a full cooler from the boardwalk when Jack's supply began to get low. Sol helping Jack, running to the customers with a popsicle, making change.

The family put all its hopes into Sol, the smart young baby of the family. Sister Helen, two years older, was expected to be pretty and pleasing and to marry a nice Jewish boy. Al or Jack or Sol might marry money. In the meantime, they all lived in a small apartment in the Bronx, near the synagogue where Mama Gussie's life was centred. She had come from Russia when she was seventeen, to marry her Sam. She spoke only Yiddish, except for the few phrases she had learned in order to satisfy the social requirements of the small town in the south where she and Sam had lived in the early days of their marriage. The only Jews in town. Pride was everything. You must keep your pride, in the face of the prejudice and barriers of society. Pride and good manners.

But Sol fell in love with me – my Canadianness, my shiksa-ness was exotic for him. And I was so young, only sixteen when we met. He used to stare at my face when I talked. Bewildered by the way my mouth moved, by the 'refined' Canadian accent. The 'delicate' movements, the polite manners.

For most of my childhood I must have been looking into pale eyes. Blue. Grey. And skin was pale, and hair, blond or barely brown, thin, limp perhaps. That was a reality of life in Western Canada and in my family.

But here was something new. Looking into eyes that are a bright brown, skin slightly olive, hair that stood up and bounced around.

It was a very happy time for me. I finally had a boyfriend, and the warm expressive Jewish culture was just what I needed to draw me out of all the old childhood fears.

In part I learned the culture through food. The week before Passover we went to a Jewish bakery for macaroons – crunchy ragged hills of sweetness. A bite crumbled shreds of coconut against my tongue, and the sugar shrieked to each little cell, 'Wake up, wake up.' Much of our time together centred around a good bakery – Danish and bagels and poppyseed cake.

I appreciated the time I spent in a Jewish world. Especially at holiday time and shared rituals. The fasts of Yom Kippur and the crowded mealtime in the restaurant on Twenty-third Street after sunset. Shopping for chocolate-covered matzohs at Barton's, and little jelly candies, kosher for Pesach. And Passover seder at Mama Gussie's, with the salt and bitter herbs, and Sister Helen so nervously trying to get everything just right.

Sunday mornings at Rappaport's, down Second Avenue, eating scrambled eggs and lox, with the big basket of rolls and slabs of butter, and the table full of wonderful food. The enormous amounts of food shocked me then; I was still a Depression child. United Dairy on Fourteenth Street near Broadway, where I used to go for a lunch of boiled potatoes and sour cream, or cottage cheese and sour cream with spring salad – the small chunks of onion and radish and cucumber. Walking through the streets on the Lower East Side and buying knishes; I held them hot in my hand, with a soggy paper napkin, and tried to bite through the crust to the kasha filling that was my favourite.

Mulberry Street, long before Dr Seuss made it famous. Our apartment
was two blocks north of here. (Photo: Brian Merlis)

At Camp Beacon, New York, in the summer of 1947.
That's my mother on the left. The dog is a new one, she
called it 'Cappy', for Captain, she said.

35. MULBERRY STREET

The afternoon after my Times Square date with Sol, Ellen and I took the crosstown bus and walked a few blocks to Mulberry Street to see the new apartment. Well, fancy that. Here we were back in Little Italy again. Not far north of our first apartment on Grand Street. This was our fifth apartment in just over a year.

We were happy to discover some downward mobility and then a little upward: after our fifth floor walkup, then the basement bog, we found the ground floor on Mulberry Street. It was a small building, only two floors: the landlord occupied the upstairs apartment. The living room had a fireplace! (Not to be used, the landlord said. Oh well. It looked pretty.) Irving and Henrietta generously offered to give back those chairs we'd so lovingly painted. We found an old dining table. We built a bookcase to fill one wall: it was easy. Ellen ordered the planks cut to size: all we had to do was hammer in some nails. As soon as we put the books in, the bookcase collapsed. We sat on the floor amid a mountain of books, laughing till we cried. Home again!

At Christmas my mother invited Sol for Christmas dinner. She was still checking him out, really. He was a lot older, about halfway between my age and Ellen's, and perhaps Ellen hadn't figured out what he saw in me beyond the obvious. At that point I hadn't either. What I saw in him was a warm cuddly guy, very polite, and very smart.

Ellen had bought a small chicken for the three of us. So we both had a moment of panic when Sol showed up with a friend in tow – Leslie, one of his colleagues. 'Are you sure you don't mind?' Sol asked. I knew Ellen wouldn't turn him away. Christmas dinner would certainly be more interesting with two men and two women, which might have been what had prompted Sol to bring him along. Perhaps Sol was nervous about making conversation with my mother all evening. Ellen thought the little chicken could be stretched. And Leslie contributed a bottle of wine, so that was a bonus.

This was long before Dr Seuss made Mulberry Street famous and long before the area became trendy SoHo: in 1947 it was Little Italy, a neighbourhood of mama-and-papa bakeries, butchers and grocery stores, with a few small Italian restaurants, affordable and homey. In summer and fall every few weeks brought a Saint's Day and its obligatory street fair, when the penetrating aromas of sausage and garlic, of onions and tomatoes and peppers spread through the area from the street vendors. Rotund politicians made speeches from the bandstand – Big Al from Chicago. Why here? Who knew? It had some kind of New York logic. Robust opera singers launched aching arias over the heads of the crowd long into the night, lights flashed, music soared over the tenements, someone played an accordion on a fire escape. People milled about in the streets jostling each other, eating, dancing, playing games. We loved every minute of it.

We didn't have much money, but we managed. That was what we said all the time, 'We'll manage.'

Here in a low building on Mulberry Street, technically not a tenement, we had two large rooms with a small room like a hallway separating them. This is what New York called a *railway apartment*, named for the long line of rooms, each leading into the next. The living room at the front faced the street, with the charming but non-functioning fireplace on the outer wall. Ellen's bed, as always, doubled as a couch, and making a successful repair, we had built rather rudimentary bookcases in the alcoves on each side of the fireplace. From the large kitchen at the back a pair of tall windows gave a view of the caboose – a back yard full of broken boxes and machine parts. The hallway between the two rooms was, on one side, my bedroom and on the other side, our closet, where coats and dresses hung on walls beside a low chest of drawers.

Some time ago the City of New York Building Code had decreed that bathtubs must be provided for tenants. Throughout the city the landlords had responded by installing bathtubs as simply and cheaply as possible – in the kitchen, right next to the sink. There is nothing quite like a bathtub to provoke thoughts of nakedness. It's quite possible that these new bathtubs were responsible for the greatly increased birth rate in Manhattan the following year.

Ellen and I found it all hilarious. The usual slab of wood provided useful work space when the tub was not occupied by a naked body. After I left for school in the mornings, Ellen would lift the slab off the tub, climb over the curled edge, and find herself looking at a kitchen sink full of breakfast dishes. To our friends from Canada the bathtub lent a certain Bohemian air; visitors were all unaccountably eager to bathe. Less charming was the unheated toilet out in the hall, where we had installed a strategically placed heat bulb, to be activated when the room was occupied.

In our living room on Christmas day, Ellen and I sat with Sol and Leslie, telling them the story of making our 'collapsible' bookcases and trying to put Leslie at ease. When the phone rang it was at least a happy distraction, a friend of Ellen's from work. Her family visit to Syracuse had turned unpleasant and Nona was now at Grand Central on her way to visit us. Today? Yes, today. Now. For Christmas. Wasn't that exciting?

Well, one girl. 'Perhaps she has a small appetite,' said Ellen.

Nona had no sooner arrived than the doorbell rang. There on the doorstep stood Reuben and Pearl, old Party friends of Ellen's from Toronto. They'd come to New York to visit Rube's uncle. His rich uncle, they always said. But they'd forgotten how thrifty the rich can be. 'My uncle's house is colder than Canada,' Rube said. They knew they could get warm at our place: hope we didn't mind them inviting themselves.

It was just as Rube and Pearl arrived that the snow began.

How simply marvellous, how picturesque, a white Christmas! Everyone rushed to the living room windows to watch the lovely soft flakes drifting down. Our cocker spaniel puppy was ecstatic: all those faces to lick. Our cat sullenly retreated under the couch, from where she stared out through the forest of legs.

We also had a visiting cat for the holidays. The poor thing had holed up in a corner and made herself as invisible as possible, hoping to escape the notice of our own cat, who glared at her, growling evilly.

The snow was coming down more heavily now. Beautiful big slow flakes.

In the kitchen, Ellen and I took inventory of the pantry. There was a can of tomato soup. We'd have that to start with, stretching it for seven people. And that pathetic chicken she'd bought to serve three people was now, like the biblical loaves and fishes, somehow going to have to satisfy the hunger of the multitude. Ellen doubled the stuffing recipe, using up the last of our loaf of bread. I cut up great quantities of vegetables. Lots and lots of mashed potatoes, lots of gravy; Ellen always made marvellous gravy, caramelled and rich. We'd get by somehow. And we had the Christmas pudding and some fruit cake that my grandmother had sent from Calgary.

The snow showed no sign of stopping. It was exquisite in the view from the windows. The back yard behind the kitchen relinquished its chaos to the serenity of a snowy blanket.

We pulled chairs and boxes from everywhere and all of us managed to sit at the kitchen table, having a merry old time. Reuben and Pearl and Ellen talked about friends and politics back in Toronto. Nona and Leslie very willingly shared a chair, and Sol and I nuzzled at each other right in front of my mother. We didn't have enough plates, of course, or glasses or cups, but we improvised. And Leslie's bottle of wine just nicely served all of us, even me, and I wasn't even of legal drinking age.

And outside in the darkness the snow fell gracefully.

The radio told us we were in the middle of what was undoubtedly going to be the heaviest snowfall in New York's history. Cars clogged the streets. Buses and taxis had stopped running. Even the subways had stopped. The radio warned everyone: Stay where you are; wherever you are, just stay there.

Our visitors had no way of getting to their homes, wherever those homes might be. We were stuck with them. They were stuck with us. We were among friends; what more could we want on Christmas day, sitting on the floor in the living room with fruit cake and coffee, warm and full of food.

We had two beds, counting the one doubling as a couch in the living room. Seven people had to sleep somewhere or at least lay their heads down for some part of the night. My mother claimed the right to sleep alone and in her own bed. Rube and Pearl suggested they'd take the kitchen floor, using cushions and coats for padding. Nona and I giggled at the thought of the one bed left, the four people. Sol and Leslie looked at the ceiling. The four of us bedded down horizontally across my bed in the hallway.

There wasn't much sleeping done that Christmas night. My mother pleaded desperately from time to time: 'Would you people please settle down so I can get some sleep.' Let people sleep who wanted to sleep, she said. 'Stop horsing around.' But to us sleep was far less important than fun. In the kitchen, Rube lay on his back and snored serenely through it all. Now and then Pearl gave him a punch and he'd snortle. That would start us off giggling again. Giggling and groping under the blankets, whispering, perfectly safe in a crowd.

And intermittently throughout the night, the visiting cat would venture out of her corner, hoping to sneak into the kitchen for food; our cat stalked her and the puppy followed, eager to see what was going on. Pet pandemonium: snarling and snapping, snivelling and cringing, yelping and hissing.

In the morning the snow was still coming down. All through Manhattan not a wheel was turning. Hills of snow marked the location of abandoned cars lining the curbs, and some in the middle of streets. The radio announced that there would be no deliveries to stores throughout the area, no bread and milk, no meat, no anything. And in our small apartment on Mulberry Street, seven hungry people awoke yawning, and hoping somehow to be given food and sustenance.

This was before everyone had a freezer. Most people bought their food on a day-to-day basis and kept a few canned things for emergencies. Our cupboard was bare. And Ellen had no money anyway. The stores weren't even going to bother to open their doors, the radio said.

Ellen made coffee and called a conference around the kitchen table. She was not only the oldest adult and official proprietor of the house, but she was used to taking charge in times of hunger – a holdover from our Depression days. She suggested we deploy two foraging teams. Each would explore the surrounding streets in the hope of finding an open store. Tactful Sol said we'd need to take up a collection to see what money we had for food. A dollar here, a dollar there, a few stray quarters: enough for eggs, milk, bread and butter.

Rube and Pearl stayed with Ellen to talk about the political situation in Canada, a bit tense these days of spy stories. Leslie and Nona went westward, with orders from Ellen to send a runner back to her at Mulberry Street in fifteen minutes to report their findings. After a cozy night under the blankets they were happy to go off to find their own way of improving the morning. Good spirits prevailed. Sol and I bundled up and plodded off toward Third Avenue, plowing through snow that came up above our knees. Calm white avenues opened in magical silence before us. We walked in the middle of the street, through the unblemished snow. New York had never looked so clean, so pure. Had never been so quiet. The bars were dark, the pawnshops closed, the office buildings and bridal shops lifeless. And *grazie, molto grazie*, a welcoming OPEN sign glowed from a corner deli.

36. WEST 103RD STREET

Marty had happened into the writers' studio on New Year's Eve, had found Ellen there and apparently didn't want to lose sight of her. They came home from their first date while Sol and I were at the Mulberry Street apartment. We were just picking up a few things to go for the weekend to stay in an apartment one of his students was lending him. So we met Marty, and no one seemed at all surprised or at all regretful when we said, 'We're just off for the weekend. Back tomorrow afternoon.' Sol and I left them to get on with their date.

Marty was always around after that. Except when he went off on one of his sea-voyages. 'Martin Phillips went to sea, in a beautiful pea-green boat,' Ellen teased. He was a pretty good guy, I thought, and obviously Ellen thought so too. He was a lefty who fit neatly into Ellen's group of friends – the writer friends and the Party friends. Marty was an electrician who did his work on ships. So he was away sometimes for a month or two, then back in New York until he needed to ship out again. Dark hair, brown eyes, warm, expressive, Jewish. It was a pleasure to see my mother happy. And when Marty was around, she didn't pester me. I could stay away for a couple of days at a time with Sol and she didn't much seem to care where I was, as long as I did well at school and was home on school nights. But when Marty was gone she always wanted to know where I was going and when I would be home.

At Ellen's Party meeting one night, with five or six people scattered about in our living room, one of the men had a problem: 'At the office today they passed out a paper we all have to sign, all the employees. It's the new loyalty oath. Everyone who works for any branch of government has to sign it. Listen to this: *I am not now, nor have I ever been, a member of any organization that supports or advocates the overthrow of the government by violent means.*'

Ellen said, 'I had to sign that when I immigrated.'

'You did? You mean you signed it?'

'Of course I did. The Party doesn't advocate the violent overthrow of the government.'

'Well, *I* know it doesn't. But the U.S. government thinks it does.'

'But do they have a right to ask about political opinions? Shouldn't politics be private business?'

'Of course. But that's not how the government sees it now. They're afraid of communists everywhere. Afraid we're propagandizing the whole country. Helping the Russians. That's how McCarthy sees us.

'Should I sign? If I sign it, it seems to me that I have accepted their right to ask me. And by their terms, I'd be lying. And if I don't sign it, I'll get fired.'

'You'll get fired? They told you that?'

'Not exactly that. They said *it's a requirement for continued employment.*'

'Same thing.'

'Right.'

I went back to my room to finish my homework. Grown-up stuff. No concern of mine, I thought.

Years later, when the FBI decided that poor innocent Ellen was an international Red courier and a threat to the government of the United States, they tried to prompt me to remember the names of the people in the group. 'I was just a kid,' I told them. 'I wasn't paying much attention.'

But in the week before graduation from Washington Irving High School, the loyalty oath was passed out to all the students in the graduating class. Sign it. *A requirement of graduation.* Well, well, so it was a concern of mine. I signed it, knowing that the 'authorities', whoever they were, had no right to ask me. But I didn't tell my mother. I was ashamed of having signed it so meekly. I should have protested, shouldn't I?

But I hadn't the courage to be a tough political fighter. I still felt small and afraid, still longed for some safety in this hazardous world. In the politics of the Depression, communists had been the heroes, the good guys of my childhood. Now, post-war, it was all more complicated. I was proud of my mother, admired her convictions and her courage, but I felt detached from the details of her politics.

An active life of politics held no appeal for me, filled me with dread. Security and stability beckoned. I was trying to think for myself, though not yet doing a very good job of it.

At my high school they told me that for graduation I had to have a white dress. Didn't anybody know that some things were impossible for some people? There was an announcement that financial assistance was available. 'See the guidance office.' They let me know that they could give me ten dollars for a dress if I needed it. But when I told my mother, she would have none of it. 'You can't buy anything decent for ten dollars,' she said. Besides, I'd probably never want to wear it again. What a waste!

Bobbi came to the rescue: I could borrow her wedding dress. It was, I see now looking back, a very 'Bobbi' sort of dress – dipping low in the front, short puffy sleeves. We wrapped a lace scarf around my neck, fastened in front with a tiny rose brooch that came from Ellen's grandmother. It worked.

My mother was there for the big event, of course, with Marty. Sol came to watch me get my diploma. He and Marty were nearly the same age and got along well, came from similar backgrounds. Marty treated us to a feast at La Bilbaina afterward, to celebrate.

Now that we both had men around, the little apartment on Mulberry Street didn't suit our lives. There was no privacy: no bedroom doors, the bathtub in the kitchen. And the toilet out in the hall, warmed all winter with a heat lamp, became increasingly less charming. Some of the charms of the Bohemian life were wearing off, especially for Ellen, who was glowing in the romance of her love for Marty.

Early in the spring we moved again, away from the charms of lower Manhattan. The apartment that Ellen found, through a friend who lived in the building, was on 103rd Street, just west of Central Park. It was a tall, thin, probably once elegant brownstone, converted for apartments – two on each floor. One at the front, one at the back. But the rear apartment had to maintain open access to the fire escape, so the hallway was officially public property, a sort of right of way.

Opening onto the hallway were two bedrooms – Ellen's still disguised as a living room during the day – with a connecting door knocked through the wall between them to give the place some semblance of an apartment. The kitchen was down the hall at the back of the house. But because the fire escape was off the kitchen, this 'apartment' could have no real doorway, just a curtain hung out in the hall. And up the hall toward the front, a wonderful bathroom, large and clean, warm – but which we had to share with the people in the front apartment.

I had taken the entrance exam for one of New York's free universities and had been accepted into Hunter College. Total cost, including books, was $85 a year – about three weeks' salary for a modest job. I worked after school down in lower Manhattan, at a toy store in Knickerbocker Village, where Ellen and I had lived with Louise just over a year ago. Four apartments ago.

I suspect that my mother got Mel's name from someone in her Party group, but I didn't ever know for sure where the connection came from, only that I got it from her. But I did know that Mel was a comrade, and I thought that gave me a slight advantage in the job I was applying for. Mel had a toystore, right there on the western side of the housing project. It was a good job and I liked it. The little kids would come in after school with a dime usually, and I would show them where the special section was, full of little ten-cent treasures.... Wax lips, marbles, itsy cars and dolls, yo-yos and puzzles, chalk and crayons, lots of things for a dime. Saturdays were sometimes a bit crazy during the day, but evenings were slow. As long as I took good care of the customers I could do my homework while I was at work.

Ellen sometimes worked at home, sometimes at the office of Contemporary Writers. Editing and writing. Both of us had part-time jobs, and we managed financially somehow. I was at school during the days. Hunter College had a beautiful campus, some old Gothic-style buildings, lots of trees and grass in the spring, after the winter winds whirling across the campus in February, when I started. Hunter used to be an all-girls' college, but when the soldiers came home from the war and were given free tuition and a living allowance the spaces at all the other schools filled up, so then they opened Hunter to men also. There was a downtown campus, but most freshmen went to the Bronx campus. That was me. A freshman. Lots of time for reading, on the subway up to the Bronx in the morning, on the subway after school down to my job at the toy store, on the subway back home. Our apartment on West 103rd Street, with two bedrooms, convenient for visits from Sol and Marty on the weekends.

There are two old black-and-white photographs of Marty that survive. In the first one he and Ellen are somewhere near a dock; there is part of a boat in the foreground. A small shaggy Yorkshire terrier is sitting on top of the cabin and Ellen is scratching its ear, leaning in to say something into the dog's face. Behind the cabin, behind the dog, is Marty. The top of his head, one eye, and a one-sided smile. Half present. The other photo is taken in our apartment, just a blurred murmur of a picture taken without flash. He's slumping in an armchair, one foot up on the cushion, wearing only undershorts. There's a lamp at his left on a low bookcase, a book up to his face. Here he is again. The top of his head, one eye, a slice of nose and in the haze a piece of chin.

My brother Andy came to visit while we lived on 103rd Street, giving us a bit of a scare. As was always his way, he just appeared out of nowhere. It was probably a Sunday morning when he arrived – Ellen and I were in our separate rooms with our guys – and knocked on Ellen's door early in the morning, announcing himself. 'Surprise! It's Andy.'

It was lucky that we had a connecting door, because Ellen just about went crazy when she heard him. 'Just a minute, just a minute,' she told him. 'I'll be right with you. I was sleeping.' She started whispering to Marty and shoving him and pushing through the door to my room. Hissing at me, 'Laurie, Laurie, get up, Andy's here. Get up. ... Get in here, come on.' And she herded me into her room, Marty into my room with Sol. Lots of whispering to them, 'It's my son. My son is in the hall.'

So the two of us, chaste females to be sure, went out in the hall to greet him. It was our first meeting since he had left for naval school over two years before. We were not a family that hugged each other, and I don't remember any emotion being expressed, although there was surely some pleasure in the reunion. Wasn't there? A lot of smiling, anyway, and certainly a lot of flustering about. Ellen was more concerned about protecting our reputation than about greeting the difficult son.

Andy was working on a Greek ship, bound for somewhere or other, and had decided to jump ship in New York, letting the ship sail away without him. There were two rather enormous legal problems with that: first, that he was in the United States illegally, and second, that he'd have to get out of the country again somehow. All without getting caught. 'I'll just stow away on another ship when I'm ready to leave,' he said. In the meantime, here he was at 103rd Street for a couple of days.

We took Andy into the kitchen and made tea, always top priority, and then Ellen told me to 'go and wake up Marty and Sol so that they can meet Andy.' And they were duly introduced as 'a couple of friends who stayed over last night because we came home really late from a movie and they both live out in Brooklyn and it's such a long trip to make late at night so we put them up in Laurie's room.' Period. Andy never said anything about it, but surely he wasn't an innocent in such things.

So we all sat around our little table in front of the window in the kitchen and Ellen made breakfast. Toast and scrambled eggs. And Andy told us what he had been doing since he was de-mobilized in San Francisco. He had gone to Vancouver to visit his father, stayed with him a few days. But Lawrence was drunk most of the time, Andy said. 'Passed out and pissing his pants,' so Andy left. 'Stayed with Uncle George for a while,' he said. 'Tried to find a job. Worked here and there, but nothing fit, so I signed back on the ships.'

He and Marty had that in common. The merchant ships. Conversation in the kitchen would have been difficult, but we all seemed to have the sense to just let Andy talk. He was nineteen; perhaps he'd come to see whether there might be a place for him here in New York with us, a home. If he had that in mind, he soon gave it up. There was no home with our father, and none here either. Ellen wasn't feeling maternal. In my mother's mind, a nineteen-year-old man was expected to earn his way in life, and she was certainly neither able nor willing to provide any financial help to him. And Andy seemed to have some of our father's prideful and arrogant disposition, enough to create tension. On top of everything, now there was the mess of his illegal status.

He told us he wanted to explore New York and try to find some of his friends from his naval days here at the end of the war. He decided to take in the sights of New York. He stayed with friends, sleeping on the floor here and there, phoning now and then to let us know where he was, visiting for dinner now and then.

Sometimes it seemed to me that he must have fallen on his head when he was a baby. He had such odd ways of doing things, inventing brilliant methods for ordinary things, little labour-saving devices. Like the day he decided to heat up a can of corn for his lunch. Why bother to put it in a pot? Why not just take the paper off the can and put the can over the gas burner? Why not? It was so easy. No pot to wash. No plate to wash if you just eat it from the can, right? Everyone always made such a production out of everything, when there were easier ways. When the corn got hot, the can exploded of course, spraying creamed corn all over the kitchen walls. He left after that, with my mother yelling at him. No one likes to feel like a fool with other people around. Better to go off and brood in private. 'How was I supposed to know it would explode?'

Guess who cleaned the walls? You could make pretty good glue from creamed corn, did you know that? Like the old-fashioned library paste, white and gummy.

One day while Andy was still in New York there was what passed for a knock on our door – we had no door, of course – it was a sort of scrabbling at the wallpaper in the hall. Two men in suits, their shoes neatly polished. 'Hi! We're looking for Lawrence. We're old friends of his.' It was Andy they were after, of course. We knew they weren't looking for my father. He had no American presence, no involvement here. But no one ever called my brother Lawrence, even though that was his first name. Named after his father, of course. The firstborn son. But everyone called him by his middle name, Alan, or Andy, his nickname. So my mother knew right away that they weren't really friends. FBI, no doubt. Of course Ellen told them she didn't know where he was. 'Sorry. He's unpredictable, you know. I have no idea where he is.' After they left she phoned the place where Andy was staying: 'Time to leave. They're on to you.'

He said he had already talked to the FBI a few weeks earlier, before he left Halifax, playing at playing 'double agent' in the hopes of gaining some freedom, some leverage. Why would anyone trust him now, on either side of the Red line? He was cut adrift politically forever. And he stowed away on a ship to England, with no fond farewells. Off again for a few years.

Sol lived in the Bronx with his family, and later with a group of friends on the Upper West Side, 107th Street, I think, in a fairly large apartment. A reasonably efficient kitchen at the back of the straggle of rooms, overlooking nothing but more roofs. Then a bathroom off the hall and a decent size room with two couches and an assortment of easy chairs, tables and desks. This became the main gathering place – a kind of communal room, near the kitchen, of course – and also theoretically a place for 'occasional' tenants, there for a week or so. Leslie had begun to make his presence permanent though, camping out on one of the daybeds. There was a long hall, with the entrance to the apartment about mid-way down it, and at the front, a large room that had originally been intended as the principal room. It had been converted to a bedroom and office for Frank and Mary Ann, who paid the most rent. There were a couple of rooms off the hall, on the airshaft. Sol's and Mike's. All of the permanent residents taught at Columbia or NYU and were struggling with MAs or PhDs – all of them in sociology or psychology. Social Psych. They were all about Sol's age, all of them eight or ten years older than I was. All good-naturedly leaning to the political left, supporting the left during the fearful days of the political witchhunts. Trying to play it safe, but to do what was right. A hard job in those days, when expressing your opinion could get you fired.

This was also a time when Ellen and I began to have problems with each other, a time when I began to draw away from her into a separate life and psyche. Part of that was just a normal growing-up process, but part of it was because I began to have, if not my own ideas, at least a different perspective on life which I was picking up from Sol and his friends. Ellen was very bright, very knowledgeable, very well-read, but she had no respect for people who seemed to her to be in ivory towers, away from the difficulties and hardships of working-class life, or the life of most working people. She had a lot of real antagonism toward Sol's friends, and eventually toward him. Perhaps part of that was because she felt that he continued to draw me away from what should be the normal life of someone my age. What that was, I didn't know.

When had my life ever been normal? I felt as though I had never fit in anywhere, rarely had friends my own age, and couldn't get along with ordinary kids. In drawing away from Ellen I did feel that I was beginning to make my own judgments, to have opinions that did not necessarily match hers. More and more I felt that she was insulting toward my friends, Sol's friends. Disrespectful. Disdainful.

She seemed disdainful of everything about them. Their politics weren't far enough to the left. Their profession as sociologists involved years of research to prove things that were obvious to her. They didn't participate in life, they stood apart and looked at other people's lives. Their writing was stilted and academic, never using one word when four long ones would do. They lived in communal squalor pretending to be poor while pulling down decent middle-class salaries as teachers. For me the cumulative weight of her judgments lay heavily on my heart. In defending my friends I seemed to be defying her.

I have a very clear memory of one occasion when I stood leaning against the wall at the group apartment, just at the threshold of the common room, lazily exchanging bits of conversation with two or three people in the room, leaning on the wall, not committed to entering that room, holding back and yet participating. It was at about this time that I began to call my mother by her first name. Everyone knew her, and we sometimes talked about her, especially in connection with the political climate, the fears and secrecy of those days. I felt terribly childish saying 'my mother' all the time, while they said Ellen, so the switch came quite naturally to me.

That summer, I finally turned eighteen. This was a very big event, you have to understand. Mainly because up until then I was still 'jailbait', and Sol was very nervous about that. His family was terribly worried about him getting into trouble, after everything they had done to push him along out of the Bronx ghetto. They were good, law-abiding citizens. I know that Sol was nervous about our relationship, but I tried to kid him about it. Kid him out of it. But here was the big day. I was having a birthday and therefore could be legally bedded. We thought we might make an occasion of it, a sort of honeymoon, I thought. So Ellen arranged with a friend of hers who lived in the building to let us use his apartment for the night. We'd go out to dinner with Ellen and

Marty, then come back to our very own private apartment. Private for the night, at least.

Great expectations. Too much work, too much wine. Sol was asleep and snoring before I even put on my brand new nightie.

37. YOU CAN'T GO HOME AGAIN

In the summer of 1948, when I was almost eighteen, my granddad on my father's side died back in Vancouver. Ellen asked me if I wanted to go to the funeral, then got tickets for me, across the continent and back. By plane to Vancouver, then by bus home to New York. I don't know however she got the money.

My aunt Alice, my father's sister, met me at the plane with her husband Harry. 'A big horsey woman', my mother called her. My dad's car was banged up, she said. Aunt Alice and I had never really known each other well, and because she had a daughter about my age there had always been a kind of tension in our relationship in that competitive family. Hearing about her daughter Joan, I knew I was being told that she was a much better person than I was or could ever be. I readily conceded defeat. I expressed my complete admiration for every one of Joan's achievements that was presented to me on the drive from the airport.

However, it was all a fake. I thought I was a pretty sophisticated young woman then. I'd been to see shows on Broadway, like *Oklahoma!* and *Carousel*. And *Streetcar Named Desire*: Brando. I'd been to Carnegie Hall and the Met. I'd eaten *shashlik* in Armenian restaurants and could say *'l'chaim.'* I was in first year at Hunter College, on campus with the GIs now home. I had an after-school job and I was 'going with' someone. I guess I thought Manhattan was the centre of the world, and I was one of its star citizens.

But the relatives gathered at my grandparents' house, now Grandma's I guess, had an easy way of not caring about anything like that. Why should that family of hard-working men and women care about this odd creature, the offspring of a marriage that was completely broken? My father was at the house with all the other relatives and he was glad to see me. 'You're quite the young lady now, aren't you, Laurie,' he said, looking my body, my figure, up and down. 'And how's your mother?' he asked. 'Is she ready to come home yet? Har-har.'

My uncle Davey drove me somewhere during those two days. I should have known better, but I thought he might have smartened up. I certainly had. He had a good job as a fireman, I heard. There wasn't any of his old adolescent groping, he just stuck his arm around me and asked, 'Heh, heh, you wanna do it, Laurie?' Stinky, rumpled old man, even then, at about thirty.

I don't remember the actual funeral, only the family gathering at the house afterwards, the small quarter-sandwiches on white bread, the rye and ginger for the men, two big pots of tea, and my grandmother, my darling grandmother. Grandma Charlotte had always liked my mother, liked her spirit of independence, and I think she was secretly very happy, proud even, that Ellen had escaped. 'Will you tell your mother I asked about her,' she said. 'Tell her that I wish her well in what she's doing, and I'm proud of her.' This was so unlike the rest of the family, who thought that Ellen had brought shame on them, running away from her husband like that.

Oh, I hugged my grandma and I cried. 'I'll tell her what you said, Grandma, of course I'll tell her.'

For the trip home I had my bus tickets and $15 in American money to buy sandwiches along the way, with some packed sandwiches from Grandma Charlotte to see me to my next family stopover. From Vancouver I travelled by bus through the Rockies, stopping in Alberta at Macleod, now Fort Macleod – population then I think about 500, or at least that's the way it felt to me – to visit relatives on my mother's side of the family. I had a grandmother and an aunt and uncle and a whole lot of cousins there. It was a big adventure, travelling by myself.

My mother never got along well with her big sister Gertrude, seventeen years older. But Aunt Gertie wanted me to stay at her house, not to bother my grandmother – this grandmother never called Grandma Julia – and her husband Charlie. I slept in Cousin Margie's room, my suitcase propped open on a yellow chair under the window, the curtains blowing into the room with all that sweet-smelling prairie air.

On Friday night the whole family was there at the Cleaver house, all gathered together at the long table – my grandmother, her husband

Charlie, Aunt Gertie and Uncle Harry, and all their children – Roy, the eldest, then Norman and Margie, and Brian, the youngest. We ate roast chicken and mashed potatoes and it was delicious, delicious. And Aunt Gertie made a chocolate cake, specially, she said, and a fruit-berry pie.

My cousin Roy was five years older than me, and maybe he was a bit bored with life in Macleod after his time in the navy. Or maybe his mother had told him to entertain me. On Saturday he asked me, 'Would you like to go out dancing? I expect there's a dance down at the Legion tonight.' He was so polite, looking at me with hazel eyes that seemed to change colour – brown, gold, green. There wasn't much else to do in town, he said, but he'd try to make sure I had a good time. Surprised, I said yes. But I was embarrassed to be on something like a 'date' with my cousin.

Main Street in Macleod ran east and west for about six blocks. Then there was prairie. 'There's nothing out there but gophers and Indians,' said Roy. That one street had all the stores any town would need, mainly two-storey buildings with offices and apartments upstairs and shops at street level. A grocery and a hardware, probably, and a barbershop and beauty parlour, a clothing store. I know there was a coffee shop, too. The entrance to the Legion Hall was between the barbershop and the drugstore.

The wide wooden stairway up from the street was dusty and worn. It cracked and creaked as we walked up. The walls were grey, painted just two years ago, Roy told me, at the end of the war. 'All across Canada there are millions of gallons of paint left over from the war – all of it battleship grey. You can buy it at surplus stores for practically nothing. You remember we all went for years without paint – first from the Depression, then from the war. So this is at least something. We painted everything in sight.'

So, across Canada in those years, meeting halls got new coats of grey paint. It didn't wear out, you know, not ever. So if those buildings hadn't been torn down to make room for the downtown hotels and shopping malls, you could see it still.

Roy wore his suit, a nice dark blue one, with a white shirt and a striped tie. I wore my light blue crepe dress. It curved over my hips and made my breasts look good. I was wearing my high heels and nylons of course. So Cousin Roy had a good look at my seams as we walked up the stairs at the Legion Hall. They probably weren't straight. They never were.

Before the war, if you had money (which most people didn't) you could buy silk stockings, but once the war started you could forget about that. And nylons just weren't available. We used to paint our legs and draw a line up the back for the seam. (After the war, when nylons first appeared at Eaton's, I stood in line in Toronto for three hours waiting to buy a pair. 'Are you crazy?' my mother said. Weren't we all?)

Roy and I went through the big double doors at the top of the stairs just the way they did in Hollywood. Pushed them open and stepped right into the big room.

The windows were full of the prairie sky at first, then as it got dark, turned into a reflection of ourselves, changing the hall into a ballroom. There was a gramophone up on the stage, opposite the windows. Wooden chairs against the walls. In their workaday lives they lined up in neat rows facing the little stage, holding the sturdy backsides of the Legion members. But tonight some of them supported the healthy young people of the area. Some stood stiffly empty at the edges of the room, occupied by the spirits of all the mums and dads, aunts, uncles, and grandparents who had cheered themselves up in this very room in the past thirty or so years.

The gramophone played and there were maybe twelve or so couples dancing. The music was Guy Lombardo and the Royal Canadians. Smooth and easy dancing. No boogie. No jive. Nothing like that here tonight. On the dance floor Roy and I touched in proper foxtrot style. Hand to hand, held high. His right hand around my waist, my left hand on his shoulder. In the centre of the room a few other couples shuffled carefully the same way. Nowhere else did their bodies touch. No body heat felt through clothing, no bodies moving against each other. The young men and young ladies of Macleod had checked their hormones at the door, at least temporarily.

I was trying very hard to be 'normal', whatever that might be. I didn't want to shame Roy by being strange. And yet, I was proud, pleased, to be different. I thought I was not like my relatives who had stayed put, who hadn't felt the need to run as Ellen and I had, to what was for us a mixture of escape and adventure, with all its consequences.

I was just about as tall as Cousin Roy, and I felt awkward when we were dancing together. All my mother's family are small people – not only short, but small-boned, thin. So when I was growing up I thought I was getting huge. I weighed about a hundred and five pounds and was five-foot-two-eyes-of-blue, but reality has no place in the mind of a teenager. I was afraid I might grow up to be like my Aunt Alice on my father's side.

That's why, when Roy and I sat down for a bit and he brought me a glass of lemonade, I took my shoes off. Just so I wouldn't feel so big, next to Roy. After that I danced in my stocking feet, snagging my precious nylons on the wooden floor. Cousin Roy seemed uneasy, looking around. But he was – and still is – a really polite man and he didn't say anything to me about it. Everyone was looking at us. It was as if I'd taken my dress off or something. Shocking, anyway. So much for trying to be normal.

We kept on dancing until closing time. One a.m. Then we went home to my aunt and uncle's place. And I sat on the bed in Margie's room, just thinking it all over, trying to find my place in this world of the prairies, where I had grown up. On Monday morning Roy took me to the bus station – really just a place where the bus stopped, behind the café. We sat at the lunch counter on chrome stools and had a cup of tea while I waited for the bus to Billings, Montana. Roy bought me a ham sandwich to take with me.

When the bus took me away I looked back and waved at Cousin Roy, with his green eyes saying goodbye.

From southern Alberta, the Greyhound route crossed into Montana, and on to Minneapolis, Chicago and New York.

At the end of the week, when I arrived back in Manhattan, there they were, my mother and my boyfriend, Ellen and Sol, both there at the bus terminal to meet me. The only thing really on my mind was having a bath. I'd been sleeping in my clothes on that bus for about four days. Of course I should have gone home with my mother. Of course I should. And that was what I really wanted. But Sol's friends were having a party and he wanted me to go with him. I didn't want to go, and I thought he was really insensitive (which was a kinder word than stupid) to have asked me. I don't know why I couldn't just say no. Giving way. Was that something I had learned from my mother? The art of appeasement? Giving in to the strongest force field? Tired and grubby though I was, I went off with him, unable to say no. Did I expect Ellen to fight the battle for me? If she had, would I have accepted it? Stupidly, with barely a thought, I said goodbye to Ellen and walked away with Sol. I probably gave her my suitcase to carry home.

38. EAST NINTH STREET

Our odd apartment on West 103rd Street was apt to be crowded on weekends, when Sol and Marty were both around, so I began staying with Sol at his friends' apartment occasionally. It didn't give us much more privacy, but it helped Ellen and Marty. Marty lived with his mother – in Brooklyn, I think – but as he and Ellen got closer, they seemed to want to settle down in something more like a home, so Ellen began apartment hunting again. She found a nice clean place with two real bedrooms, a living room, and a tiny kitchenette. I know that the landlord wanted 'key money' – how much? Two hundred dollars, maybe. Plus first and last month's rent. But Ellen, with her amazing landlord-slaying charm, talked her way into it with nothing more than the first month's rent. The apartment was in a four-storey building on East Ninth Street, near Third Avenue. Not bad. The Lower East Side, yes, but not too lower and not too east.

This was the first apartment that felt real to me. The first that seemed not doomed from the start by our poverty. Ellen bought a double bed as an act of hope, and Marty moved in, probably sharing the rent. They read and talked and shopped and cooked together. The kitchen counter would be piled with fresh tomatoes, onions with the stalks still on, little bags of spices. And Marty liked to cook. Now that was a real treat to Ellen. Not because it spared her the work of cooking, but because cooking together became another shared activity, another way of exploring sensuality, perhaps. Marty had travelled to many parts of the world, experienced and enjoyed exotic tastes and smells. He cooked spicy shrimp *diablo* in the Mexican style, and paella. He introduced Ellen to avocados. It was lovely having him around the apartment, and lovely to see my mother happy.

I began looking for a real job for the summer. I wanted something better than the toy store. I checked the 'Help Wanted Female' ads in both the *New York Times* and the *Herald Tribune*, scanning through all listings, since I had no particular job category in mind, and no particular skills: Asst everything, clerks of every kind, cashier, energetic ..., friendly ..., hairdresser, receptionist, salesgirl, waitress, young woman to help....

I measured each job description against what I thought were my skills and inclinations, and settled on 'Receptionist at Public Service Organization'. It sounded good, even though the ad specified typing and switchboard. I thought 'some typing' might reasonably describe my slow search and stab system. 'Switchboard' was beyond me but I thought I could learn in a hurry. One of my school friends was working in an office so I asked her to give me a demonstration, just in case. She gave me a quick lesson at her switchboard, but told me, 'This is a plug board, but there's another kind. Newer, different, called a monitor board. I don't know how those work.'

I phoned and arranged an interview. Down on West Fortieth Street, just off Fifth Avenue, across from the library. Nice area. The thin well-dressed woman, crisp in a brown linen suit was very pleasant, smiling. Her neatness was so smooth and sophisticated that it made me feel clumsy and awkward, sure that my slip was showing, or that my stockings had developed a run. She asked about my work experience and about school. 'This is a full-time job, you know,' she told me. Yes, I said, I realized that, but I needed the job and didn't plan to return to school. That was one of those lies that became prophetic.

I told her I could type 'a bit'. I hadn't yet learned to be careful of the lies I told. You have to watch it. They can come back and clobber you. And when she asked me about operating a switchboard I asked, 'Is it a monitor board or a plug board?' The question was a good one, because it showed her that I knew *something*. When she told me it was a monitor board I said, 'I have more experience with a plug board.' That wasn't a lie, after my ten-minute lesson the previous day. But I had to take a typing test, which was very humiliating. It taught me just exactly how well I did *not* type. Pitiful. I was just pitiful. She said she had other people to see. Well, I never thought I'd get the job, not after that horrible typing experience. My score was probably ten words a minute, by the time I finished correcting all my mistakes. But she phoned me a couple of days later to tell me I was hired. 'You seem to have a good personality for the job, and that's what's important. You can learn to type once you're here.'

The building was called Freedom House, and Willkie Memorial Building, named for Wendell Willkie, a former president of the United States. And the tenants were all the good interracial progressive organizations: National Association for the Advancement of Colored People, United Jewish Appeal, B'nai Brith. And I did real work, talking to people who came into the building, directing them to offices, answering the phones – learning the monitor board. 'Freedom House, may I help you?' Earning money, enough to share the rent. All through the fall, Bryant Park across the street a place for lunch when the weather was good.

I got an instruction manual and worked at learning to type. Punching the keys through the frequently-used combinations of letters: the the the, ght ght ght, my left hand flying up to fling the carriage back at the end of every line. Line line line fling fling fling. End end end.

On the balcony of Freedom House, opposite Bryant Park in New York. This is the blue crepe dress I wore to the dance with my cousin Roy when I travelled back west (1948).

I worked through the summer and registered for the next term at college, not telling anyone at work that I had done it. I wandered into the Henry Street Playhouse one evening and worked on a couple of plays, finding props, making thunder, standing in for the director's wife in the star role. Soon I was there almost every night. Marty had an old car, a coupe, with a rumble seat. Sometimes we'd all go out together. They'd cuddle in the front seat and I'd be out there in the back, wrapped up in a blanket, waving and yelling out into the darkness of Manhattan.

But Marty was a seaman. He got bored just 'hanging around' in New York. He couldn't find, or perhaps didn't want, a shore job. He began to be glum, sitting about. 'I'm bored,' he said. 'With me?' my mother asked. 'Of course not with you, silly. I just need to have a job, I need to ship out again.' The vanishing man. And he'd come back a couple of months later, all smiles and souvenirs. Shalimar perfume for Ellen, always.

Then he vanished once too often for Ellen, off to sea again. She had told him. She had warned him: 'If you go off again, I won't be here when you get back.'

I was barely noticing, completely wrapped up in my own life. A job, a boyfriend, evenings at the Playhouse. What else would I even notice? When she said, 'I'm going to England. Do you want to come?' I hadn't the faintest idea what it was all about. Only that she wanted to move again.

There was no money, of course. How could she afford the fare for herself, let alone for me? That's one excuse I could use.

And we had grown too distant, a bit antagonistic over our choices of men, perhaps. Or she with mine, at any rate. We had moved too often and I was desperate for roots. I think I told her that. We had lived in New York for two years, in eight apartments.

'I need to put down some roots. I'll stay here.'

It seemed to me much more practical for me to stay here in New York, dibbling my way along in my uncertain relationship with Sol. Ellen told me I could have my bed and whatever other furniture I needed – a lamp, a dresser, a bookcase. The sewing machine, of course – and she sold the rest to a neighbour to pay for her fare.

So suddenly I became the one who had to find an apartment, had

In Bryant Park, behind the New York Central Library on
Forty-second Street, 1948.

to learn the landlord-slaying style. In this case a landlady. I went back to the building at West 103rd Street, asking if perhaps there was a vacancy. Nothing, really. Except the place in the basement which she was just thinking of renting out. I could use the basement entrance, downstairs from the street, through the hallway and into two rooms. I'd have to share the bathroom on the first floor. The rent was only $23 a month. I could do it. I could manage that. And she said I could use her telephone, which was another great blessing. And so another stage of life was ready to begin. I would keep my job and try to go to school too. Perhaps I could manage if I just juggled my hours, worked at night maybe.

Ellen never doubted that I would find a place to live, find a job. She knew I was capable of whatever was necessary. She had taught me well. The movers came and took away the furniture that was now mine: anything tied with a yellow ribbon was to go to my apartment. Everything else stayed for the neighbour she had sold it to.

Sol and I saw Ellen off on the *Duchess of Bedford*. We taxied down to the dock on the West Side, walked with her onto the ship. She looked already so British in her tweed jacket. I thought she must be the most sophisticated woman in the world. Sophisticated Lady, holding her head high, chin defiantly forward. Whoever would have known that she was wrapped in the misery of the failure of love? Certainly not me.

There was so much glamour in travelling by ship. Ellen had bought a steamer trunk for her clothes and other shipboard necessities, and all the other things she was taking with her had been packed in boxes marked *Not Wanted on Board*. All those things she could live without for a week, books mostly, including the massive twenty-pound Merriam Webster dictionary that would travel with her for the rest of her life.

Sol and I went with her, following the purser to the tiny cabin she would be sharing with another passenger. The other woman was clearly more experienced at this particular kind of farewell. Her friend had brought a bottle of champagne and the purser provided glasses for all of us. We toasted the two women, clinking our glasses, feeling all the cameras of Hollywood recording this glamorous moment. The cabin was so tiny that the five of us couldn't stand up at the same time, so each of the travellers sat on her own bunk while the rest of us

Don't I look confident? However, I am perched precariously on a chain, smiling and poised. This was taken in 1949, outside of Stuyvesant Town, where friends of Sol's lived. I think my mother gave me this dress when she left for England, and it is certainly her jacket.

stood shifting our feet. Awkward at the unaccustomed closeness of strangers encroaching on our private space.

I was relieved when the purser came through the corridor calling out the traditional warning: 'All ashore that's going ashore.' And I was momentarily filled with panic at the idea that I might get stuck on the ship and swept away again into Ellen's uncertain world. 'All visitors ashore', we were warned again and again. I have no memory of saying goodbye to my mother, only the vastness of the void as I stood at the dock waving as the ship's horns sounded, waving to someone somewhere in that crowd on the decks, waving as the *Duchess* moved elegantly from the pier.

39. GRAND CENTRAL AGAIN

I don't even know how long Ellen was gone, that first time. She went off to England, and when Marty came back from his sea-job, he realized that she had been serious about 'me or the sea'. Marty went chasing after her to England, and a few months later she came back to New York. Marty found an apartment for her – in the West Seventies, I think. At least that's my memory. A brownstone, with a wide flight of concrete steps leading up to the main door. Was her apartment at the first floor front? No. First floor back. I know that she contacted Bobbi and Julie again, and all her friends and the Party. She was going to try again. She got a job editing something, somewhere. I continued my job at Freedom House, learning how to fit into the work of receptionist, living in my basement apartment on West 104th Street. No room there for my mother. Just me and the mice and the coal chute.

But she wouldn't live with Marty, perhaps trying to maintain some emotional strength, as he went off to sea again. It was what he did, after all. It was his work. And the political situation was becoming quite frightening, with 'loyalty oaths' and 'security clearance' and the sense among all the lefties, whether communists or not, that they were under attack. Their jobs were threatened.

The FBI was everywhere, wiretapping, using spies and stoolies. Ellen knew that she couldn't live in the United States any more, and was trying to figure out what to do. Where to go, how to live. Back to Canada? Would Marty come too?

And one day, when she returned home from work the owner met her at the door. 'There were two men here looking for you today ...' And she knew it was time to get out. Her fear was that the FBI would question her. And the problem with that was not what they asked you about yourself, but what they asked about your friends. If you didn't give them names, you went to jail. Like Dashiell Hammett and a lot of others. Ellen sensed also that there would be problems about her immigration statements, about her political activities, about her friends. Not that she thought for one minute that she had done anything wrong.

She phoned Sol, who phoned me at work. (She told me later that she was afraid her phone might be tapped, and she'd rather throw Sol to them than lead them directly to me.)

He called me at work. 'Ellen says she needs you to visit her this evening. It's urgent, she says.'

And so I went to see her, right after work. She heated up a can of soup, made toast, and we talked about the situation. She was sure the apartment was being watched, and that the 'two men' would be back in the morning. She had to get out of the United States without being caught, that was the key. Because if she were caught it would cause trouble for Julie and the others. She knew too much, perhaps. It was not a question of communist 'spying' or any sort of espionage. Merely *being a communist* meant that you would lose your job. Naming names was something she wouldn't do.

And so, we worked out a plan. She would leave the apartment innocently in the morning at her usual time, as though to work, carrying only her handbag. But she would be wearing extra layers of her clothes. I put on some of her clothes ... several layers, actually ... under my coat. So when I left the apartment I looked about twenty pounds heavier, I'm sure. I carried her typewriter and stuffed as much as I could into my handbag, packing it tightly with her passport, papers. In the morning she would go to Grand Central, where I would meet her with typewriter, a suitcase, and some money. Forty or fifty dollars, anything I could spare. I gave her my last twenty right then, just kept subway fare to get myself home.

Back at my apartment, I went upstairs and used the landlady's phone to call Sol and ask if he could come by and lend me some cash. I didn't tell him what was going on, just that I needed forty dollars or so, for a couple of days, just until I got paid on Friday. 'Just something I have to do for my mother,' I said. I think he borrowed some cash from his friends.

I knew that I couldn't tell him anything, because he might be asked about it later by some committee. He might be investigated. So it was better if he didn't know anything. Sol and most of his friends were 'liberals', not anything more serious than that, politically. Well, except, except? but that was long ago, and everyone's dead now, I'm sure. But even now, there are names that I won't name. Everyone knew that it was better not to ask, and not to tell. Secrets kept you safe, it seemed.

After Sol left my apartment, about ten o'clock, I packed Ellen's things into my small suitcase, then tried without much luck to get to sleep. At eight o'clock the next morning I was there in Grand Central, under the clock, which was where everyone met, somewhere under those sparkling stars in the great dome. She had already bought her ticket on the morning train to Toronto, and we began to walk sedately to the track together. But she worried about being seen together, afraid that if 'they' caught her, 'they' would get me too.

'You go,' she said. 'You go. Don't make a fuss. Just go. I'll phone you tomorrow at work.'

And so we became actresses again, just smiling and walking away from each other, waving goodbye under the silver stars.

On my way to work I walked across Forty-second Street slowly, dawdling in front of the library lions for a bit, trying to get my bearings, sitting in Bryant Park with the pigeons until it was time for me to show up at the office across the street. Bewildered by politics. Bewildered by this surge of love for my mother, by pride and principles. I was barely getting to know her, I thought. The adult Laurie, beginning to know myself, trying to make a connection with the adult Ellen. That person who was more than and different from the mother who had rescued me from troubles, even while she was trying to rescue herself. And who was still trying to find a safe harbour, a happy harbour too, if possible.

Later in her life, after many more moves, I said, 'You always seem to think that happiness will be in the next place you move to.' 'No,' she told me, 'I just know it's not here.'

40. HUNTER COLLEGE AND THE TOYSTORE

After I heard from Ellen that she was safely in Canada I went back to her apartment and packed up the books, the remaining clothes. Luckily she hadn't been back from England long enough to acquire furniture – the apartment was mostly furnished – so I didn't have to worry about shipping a lot of things, just a couple of boxes. I took the bits of groceries and oddments back to my apartment, still the Depression baby, never wasting anything.

And life went on. I saw Sol on weekends, at the friends' apartment, mostly. Sol still lived with his mother, Sister Helen, Brother Jack, and Brother Al. But Helen, at long last, was engaged. The family began organizing for the wedding. A giant affair at one of the hotels. I bought a long dress, lilac satin with a small train at the back, and looked very glamorous, surprising Sol's family, who still thought I was a mouse.

The next summer Sol decided to have a serious talk with me about my future (not *our* future, *mine*). He thought I should think about going back to school. I'm sure his friends had been after him.… I was clearly a bright girl, I shouldn't spend my life doing office work. And I was certainly beginning to be bored with being a receptionist, pasting newspaper clippings in the scrapbook, ordering egg salad on brown toast to be delivered for lunch. I couldn't afford school, of course. What would I live on if I quit my job and went back to school? I had saved a little money – very little on my salary of $44 per week. But the rent on my apartment had actually been reduced from $27 a month to $23, by some City of New York rent control board. I could keep the apartment, go to school, work part time, and Sol would contribute some money to help out.… It all seemed very possible. There was no real problem about tuition costs, since undergraduate tuition at any of the subsidized New York City colleges remained at about $85 a year (including books).

I took an afternoon off work – 'doctor's appointment' – and talked to the admissions office at Hunter College. My previous marks were good, but there was now a special problem. By state law, since I was under twenty-one my legal residence was with my parents, and since neither parent lived in New York State I was not eligible for subsidized tuition. I talked and talked to the Dean of Women, trying to work out some way to be accepted. 'It's just not possible,' she told me. 'You aren't a legal resident of New York City.'

I persisted: 'I am almost twenty years old. My mother lives in England, my father lives in Canada. I have been living on my own for two years. I pay state and federal taxes....' And I had said the magic words, it seemed. Taxes became the key to the problem. If I paid taxes, clearly I was a legal resident. The Dean went into a huddle with other administrators and when she came back she was laughing. 'I guess we'll have to call you an emancipated minor,' she said. And so the first hurdle was past.

I worked through the summer, then gave two weeks' notice and left the job. When I left, they gave me one of the old typewriters from the office, a metal typing table, and a good leather club chair with a little tear on the seat that I never could fix. These were great additions to my apartment, which was just one room for living in and another room with a sink in it, and a fridge and stove too. I had bought some furniture – a kitchen table and four chairs at the secondhand shop on Amsterdam Avenue. I hung a bamboo blind down the middle of that room and put the table and chairs in front of it. A Chianti bottle with a candle in it, a couple of copper pots of philodendron – they were perfectly happy to be in the dark basement, it seemed. Very elegant, I thought. I'd do my reading in the living room/bedroom, and then if I was working on a big project for school I'd put the typewriter on the kitchen table and work most of the night, papers spread out on the table, and eating baloney sandwiches at one in the morning.

I cooked all the family recipes of potato soup and as a special treat, hamburgers with mushroom soup and carrots. Lived on Kraft Dinner at seventeen cents a package, and baloney sandwiches to take to school.

I had contacted Mel at the toystore where I used to work and he was glad to give me a job working nights and weekends. And so my life underwent a big change. Living in my little apartment in the basement, going to Hunter College – now at the downtown campus, which saved me that long subway ride up to 198th Street.

I made friends at school, including one girl who was about as poor as I was. Beverley Atkins. We would buy a package of frozen fish for fifty-nine cents, thaw it a bit, and share the fish fillets, peeling them apart and wrapping our shares in waxed paper. Sometimes we had dinner together at my apartment or at hers. We bought lamb ribs for nineteen cents a pound and 'barbecued' them under the grill, slathered with catsup and mustard and a lot of herbs. They were almost all fat, but we managed to gnaw a few shreds of lamb from them.

(We told each other stories of our lives. Her father was a minister somewhere in New England. She showed me the scars on her breasts where he had burned her with cigarettes as punishment for her bad thoughts. Eventually she married her psychiatrist and they moved to Switzerland to go to med school. But, as it turned out, she had a baby and he was the one who continued at med school. When they came back to the States, he got a job in New Rochelle or some place like that, and she tried to be a good faculty wife.)

In my second year back at school, a great calamity struck, in the form of a City of New York decree that my apartment was 'unfit for human habitation.' And that was that. I would have to find another place. But nothing would ever be that cheap. Sol and I talked about it and decided that perhaps we might live together. In 1950 this was very daring. He was teaching at the girls' college, surrounded by rich young women ... and he delighted in making them jealous by extolling my virtues at great length. How smart I was, perceptive, kind and compassionate, sensitive, well-spoken, polite. I think he drove them quite mad, just to tease them. We lived together for almost a year ... a little apartment on Seventh Avenue near Twenty-third street.

I think that I started working at the toystore again in the fall of 1949, to help out during the Christmas rush. As Christmas approached, Mel put up a notice about buying presents on 'the lay-away', paying a bit every week or every month, so the gifts would be paid up by Christmas. These were the expensive things: bicycles and tricycles mostly, but sometimes expensive dolls and doll carriages. The bikes would arrive in cartons, but they all had to be put together. Usually Mel did that in the basement storeroom while I took care of the store.

Mel also sold a few books in the store, not enough to be considered a real bookshop, but enough that you could find a gift for a friend. He didn't sell paperbacks though, just hardcover books. This was at the beginning of the Book-of-the-Month Club, and Mel had a couple of friends sign up for membership. I was one of them. The B-o-M would send the month's book selection to you if you didn't tell them not to, and the price was a lot lower than it would have been in a standard retail edition. So Mel would pay the B-o-M invoices and sell the books in the store. It seemed to be a good deal all around, although it might have been a little devious.

Sometimes Mel let me go down to the basement storeroom and help put together the tricycles. I really enjoyed that. I had a bit of a mechanical side, and my brain seemed to know instinctively what part went where. It was always exciting to see the bikes and trikes crowded together in the basement, waiting for the magical day before Christmas, when the moms and dads would come and pick up their treasures to surprise the kids on Christmas morning.

This job paid better than ushering at the movies, but a lot less than my job as a receptionist. But I enjoyed talking to the customers and the kids. Well, most of them, anyway. Mel needed an assistant in the store and I needed a job – all through the winter I worked after school and all day Saturday. Then once my classes at Hunter College finished for the summer I was able to work longer days. The store was open until eight at night, so I could work from four to eight, then take the subway home to my apartment on West 104th Street.

Mel and his wife, whose name I think was Elaine, lived on the top floor of the project, the 'penthouse' floor. Sometimes, not often, I would have dinner with Mel and Elaine and their two daughters. It was a bright apartment, with big windows looking out into the Manhattan skyline, and there was a place on the roof where they had a few plants and some outdoor furniture. It seems funny now, to think of the word penthouse attached to a subsidized housing development, but I thought it was splendid at the time.

However, it was not nearly as grand as the penthouse where one of Sol's students lived. Sol and I visited her place a few times. She was allowed to have parties when her parents were away. So there would be a lot of the girls from the college where Sol taught ... the Anne Reno Institute. That penthouse had huge rooms and even 'maid's quarters', which Sol showed to me. And the outdoor roof areas were very grand – big urns full of plants, lounges, tables and chairs where we could sit and talk outside in the nighttime of Manhattan.

At Knickerbocker Village there were, I believe, a few other stores around the perimeter, although I don't remember them. There were a couple of good Italian restaurants up the street, and there must have been a handy grocery store. It was a family neighbourhood, where people could walk easily to the stores and to the subway.

I don't know whether Mel knew that the FBI had been around to question Julius Rosenberg that summer. I don't even know if Mel knew that Julius was a communist. Just because they were neighbours didn't mean they knew each other's politics, especially in those days of secrecy. And when my mother and I lived there in 1947 we certainly didn't know Julius and Ethel, even though they lived in the same building. But the spy scares were getting frantic, and the great fear was that secrets were being given to the Russians – that Russia would learn how to make the atomic bomb (and that it would someday be used by communist Russia against capitalist United States).

But I was there in the toystore that Monday, just getting the last of the pre-dinner customers out of the way and before the evening customers came in, and Mel came dashing in from the inside hallway.

'Get away from the door,' he said. 'Get away from the windows.' He pushed me away. He was quite odd, frantic. He went to the door, opened it, and leaned out to look up the street. Then slid back again and closed the door. 'Get away, get back,' he said. 'Don't let them see you looking.' I caught his fright, even though I had no idea what on earth was going on. 'The FBI, they are arresting Julius.' I know that's what he said. I crowded beside him at the door and we peeked up the street, and drew back. Alternating ... needing to know but afraid of being seen. Was it dangerous to look? Dangerous to be seen looking? Mel, of course, could perhaps reasonably have been afraid that they might pick him up as a commie, although he certainly wasn't a spy. Was he? Little grey-haired Mel? Impossible. Although perhaps people said that about Julius.

It was nearly two month later that we heard that they had picked up Ethel, but not from home. They got her at work. Her children were with a neighbour, probably. That's what people did then, for baby-sitters. Robert, the youngest, was only four. Michael was eight, so he was probably at school. I worried about the children, then and later.

The trial was fast and furious, really, with Ethel's brother testifying against them. Oh, the political situation was scary. The hunt for hidden communists became more widespread, and I was glad my mother was safely out of the country. Of course I believed Julius and Ethel were innocent, that they were being accused of spying just because they were communists. In the end – oh my, the trial was fast – they were executed less than two years later. Whatever Julius had done, surely Ethel's role was minor, I thought. Why did they have to execute her too?

In Ellen's apartment on Avenue Road in Toronto, just before she left for England again. She is forty years old, and I am almost twenty. The print on her couch was extremely modern, now a recognizable 1950s graphic.

41. CLOSER AND CLOSER, AND FARTHER AWAY

My mother, back in Toronto, seemed to have achieved a touch of security in Toronto, working for McClelland & Stewart. She got along well with Jack, she was a skilled editor, and was apparently much admired by her co-workers, Ann and Florence, to whom she represented 'the new woman'. Marty had been to visit her in Toronto and there was talk of a wedding.

I could almost hear her laughing when she sent me her version of a 'marriage contract':

Do you Martin Phillips solemnly swear not to exist all day on noshes? Do you solemnly swear you will clean your teeth immediately on arising? Do you swear to cease wasting your time on crappy movies? Do you promise to assume your share of the rent regularly, once a month, and likewise the phone and electric bills and any other such? Do you solemnly swear that from now on you will wear house slippers in the house, and slacks, instead of going around in bare feet and shorts like a broken-down beachcomber? Do you promise to quit nagging and teasing, and cultivate the gentle art of talking sensibly at least once a day?

Do you, Ellen, solemnly swear that you'll quit this skittish kicking over the traces and make a determined effort to behave like a woman? Do you promise to love and honour (we won't even mention obey) this man who is so doggone lovable and honorable? Do you pledge to cut out your bitching and nagging and your moodiness and your hysterics, and settle down to a placid, good-humoured existence so that both of you can extract a little joy out of this business of living? Do you swear to settle down emotionally and do some writing, considering your life to be divided into three main interests, to wit, your job, your hereby-to-be-husband, and your writing, not necessarily in that order?

That was a good summer, both for me and for her.

So I was surprised, just a few months later, to get a letter telling me that she would be returning to England permanently, so if I wanted to see her, I'd better come now. I arranged a few days of vacation from work, and took the train to Toronto, where she had a compact little apartment on Avenue Road, across from Yorkville. She had a farewell party, and I met her friends from work – interesting attractive women. After they left, Ellen and I finally had a chance to talk, and we actually did. A rarity for us, always. We never talked about what was happening in our lives, especially about how we felt.

She told me about Marty. He had come to Toronto and stayed for a couple of weeks, while they adored each other and talked about their situation. Would he be willing to emigrate? Would he leave his family behind and move to Canada? Could he? But the major problem, as always, was his restlessness and the need to go to sea. But ... oh Ellen.... She sent him away again, in another fit of exasperation, arguments over money.

He went off again, she told me, and phoned her from New York a month later, when he got back.

'I've brought you some Shalimar,' he said, 'and I'll be up there next week.'

'Well, you can just give it to someone else,' she told him.

Oh, she cried when she told me that. I'd never really seen her cry. She told me she had written a long letter to him, trying to retract, but the only address she had was at his mother's. He probably hadn't received her letter, because he didn't ever get in touch again.

And then, only a couple of months later she got a letter from Eve: 'Well, guess who just got married!'

She told me: 'I'm glad for him, and for whoever-she-is. She's one of the luckiest people in the world. I hope they'll be happy – I'm sure they will. Only a silly bitch like me could not be happy with Marty. I used to sit in the bathroom and watch him shave. He used to drink from my glass and eat from my plate. And the first time he left me to go to sea, I couldn't put his dirty towel in the laundry. I kept it and used it until I couldn't any longer.'

That was when she decided to move to England. She couldn't stand to be on the same continent with him, she said, to be that close to him now that she had thrown him away, now that he was permanently gone from her life.

'I'll go to England at the end of January,' she said. 'After that, who knows?'

Oh, it was a sad time, all right. But she seemed, as always, absolutely certain that what she was doing was the right thing. When you can't cope, just leave.

Me too, really. I was almost ready to join her in England. Politics again separated me from Sol. The McCarthy witchhunts in the United States began to focus on teachers, on the moral influence they had on their students. Every teacher was expected to be above reproach, with proper political ideas and a proper moral life. Several teachers were charged with 'moral turpitude', and the hunt was on. Of course Sol and his family were afraid, worried. All their life's ambitions centred on Sol, and here he was, clearly 'living in sin'. The political climate didn't push us into marriage, which would have been the obvious answer, but that would have been even harder for his family to bear. Marriage to a shiksa! Impossible!

And Sol asked me to move out of the apartment. After 'going together' for four years, we were separating. I was fretful, angry and wounded.

For months I lived with Leslie and Nona just a few blocks away, I flirted with other guys. Necked on a stairway and listened to Rachmaninoff. I have no idea what Sol did. I had assumed we had a monogamous relationship, though I later learned it was one-sided monogamy. But Sol and I were still connected. He came to see me to try to soothe me. I'm sure he felt guilty, but felt he had had no choice. 'It's the politics of these terrible days,' he said.

He began to pressure his family to invite me for Passover. I began talking to the rabbi in New Rochelle about conversion, and slowly, slowly, we moved closer to a wedding.

42. MIDTOWN MANHATTAN

The summer after I married Sol – it was 1951 – I applied for American citizenship (damned fool that I was) and brought myself to the attention of the Feds. I don't know what I was thinking of, except trying to 'fit in' to an ordinary sort of world. But those were not ordinary times. I submitted some routine paperwork, I thought, to Immigration and Naturalization, or whatever the department was, and then I was asked to come to the office because 'further information' was needed.

I remember the office well, the solid rectangular oak desk and the chairs – a swivel chair behind the desk for one of the men, and a couple of straight chairs. One for me. No windows. The walls were bureaucratic beige. Bare minimum. This wasn't an office, just a room. Perhaps it was in the basement, that might fit with my vague memories. But I don't remember that part. And I have no real memory of the two men who talked to me. Suits and ties, as usual. That's all I remember of them. Tall, short? Skinny, fat? No memory. One sat behind the desk, the other walked about, occasionally pulling the other straight chair to face me, sitting in it, looking at me. He was just neutral. There was no agenda that I could see, nothing to scare me, threaten me. It was just information. There was another room somewhere, with typewriters clacking.

I was a pleasant and innocent young lady, a legal immigrant since 1946, recently married to an American citizen, applying for citizenship. I just sat there in my navy blue suit, being honest about what life was like when I was a kid, when I just happened to have communist parents.

Of course I was frank and friendly about all the Canadian communist stuff from my childhood, whatever I remembered. A kid's memory. Why not? It was all open, all public knowledge, and I was quite happy to dish the dirt on my father, if that's what it was. Canada had a tradition of lots of political parties. No, I hadn't seen him for about four years, not since my grandfather's funeral. I was happy to elaborate on that, blathering on about all the relatives. All perfectly innocent, I knew that. All those aunts and uncles, those innumerable cousins back in Canada. And Canada was Canada. Nothing the FBI could do about that. What happened in Canada was Canada's business, I thought.

But when they moved on to ask about my mother it was a different situation.

'She's living in London now, in England,' I told them. 'I haven't seen her in about two years. I visited her in Toronto before she left for England.'

They asked a lot of questions about her: when did we arrive in New York, what kind of work did she do, who were her friends? I talked about Rosie, our wonderful Italian saviour, about going to high school, ushering at the movie, about Louise, whom we lived with for awhile. About where she had worked. That was all open information. And all the apartments we had lived in. I even told them about Ellen's romance with Marty the sailor. And about my husband, Sol. A clean, upright, non-political, untouchable citizen.

I was questioned for the whole morning about my mother and her activities. The Rosenbergs had been arrested but not yet executed. International spy rings seemed to be everywhere.... Apparently they thought Ellen was a courier because of her back-and-forth trips across the Atlantic just at that time. They didn't say that, but I began to worry about it.

'Why did she go to England in 1949?' I told them about her romance with Marty, and about her ambitions as a writer.

'And why did she come back to New York?'

'I don't know. I guess they patched it up. She never talked to me about it.'

'What about her other friends, her political friends?'

'I don't know. I was just a kid,' I told them. 'I was just a kid in high school.'

Hours of questions, my adolescent haze quite useful really.

'I had a boyfriend, and I wasn't paying much attention to my mother.'

All those years of not paying attention to her. How very fortunate. Names?

'Gee, no, I really can't remember their names at all. Except Marty, her boyfriend. Martin Phillips.'

When I was summoned back the following day to sign the statement they told me, 'There were a couple of questions we forgot to ask you. We just added them at the end, and we put in what we thought your answers might be.'

The first question they had forgotten to ask me was whether I would testify against Ellen if she were ever on trial. They had given my reply to that as something like 'Oh, I wouldn't want to do that ...' And the second question was: 'If you were subpoenaed, would you testify?' To which they had predicted a reply: 'I guess I would have to, wouldn't I.'

I was shocked. Suddenly, at last, I was afraid. And I very rapidly thought I knew the danger ahead.

That fear zipped through my body, as it had when I was a child. I remembered my encounter with the RCMP, and unthinkingly reached into my childhood, into that desperate emotional bank, where all the emotions went in and nothing ever came out until it burst. Out of the pain came a great wail: 'But she's my *mother*! I couldn't ever testify against her. She's my *mother*!'

It was different this time. I was old enough to know that no little-girl tears were about to turn the trick with the FBI. And it would take more than a few tears to give me strength. It had to come from somewhere else.

I kept saying it. 'I'd never testify against her. Never. She's my mother.' Over and over. 'Never, never. She's my mother and she hasn't done anything wrong.'

And eventually, the statement was duly sent out to have the last two pages retyped. When it came back I dried my eyes and signed it. It seemed to me that this time it wasn't about weakness, but about strength. Whatever came, I was strong and she was my mother. I could do whatever it took, and she'd be proud of me.

Released, upset and shaken, clutching my handbag and a wad of tissues, I pushed open the big glass doors and stepped out into the afternoon of midtown Manhattan. Taxis, people, noise. Air and sky. The world had held its breath for me, and now was sighing with something like relief. What had been disconnected was connected again. Rediscovering my mother, courtesy of the Feds. I felt I had I rescued both of us that day, my mother and myself.

The rough voyage of childhood was over.

ACKNOWLEDGEMENTS

I'm an old lady now, and of course I want to thank everyone who had a hand in getting me to this point in my life. But that's not, I know, the purpose of a book's acknowledgements.

My family comes first on my thank-you list. I have been helped by the constant support and encouragement of my daughters Amanda and Delvalle, and my son-in-law, Tim Wynne-Jones. In particular, Amanda has been my first reader during this book's rather long gestation. She continues to give me valuable advice and assistance, and appropriate splashings of Prosecco. The encouragement I have received from the writers' community in Kingston has been generous and astonishing. In particular, Carolyn Smart, Joanne Page, and Maureen Garvie encouraged me in my early writing days, and from farther afield came the energy and enthusiasm of Mark Abley and Sheila Fischman. Carolyn Smart has continued to be my guru and a source of strength, of advice, of inspiration, of unfailing honesty and loyalty. Over the past ten years we have collaborated in publishing the work of her creative writing classes at Queen's University, through Artful Codger Press.

Editor Doris Cowan has been strong, insightful and affectionate, pushing and pulling me along as needed. The day she and Tim Inkster said 'yes' to *Little Comrades* was the beginning of a new life for me.

My mother, Ellen Stafford, who is very present throughout this book, would have been one hundred years old now. When she was eighty, the age I am now, we once again began to co-habit. I can't truthfully say that she encouraged me to write, although she probably meant to, and I must acknowledge that our memories of specific events were different. But one of the best things she ever did for me was to say, that day in my early teenhood, 'I'm leaving. Do you want to come?' And we got the hell out of Dodge. Perhaps I have not always been able to capture the parts of our lives that were fun, being distracted by distress, but nonetheless … we were there, and we did what we did. And we both survived those days. Thanks, Ellen.

And I gratefully acknowledge the support of the Ontario Arts Council for a Writers' Reserve grant, which provided great assistance during the writing of this book.

ABOUT LAURIE LEWIS

Laurie Lewis is a Fellow of the Graphic Designers of Canada and is Editor of *Vista*, the publication of the Seniors Association in Kingston, Ontario, and director of Artful Codger Press.

Laurie began her career in publishing with Doubleday in New York in 1961. She returned to Canada in 1963 to join University of Toronto Press, where she worked in production and design of UTP publications, becoming Head of Design. During her thirty years in publishing, she also taught book design in Guyana, the Philippines, and at Ryerson University in Toronto. She moved to Kingston, Ontario, in 1991, where she founded Artful Codger Press.

Her written work has been on CBC and has been published around and about, including *Contemporary Verse 2, Queen's Feminist Review, Kingston Poets' Gallery* and *The Toronto Quarterly*. A chapter of this manuscript was shortlisted for the 2007 CBC Literary Awards in Creative Non-Fiction.